REPUBLICAN RELIGION
The American Revolution and the Cult of Reason

EXPLANATION OF THE FRONTISPIECE

1. "The Sun, the emblem of Truth and Reason."
2. "The School of Science, where the pupils are represented of puerile age. . . . The King, at the head of the table, marks, by his actions (of pointing to the trifling pursuits of literature, and directing his guards, at the same time, to put chains upon the legs of the pupils unobserved), both the use and abuse of power. The Priest, at the other end of the table, points the attention of the pupils to metaphysics, and at the same time hoodwinks them, that they may not look towards the light, or study of Man and Nature."
3. "A Curtain upheld by a King and a Priest" to conceal the "study of Man and Nature. . . . The Author, with the scroll, or work of the Opus Maximum, lifts up the curtain (which the King, with his sceptre, endeavours to keep down), in order to let in the light of the Sun of Truth and Reason."
4. "An emblem of the world and its inhabitants, represented by a Woman with many breasts, sitting upon a globe weeping, with dishevelled hair. Her Children in the dark part, shaded by the curtain, have all left the upper breasts, and cling to the hair, swinging backwards and forwards, scratching and biting one another, as they feel the rod of the Priest, or the spear of Mercury which goads them on either side. The rod of the Priest represents religious persecution and cruel bigotry; and the spear of Mercury represents the cupidity and fastidious wants of luxury, the seed of destruction to civilization, and the great empediment to human perfectability. The Children on the breast, illumined by the rays that pierce the curtain, are all sucking in tranquility and peace."
5. "The School of Sense illumined by the rays of disciplined Reason, and contrasted with the School of Science." In the former, man is taught to use his mind independently and constructively; "while in the School of Science it is made a mere repository of memory, or an overstuffed sack," to contain only the ideas of other men. In the School of Sense man is conducted "to a state of virility, as represented in the adult figures of the pupils; while that of Science retains Man in a state of intellectual puerility, as represented by the stature of boys at the table." The School of Sense is taught by a philosopher, not by a king and priest.
6. "The Colony of Manhood, which represents the apex of human perfectability, where all individual power being united in one public capital or community, the personal stock of each in pleasure, power, and well-being, is multiplied in an incalculable ratio." In this happy state the individual attains the greatest personal well being and happiness by living in the most harmonious relationship with his fellow men. "On the top of the column we observe a Beast supporting a Sun, which is a symbol of the triumph of Reason over Instinct."
7. "The School of Metaphysics, represented by a group of Infants seated round a table, to read books of unmeaning sophisms and phantasms; while metaphysical doctors point their telescopes into an invisible medium of darkness. . . . In the back-ground we observe an Altar, surmounted with the head of an Idol, into which a Priest is seen creeping below, to deliver, in the School of Metaphysics, those supernatural, or rather unnatural oracles of inspired intercourse, which have obstructed the discipline of human reason."
8. "The figure of Twilight, to represent those obscure intellectual operations of conjecture which pass beyond the boundaries of experience."
9. "The figure of the River running through the Twilight typifies the universal transmutation of all matter."
10. "This figure of cloudy and impenetrable Darkness, . . . marks the boundaries of intellectual power, . . . and proves, . . . that human reason can have no power, and consequently no interest beyond intelligence or conceivability."

—John Stewart, *Opus Maximum* (London, 1803), pp. 3-15.

ALLEGORICAL REVELATION OF THE MORAL AND PHYSICAL LAWS OF INTELLIGIBLE NATURE

(Reproduced through the courtesy of the New York Historical Society)

REPUBLICAN RELIGION

THE AMERICAN REVOLUTION AND
THE CULT OF REASON

BY

G. ADOLF KOCH, Ph.D.

WIPF & STOCK · Eugene, Oregon

Wipf and Stock Publishers
199 W 8th Ave, Suite 3
Eugene, OR 97401

Republican Religion
The American Revolution and the Cult of Reason
By Koch, G. Adolf
ISBN 13: 978-1-60608-587-5
Publication date 4/9/2009
Previously published by Peter Smith, 1933

To

DAISY A. KOCH

CONTENTS

PREFACE

WHEN the Abbé Van Becelaere wrote his slender volume, *La Philosophie en Amérique depuis les origines jusqu'à nos jours (1607-1900),*[1] at the beginning of the present century, he anticipated the present-day interest in America's cultural and intellectual heritage. At that time few at home or abroad were aware that there had ever been any philosophy in America. It can be said of our intellectual and religious heritage, as of the Dark Ages, that it seems so dark because we know so little about it. The recording of American religious thought and activities was left to the mercy of clergymen who, with rare exceptions if any, had not been trained in the scientific method of historiography or inspired with Ranke's scientific ideals. Objective history, perhaps euphemistically so-called, was in fact not the aim or ideal of the average denominational historian. He presented the devotion, the hardships, and the sacrifices of the fathers as an incentive to carry on the good work and to continue in the true faith. The tenor of their works is teleological—not *how* things happened, but to what end.

For this reason freethought has naturally suffered even more than have the conventional faiths from our religious historians who treated it merely as a work of the devil. This study of rationalism as a type of American religious thought from the Revolution to 1810 reflects a new attitude toward religion and a new interest in an hitherto

[1] New York, 1904.

xi

neglected phase of our culture. To the sectarian historian, for example, Ethan Allen's freethinking was a blot on the escutcheon of pious heroes of the Revolution, while the old political historian thought of him only as the leader of the Green Mountain boys and the hero of Ticonderoga. He is here presented, neither as an apostate nor as a long-neglected martyr, but as an American who expressed in writing the thoughts on religion which were a part of the intellectual milieu of the time and shared, more or less, by many of his fellow fighters.

In the French Revolution religion was scarcely less an issue than politics, a fact which was bewildering to American admirers of French liberty. To a conservative New Englander the religious aspect was the more pernicious of the two. "Still worse [than the beheading of Louis XVI]," wrote John Trumbull of Connecticut, "when the National Assembly of France, the elected rulers of a great nation, formed a procession to the metropolitan church of Nôtre Dame, which had been consecrated during long ages to the worship of God, and there in mock solemnity bowed their knees before a common courtezan, basely worshiping her as the goddess of reason, still there were those, and not a few in America, who threw up their caps, and cried, 'glorious, glorious, sister republic!' " [2]

The American liberal, while a republican in politics, was unable to accept republican religion. Consequently the religious implications of Revolutionary thought were quickly submerged and freethought became an isolated and irresponsible element in nineteenth-century America. The aim of this study is to trace the various stages in the

[2] John Trumbull, *Autobiography, Reminiscences and Letters of John Trumbull, from 1756 to 1841* (New Haven, 1841), p. 169.

degeneration of radical republican enthusiasm. The economic and political factors underlying this change have been disclosed by recent historians, notably Beard, but the philosophical and religious history still needs to be told.

One could wish for a typical eighteenth-century title for this study to define its purpose and scope more specifically. I have limited myself primarily to the movement to establish deism as a religious cult. For example, I have not attempted to explain the sources of Thomas Jefferson's liberal religious beliefs. Jefferson is important here not for what he wrote in his *Notes on the State of Virginia* but for his relation to the deistic movement. For the same reason, I have not included an analysis of Paine's *Age of Reason* or of any of his other works, all of which are readily available and about which much has been written, but have confined myself largely to the period after his return to America in 1802 when he was a member of the Deistic Society in New York.

The geographical limitation of the subject to the New England and Middle Atlantic states also needs a word of explanation. I have not included deism in the South nor the wave of infidelity and irreligion associated with the early pioneering days of Kentucky. There is no evidence in the records of the deistic societies in the East that the Kentucky movement was related to that in New York in the sense in which the Philadelphia society, for example, was. The New York and Philadelphia societies were sister organizations, inspired by the same leaders and nurtured by a common periodical literature. The Kentuckians undoubtedly read the *Age of Reason*, but neither Thomas Paine nor Elihu Palmer was associated with their activities. Nowhere in *The Temple of Reason* is there any reference to indicate that that militant deistic journal had any agents or subscribers beyond the Alleghanies. The story of Kentucky's infidelity before the days of its repentance in the Second Awakening needs to be made the subject of a separate study.

The movement to establish a religion of deism with meeting houses, services, and other attributes of a religious institution is not synonymous with the religious liberalism associated, for example, with the cosmopolitan Dr. Franklin. Historians are in substantial agreement that the second half of the eighteenth century was characterized by a kind of scepticism among the upper classes, roughly defined as deistic. It did not preclude remaining affiliated with Christian denominations, but it did tend to cool religious ardor. Deistic influences broke down the distinction between one's own "true" religion and all other "false" religions. Deists thought of the Deity as the Author of the Universe rather than as a stern judge and jealous God. They believed in immortality but not in salvation through "the blood of the Lamb." The divinity of Jesus seemed less important than the example of His life. "Natural religion" was more persuasive and more certain than revealed, and natural phenomena were easier to comprehend than miracles. There was a tendency toward anti-clericalism, and a feeling that religious dogmatism and orthodoxy led to obscurantism. Some indeed thought of the clergy as hypocritical, designing, and unscrupulous exploiters of the ignorant and superstitious.

These were the general attributes of the deistic temper. It was an attitude of mind rather than a specific creed, rather like the scientific temper of our age which is superimposed upon our religious beliefs and institutions, Protestant, Catholic, and Hebraic, alike. Similarly, too, not all men were influenced in the same way nor to the same extent, but few among the learned, lay or clerical, escaped it altogether.

The theme of this work is the story of what happened when deism spread from the intelligentsia to the common man after the American Revolution; how republicanism in politics became identified with republicanism in religion; how both were sublimated and heralded as forerunners of the millennium in the heyday of the French Revolution; and how republican politics triumphed in 1800 but republican religion was defeated by an equally enthusiastic evangelicalism.

I wish particularly to express my appreciation to Dr. Herbert W. Schneider, Professor of Religion in Columbia University, at whose suggestion this study was undertaken. He has been throughout a source of constant help and wise guidance. To Professor John Herman Randall, Jr., I owe the debt of a grateful pupil to an inspiring teacher who first introduced him to the study of philosophy, and appreciation for his careful reading and thoughtful criticism of the manuscript. It is difficult for one who has been a student of philosophy at Columbia to express his appreciation of the unfailing guidance of Professor John J. Coss, Executive Officer of the Department of Philosophy. I also wish to thank Professors Evarts B. Greene, Dixon Ryan Fox, and Horace L. Friess of Columbia University; Dr. William Walker Rockwell of Union Theological Seminary; and Professor William Warren Sweet of the University of Chicago for reading the manuscript and for their many helpful suggestions.

The research work involved in this study was made pos-

sible by the facilities of the libraries of Columbia and
Harvard universities, the New York Historical Society,
the Long Island Historical Society, the Newburgh Free
Library, the Public Library of the City of New York, and
Union Theological Seminary.   To the staffs of these institutions I wish to express my thanks for their kindness
and assistance.

G. A. K.

New York, N. Y.
January, 1933

REPUBLICAN RELIGION

POLITICAL FREEDOM AND FREETHOUGHT

"HE was eminently a friend to liberty, both civil and religious," said the Rev. Dr. Chauncy in 1766 in his funeral sermon for Dr. Jonathan Mayhew, "and if his zeal, at any time, betrayed him into too great a severity of expression, it was against the attempts of those who would make slaves either of men's souls or bodies." [1] The military struggle for American independence was still to come a decade hence, but religious liberalism had become quite common by the time the Peace of Paris in 1763 opened what we from our perspective think of as the Revolutionary Period. The same forces which made control of American political affairs from Westminster on the Thames increasingly precarious, were at work for American spiritual emancipation. A land so large, so heterogeneously settled, and, especially on its wide frontiers, so far removed from social control, was naturally adapted to the fullest religious freedom.

In his last sermon to the Pilgrims before their departure for the New World from Leyden, the Rev. John Robinson urged his brethren to be tolerant, to be ready to receive whatever new truth God might reveal to them, for "the Lord hath more truth and light yet to break forth out of his holy word." Though they were to guard against error, they were encouraged "rather to study union

---

[1] Sermon by Charles Chauncy, July 1766, quoted in William B. Sprague, *Annals of the American Pulpit* (New York, 1865), Vol. VIII, p. 26.

than division," to see how close, without sin, they might come to effecting union "with the godly party of the kingdom of England." [2] Though united by necessity, the fathers of Congregationalism differed evidently on principle and in faith.

This is especially well illustrated in the early history of Harvard College. "Surprising as is the fact," says President Quincy, "there is not, in any one of the charters that form the Constitution of this College, one expression, on which a mere sectarian spirit can seize to wrest it into a shackle for the human soul." [3] "It is possible, nay, even probable," he explains, "that the reason of the entire absence of any reference to points of religious faith in the charters of the College was, that these early emigrants could not agree concerning them among themselves, and preferred silence on such points to engaging in controversy, when establishing a seminary of learning, in favor of which they were desirous to unite all the varieties of religious belief. The right of exercising private judgment in matters of religion was, at that day, in terms at least, universally recognised." [4]

Word of American deviations from orthodox principles reached London as early as 1637 and prompted several non-conformist London clergymen to send a letter to their American brethren requesting their views on certain points of ecclesiastical discipline and order. "Since your departure into New England," they wrote, "we heare (and partly believe it) that divers have embraced certaine vain

---

[2] Sermon preached July 21, 1620. Quoted in William B. Sprague, *Annals of the American Pulpit* (New York, 1857), Vol. I, p. 4.

[3] Josiah Quincy, *The History of Harvard University* (Cambridge, 1840), Vol. I, p. 46.

[4] *Ibid.*, Vol. I, pp. 49-50.

opinions, such as you disliked formerly, and we judge to be groundlesse and unwarrantable." In the answer returned (1639), it is admitted by the New Englanders that they had introduced certain changes; not without some misgivings, for "we see as much cause to suspect the integritie of our own hearts, as yours. . . ." Nevertheless, we believe that, "Churches had still need to grow from apparent defects to puritie; and from reformation to Reformation, age after age. . . ." [5]

This spirit of religious liberalism not only survived but flourished, for the stern Puritan virtues had within them the seed of their own destruction. Hard work and frugality without frivolity made for material success in this world as well as for salvation in the life to come. And wealth, as the prophets knew of old, leads inevitably to the secularization of thought and action. The Puritans, in short, were gradually becoming urban, cosmopolitan, and civilized.

This whole liberal movement is well illustrated in the case of the Brattle Street Church which was established in Boston at the close of the seventeenth century. Its founders or "undertakers," as they called themselves before this word had become identified with a specialized activity, were influential and respected citizens who had become thoroughly dissatisfied with the old order which had but

[5] From a rare pamphlet in the Library of Union Theological Seminary: *A Letter of Many Ministers in Old England, Requesting The judgement of their Reverend Brethren in New England concerning Nine Positions. Written Anno Dom. 1637. Together with their Answer thereunto returned, Anno 1639. And the Reply made unto the said Answer, and sent over unto them, Anno 1640. Now published (by occasion mentioned in the Epistle to the Reader, following in the next page,) upon the desire of many godly and faithfull Ministers in and about the City of London, who love and seeke the truth. By Simeon Ash, and William Rathband. I Thes. 5.21. Prove all things; Hold fast that which is good.* Printed for Thomas Underhill, at the signe of the Bible in great Woodstreet. London, 1643.

recently expressed itself at its worst in the witchcraft persecution. The new charter introduced by William and Mary in 1691, weakening the political power of the clergy, made the time ripe for some innovations. These were expressed in "A Manifesto or Declaration, set forth by the Undertakers of the New Church," dated November 17, 1699.

The Brattle Street Church approved the Westminster Confession; the reading of the Scriptures in the public worship; [6] the extension of the franchise within the church to include all who contributed to its support; the repudiation of "Publick Relation" of experiences; and, in regard to baptism, the acceptance of the principle of the Half-Way Covenant, stating, "we dare not refuse it to *any* Child offered to us by *any* professed Christian [whether or not in full communion with the church], upon his engagement to see it Educated, if God give life and ability, in the Christian Religion." [7]

Strong opposition came of course from the Mathers. To admit persons "orthodox in judgment" as to matters of faith and "not scandalous in life" to partake of the Lord's Supper, said President Increase Mather of Harvard in 1697, "without any examination concerning the 'work of grace in their hearts,' would be a *real apostasy* from former principles, and a *degeneracy* from the *reformation*." [8] At that time, of the founders of the Brattle Street

---

[6] Gradually the reading of the Scriptures was adopted by other churches, but it did not become universal until early in the nineteenth century.

[7] The Manifesto of the Brattle Street Church from an original copy is quoted in Samuel K. Lothrop, *A History of the Church in Brattle Street, Boston* (Boston, 1851), pp. 20-26.

[8] From the "Epistle Dedicatory" by Increase Mather for Cotton Mather's, "Life of Jonathan Mitchel," in Cotton Mather, *Magnalia Christi Americana* (Hartford, 1853), Vol. II, p. 69.

Church, Leverett and Pemberton were tutors, Thomas Brattle the Treasurer of the College, and William Brattle pastor of the church in Cambridge. Since President Mather's words were addressed "To the Church at Cambridge in New-England, and to the Students of the Colledge there," there could be no mistaking whom he had in mind when he referred to "young profane mockers" and "scornful neuters" through whom places where God had planted His church "were all overgrown with thorns and nettles," so that the "glory of the Lord" had gradually departed. "Mercy forbid," he adds, "that such things as these should be verified in New-England, or in Cambridge!" [9]

In 1700 the Rev. Solomon Stoddard, grandfather of Jonathan Edwards, began a long controversy with President Mather in which he maintained that the Lord's Supper was a means of conversion for the sinner, a spiritual exercise of redemptive value, not to be restricted as a sacrament for the saints on earth. While predestination and "vindictive justice" remained as official doctrine, more and more churches adopted the laxer views of admission to church ordinances.

Democratic principles developed on the institutional as well as the doctrinal side of Congregationalism. When the Mathers in 1705 proposed a closer union of the churches with a view to greater control of the separate congregations by ministerial association, we find, in the Rev. John Wise of Ipswich, Massachusetts, an apostle of democracy in ecclesiastical affairs, and a champion of Congregationalism vs. Presbyterianism, whose arguments were

[9] Increase Mather in Cotton Mather, *op. cit.*, Vol. II, pp. 66-67.

as relevant for American political liberty after 1765 as for
the sovereignty of the individual congregation at the beginning of the century.   He argued that the democratic
principles of Congregationalism were nearest the divine
model revealed in Scripture and in the law of nature.[10]
". . . a furious Man, called John Wise," wrote Cotton
Mather, ". . . has lately published a foolish Libel,
against some of us, for presbyterianizing too much in
our Care to repair some Deficiencies in our Churches.   And
some of our People, who are not only tenacious of their
Liberties, but also more suspicious than they have cause
to be of a Design in their pastors to make abridgments of
them; are too much led into Temptation, by such Invectives." [11]

While the doctors of the church were thus unhappily
divided among themselves, laymen were relatively indifferent to the spiritual life.   "The former Strictness in
Religion, that Brotherly-Love, that Publick Spirit, and
Zeal for the Order and Ordinances of the Gospel, which
was so much the Glory of our Fathers," laments the Rev.
Peter Clark of Salem in his Election Sermon in 1739, "is
very much abated, yea disrelished by too many: and a
Spirit of Licentiousness, and Neutrality in Religion, of
Uncharitableness and Contention, Pride and Sensuality,
and other corrupt Manners and Practices of a World that

[10] Vernon L. Parrington, *The Colonial Mind, 1620-1800*, Vol. I of
Main Currents in American Thought (New York, 1927), pp. 118-125.
Regarding the law of nature, *vide*, Alice M. Baldwin, *The New England
Clergy and the American Revolution* (Durham, N. C., 1928), pp. 14-17.
[11] Letter, dated September 17, 1715, to Robert Wodrow, Professor of
Divinity in the University of Glasgow, in the *Diary of Cotton Mather,
1709-1724*, *Massachusetts Historical Society Collections*, Seventh Series,
Vol. VIII, p. 327.

lies in Wickedness, so opposite to the Ways of God's People, do exceedingly prevail in the midst of us." [12]

Worldliness and church policy, however, were not the only wedges to split the faith of the Puritan fathers. The revivals of 1734-1735 and especially that of "The Great Awakening" in 1740, while quickening the religious consciousness which had long slumbered under the Half-Way Covenant, in its turn led to schism, dividing the Church between the "Old Lights" and "New Lights," and to the beginnings of the liberalism which by the end of the century developed into Unitarianism and Universalism. New England Congregationalism was left hopelessly divided against itself. The "Old Lights" looked back sadly to the ideals of the Puritan fathers, while the "New Lights" were inclined toward evangelicalism. But the theological distinctions between them were not as clear as their animosities.

Perhaps even more important than its effect on the older churches, was the impetus given by the Great Awakening to newer and more democratic denominations. The poor, the uneducated, and under-privileged eagerly associated themselves with denominations whose dogmas were especially adapted to their own characteristics. Among these were the Baptists, Methodists, and Presbyterians. "In a period when the special privileges of individuals were being called in question or destroyed," says Dr. Jameson, "there would naturally be less favor for that form of theology which was dominated by the doctrine of the especial election of a part of mankind, a growing favor for

---

[12] Peter Clark, *A Sermon preach'd in the Audience of His Excellency the Governour . . . of the Province of the Massachusetts-Bay, in New-England, May 30th, 1739. Being the Anniversary for the Election of His Majesty's Council for the Province* (Boston, 1739), p. 40.

those forms which seemed more distinctly to be based upon the idea of the natural equality of all men." [13]

The Baptists seemed to fit into this scheme of things beautifully. Their untutored clergy, their informality and democracy made their doctrine increasingly popular among the poor in town and country. They were, for example, definitely opposed to the Congregational custom of assigning seats according to age, family, or wealth. This was in itself an unimportant matter except in so far as it was typical of a system which drove many men into the ranks of opposition. [14]

They wanted religious liberty from their Anglican fellow revolutionists in Virginia and Congregationalists in New England just as much as political independence from Great Britain and carried on the two struggles simultaneously. Such pamphlets as Isaac Backus's [15] *An Appeal to the Public for Religious Liberty* and *The Exact Limits between Civil and Ecclesiastical Government* and Israel Holly's *An Appeal to the Impartial* called attention to "the inconsistency of New England refusing religious

---

[13] J. Franklin Jameson, *The American Revolution Considered as a Social Movement* (Princeton, 1926), p. 157. *Cf.*, Wesley M. Gewehr, *The Great Awakening in Virginia, 1740-1790* (Durham, N. C., 1930), *passim.*

[14] Richard J. Purcell, *Connecticut in Transition, 1775-1818* (Washington, 1918), p. 73.

In the colleges it was the painful duty of the president to arrange according to social rank the list of each freshman class. In the 1760's, however, when there was a great deal of discussion about equal rights, liberty, and freedom, it is not surprising that such a system could not escape adverse criticism and had to be abolished.—Franklin B. Dexter, "Social distinctions at Harvard and Yale" in *Miscellaneous Historical Papers* (New Haven, 1918).

[15] "Though many others joined in the protest against civil control of religion and there were other leaders in the effort to secure separation of Church and State, no individual in America since Roger Williams stands out so pre-eminently as the champion of religious liberty as does Isaac Backus."—*Dictionary of American Biography*, edited by Allen Johnson (New York, 1928), Vol. I, p. 471.

freedom to dissenters who were assisting in the struggle for political independence."[16] If it is true that taxation without representation is tyranny, the Baptists were not illogical in claiming "that the taxes imposed upon them for the support of a form of religion in which they could have no part was in sheer contradiction to the principle involved in this contention."[17] So active were they in the struggle for the establishment of the principle of the non-interference of the state with religion and the equality of all communions before the law, that "So far as this work was a work of intelligent conviction and religious faith, the chief honor of it must be given to the Baptists."[18] The political struggle had in fact become a part of their religion. While at "the widow Kembrough's" in North Carolina in 1784, Francis Asbury recorded in his *Journal*, "Here I was wonderfully entertained with a late publication by Silas Mercer, a Baptist preacher, in which he has anathematized the whole race of kings from Saul to George III." The less republican-minded Methodist bishop commented, "his is republicanism run mad."[19] Unchristian and undemocratic had become almost synonymous for the Baptists.

This identification of religion and politics which was so peculiar to the Baptists in the revolutionary era is more clearly brought out when we compare them with the

[16] Richard J. Purcell, *op. cit.*, p. 75.

[17] A. H. Newman, *A History of the Baptist Churches in the United States*, Vol. II in *The American Church History Series* (New York, 1894), p. 349.

[18] Leonard W. Bacon, *A History of American Christianity*, Vol. XIII in *The American Church History Series* (New York, 1897), p. 221.

Vide, A. H. Newman, *op. cit.*, Period II, Chapter VI, "Struggle for Civil and Religious Liberty in New England," and Chapter VII, "The Struggle for Liberty of Conscience in Virginia."

[19] Francis Asbury, *Journal* (New-York, 1821), Vol. I, p. 365.

Methodists. The latter were in a somewhat delicate position because of their affiliation with the movement in England and consequently found it advisable to divorce politics from religion. The Methodists had begun their activities in New York in 1766 when Philip Embury preached to a small group in his home. The work spread, especially to the South, after the arrival of Francis Asbury in 1771, but unlike the case of the Baptists the political situation was a hindrance instead of a help to their cause. Most of their preachers were Englishmen with British sympathies who had come to this country after political difficulties had begun in earnest, with the result that Methodists were naturally subjected to the suspicion of being disaffected to the cause of independence.[20] Many of their preachers returned to England during the war. John Wesley's dictum that "We are not republicans, and do not intend to be," was of no help to American Methodism.[21]

Except for politics, however, the Methodists had a great deal in common with the Baptists. They appealed to the same intellectual, economic, and social classes and both were democratic in their theology in the sense that Arminianism is more democratic than Calvinism. Their untutored clergy spoke the language of the people and made up in emotional appeal and enthusiasm what they lacked in scholarship and culture.

More important in numbers and influence than either Methodists or Baptists were the Presbyterians. This denomination owed its existence to a large degree to Scotch-

---

[20] Nathan Bangs, *A History of the Methodist Episcopal Church* (Third Edition, New-York, 1845), Vol. I, pp. 87, 118, 139; Francis Asbury, *op. cit.*, Vol. I, p. 132.

[21] Leonard W. Bacon, *op. cit.*, pp. 199-202; Nathan Bangs, *op. cit.*, Vol. I, pp. 122-123; William W. Sweet, "John Wesley, Tory," in *The Methodist Review*, April 1922, Vol. LXXI, pp. 255-268.

Irish immigration.   Since their first migration to New England in the early part of the eighteenth century did not mix well with the Puritans, the later immigration found its way to the more congenial atmosphere of the middle and south-Atlantic states and isolated Vermont. By far the largest number settled in the frontier valleys of the Alleghanies from the Catskills to Georgia.

By the beginning of the American Revolution, the Scotch-Irish were an influential element in every colony. They were not legally established as the official religion in any colony or state and hence not on the defensive on that account.   In fact, they were themselves the most militant of all dissenters.   Being primarily frontiersmen, they were outstandingly democratic, and their political liberalism was nurtured by a boundless hatred of the British.

Their religious orthodoxy, however, was in striking contrast to their political liberalism.   Their clergy, unlike their Puritan brethren who had been schooled at Harvard or at Yale, were not contaminated by current English Arianism.   They did not experience those subtle doubts which confronted the scholarly New England minister in his well-stocked study and they resisted firmly the prevalent tendency to deviation from the articles of faith. Those ardent revivalists of the Great Awakening, the Tennents, father and sons, were typical.   Gilbert Tennent, for example, in 1734, "insisted that there should be a closer scrutiny as to the evidences of a gracious and genuine religious experience" of candidates for the ministry.[22] After one Samuel Hemphill was convicted the following

[22] E. H. Gillett, *History of the Presbyterian Church in the United States of America* (Philadelphia, 1864), Vol. I, pp. 59-60.

year of preaching "downright Deism," the Synod took decisive measures while "devouring monsters" were "numerous abroad in the world" to guard the churches against "wolves in sheep's clothing" who were "invading the flock of Christ." [23]   Their religious principles, in short, and the circumstances and conditions of their environment contrived to make the Scotch-Irish Presbyterians the backbone of the movement which was to restore American religion to orthodoxy after the turn of the century.

Whereas the Baptists, Methodists, and Presbyterians were thus a liberal influence on American religious thought primarily from the point of view of democratizing the institutional and social aspects of religion, theological liberalism was largely the result of foreign influence. "Arianism, as well as Arminianism," says Professor Walker, "tinged the writings of some of the ablest theologians of that period, both within and without the Church of England, and the books of Thomas Emlyn, William Whiston, Samuel Clarke, Daniel Whitby, and John Taylor, in which this doctrine is implied or expressly asserted, were among the most valued treatises in English Dissenting circles during the first half of the eighteenth century. . . . These works crossed the Atlantic and naturally found most welcome in eastern Massachusetts, since that region, owing to its trade, the size of its seaports, and the acquaintance of its more prominent ministers, by correspondence at least, with the leading English Dissenters, was more susceptible to current English thought than southern and western New England." [24]

[23] E. H. Gillett, *op. cit.*, Vol. I, p. 67.
[24] Williston Walker, *Ten New England Leaders* (New York, 1901), pp. 297-298.

Boston and its vicinity particularly was hospitable to every radical influence from home or abroad. By the beginning of the eighteenth century, the latitudinarian tendencies at Harvard College were a factor of moment in inducing the faithful to the establishment of the seminary of learning at New Haven. Their careers show that Harvard men had been too freely exposed to deism. The young Rev. Robert Breck, for example, who occupied the pulpit in Springfield, Massachusetts, was accused in 1734 among other things of declaring, "What will become of the heathen who never heard of the gospel I do not pretend to say, but I cannot but indulge in a hope that God, in his boundless benevolence, will find out a way whereby those heathen who act up to the light they have may be saved." [25] Since such doctrines, variously denounced by the orthodox as Arminianism, Arianism, Pelagianism, Socinianism, and Deism, were openly avowed and championed, as President Quincy says, by "alumni of Harvard, active friends and advocates of the institution, and in habits of intimacy and professional intercourse with its governors," though their religious views received no public countenance from the College, circumstances nevertheless "gave color for reports which were assiduously circulated throughout New England, that the influences of the institution were not unfavorable to the extension of such doctrines." [26] Not unnaturally, the faithful feared and exaggerated the apostasy of Harvard College, but it was probably not a mere coincidence that Ebenezer Gay, Charles Chauncy,

---

[25] Franklin B. Dexter, "Thomas Clap and His Writings" in *Miscellaneous Historical Papers*, pp. 182-183. For a detailed account of the heresy of the Rev. Robert Breck, *vide*, Mason A. Green, *Springfield, 1636-1886, History of Town and City* (Springfield, 1888), pp. 228-258.

[26] Josiah Quincy, *op. cit.*, Vol. II, p. 52.

Jonathan Mayhew, James Freeman, and William Bentley, the exponents of the liberalism that gave birth to the Unitarian movement in America, were all Harvard graduates. In fact, deistic principles were openly proclaimed in 1755 with the establishment of the Dudleian lectures for "the proving, explaining, and proper use and improvement of the principles of Natural Religion." [27]

The history of the eighteenth century with respect to deism is the story of its gradual filtration from the philosopher to the common man. In Europe this process was already advanced and as the second half of the century established increased contacts between the two hemispheres, the common man in America was brought into contact with its principles.

Writing in 1759 relative to the probable effect of the last inter-colonial war on religion and morals, the Rev. Ezra Stiles of Newport noted: "I imagine the American Morals & Religion were never in so much danger as from our Concern with the Europeans in the present War. They put on indeed in their public Conduct the Mark of public Virtue—and the Officers endeavor to restrain the vices of the private Soldiery while on Duty. But I take it the Religion of the Army is Infidelity & Gratification of the appetites. . . . They propagate in a genteel & insensible Manner the most corrupting and debauching Principles of Behavior. It is doubted by many Officers if in fact the Soul survives the Body—but if it does, they ridicule the notion of moral accountableness, Rewards & Punishments in another life. . . . I look upon it that our Officers are in danger of being corrupted with vicious principles, & many of them I doubt not will in the End of the

[27] Josiah Quincy, op. cit., Vol. II, p. 139.

War come home minute philosophers initiated in the polite Mysteries & vitiated morals of Deism. And this will have an unhappy Effect on a sudden to spread Deism or at least Skepticism thro' these Colonies. And I make no doubt, instead of the Controversies of Orthodoxy & Heresy, we shall soon be called to the defence of the Gospel itself." [28]

"Stiles was right," says Dr. Purcell. "The British regular from the barracks, where loose morals and looser free thinking prevailed, proved a dangerous associate for the colonial militiaman. The rank and file were familiar with the Anglican Church of the Georges and the officers were frequently imbued with the prevalent continental philosophy or its echoed English rationalism. Their unorthodox thinking impressed men, and their philosophy was assiduously copied as having a foreign style. Thus the militiaman on returning from the campaign introduced his newly acquired habits of thinking and of life among the humble people of his town or wayside hamlet. Judging from the reported change in the religious tone of such a town as New Britain, no society was too secluded to escape the baneful contagion. Thus the infidel philosophy of the old world gained a foothold in the new." [29]

The Peace of Paris in 1763 opened the way for the spreading of even more dangerous religious influences. France was no longer feared as a political and religious rival in the New World. "Naturally enough during the

---

[28] Letter from Newport, R. I., September 24, 1759, quoted in I. Woodbridge Riley, *American Philosophy, the Early Schools* (New York, 1907), p. 215.

[29] Richard J. Purcell, *op. cit.*, pp. 7-8. *Cf.*, David N. Camp, *History of New Britain, Connecticut, 1640-1889* (New Britain, 1889), pp. 56-57; J. E. A. Smith, *The History of Pittsfield, (Berkshire County,) Massachusetts, from the Year 1800 to the Year 1876* (Springfield, 1876), pp. 57-58.

periods of war against Louis XIV and Louis XV," says Professor Jones, "French emigration to the British colonies was small. It seems clear, however, that upon the conclusion of the peace in 1763, numerous French soldiers of fortune, hair-dressers, dancing masters, adventurers, and ne'er-do-wells came to the New World." [30]

The French language gradually came to be more widely studied. At the College at Philadelphia, it had been on the curriculum since before the last inter-colonial war.[31] President Witherspoon is believed to have introduced it in the College of New Jersey after he became President in 1768.[32] In New York, John Haumaid is said to have taught French to some of the students of Kings College, but he was not a member of the faculty of that institution. At Newport, Rhode Island, the Rev. Ezra Stiles was visited by a young Frenchman, Mr. Lewis Delile, who was planning to teach French and fencing there.[33] Later Delile is believed to have taught French in Cambridge, Massachusetts, on his own account.[34]

[30] Howard M. Jones, *America and French Culture, 1750-1848* (Chapel Hill, N. C., 1927), p. 124.

[31] Charles H. Handschin, *The Teaching of Modern Languages in the United States* (United States Bureau of Education Bulletin, 1913, No. 3, Washington, 1913), pp. 13, 21, 22.

[32] John Maclean, *History of the College of New Jersey* (Philadelphia, 1877), Vol. I, p. 388.

[33] Ezra Stiles, *Literary Diary*, edited by Franklin B. Dexter (New York, 1901), November 13, 1771, Vol. I, p. 184.

[34] *Cf.*, Bernard Faÿ, *The Revolutionary Spirit in France and America* (New York, 1927), pp. 38-39; Charles H. Handschin, *op. cit.*, pp. 13, 16. Harvard had had an unfortunate experience with the teaching of French a good many years previously when in 1735 M. Longloissorie, who had been permitted by the President to teach French in the College, was reported as disseminating "certain dangerous errors." Although the investigating committee reported that these errors had not been embraced by others, the Overseers judged it "not consistent with the safety of the College that Mr. Longloissorie should continue to teach the French tongue there any longer."—Josiah Quincy, *op. cit.*, Vol. I, pp. 394-395, 574-576.

With the establishment of the French alliance, the French language increased in popularity. At William and Mary College, Governor Jefferson of Virginia established the first professorial chair in French in America,[35] and shortly after, it was taught at Harvard "to such students as their parents or guardians should permit." [36] The Rev. Mr. Tétard, who had previously taught French intermittently in New York, became Professor of French in Columbia College in 1784.[37] In the same year Rhode Island College solicited the aid of Louis XVI for the same purpose, writing in part: "Ignorant of the French language, . . . we too readily imbibed the prejudices of the English,—prejudices which we have renounced since we have had a nearer view of the brave army of France, who actually inhabited this College edifice; since which time our youth seek with avidity whatever can give them information respecting the character, genius, and influence of a people they have such reason to admire,—a nation so eminently distinguished for polished humanity. To satisfy this laudable thirst of knowledge, nothing was wanting but to encourage and diffuse the French language; . . . for spreading far and wide the history of the so celebrated race of kings, statesmen, philosophers, poets, and benefactors of mankind which France has produced." [38]

While the study of the language, the reading of French

---

[35] Charles H. Handschin, op. cit., pp. 17, 21.

[36] Josiah Quincy, op. cit., Vol. II, p. 275; Henry Adams, The Life of Albert Gallatin (Philadelphia, 1879), p. 42.

[37] Julia Post Mitchell, "Jean Pierre Tétard" in Columbia University Quarterly, June 1910, Vol. XII, pp. 286-289.

[38] Letter signed by the Chancellor and President of the College at Providence, R. I., January 9, 1784. Quoted in Reuben A. Guild, Early History of Brown University, including the Life, Times, and Correspondence of President Manning. 1756-1791 (Providence, 1897), p. 351.

books, and the dissemination of French thought thus gradually and naturally increased as a result of the alliance,
it was in spite of the traditions and customs of long standing. In New England, particularly, the clergy had a long
record of anti-Catholic sermons. Even so ardent a Whig
and so staunch a fighter for civil as well as religious liberty
as Jonathan Mayhew had delivered the Dudleian Lecture at Harvard in 1765 on "Popish Idolatry." [39] Gad
Hitchcock's "Discourse on the Man of Sin" (Boston,
1770) was typical of the Puritan tradition of abusing the
Pope and with him, France, his faithful ally.[40]

At Yale the students debated in one of their clubs,
"Whether the Alliance with France will be beneficial to
the Inhabitants of America." This was in July 1780.
Simeon Baldwin of the Class of 1781, speaking for the
negative, foresaw lamentable consequences. "Though the
Inhabitants of America will never introduce the Popish
Religion" of themselves, he said, the alliance will lead to
its introduction here, "& when once it has taken root; the
Liberty & Licences that are allowed, are so captivating it
will soon spread with universal acceptance among the
lo(o)ser & more vitious part of the People, & from them
to others of more note till great part of the Inhabitants
are tainted with it." A true son of the Puritans, he regretted the sad necessity of "introducing Foreigners who
deprive us of our Sacred rights & Religious duties, & lead
us on to Popery & destruction; who take away what little
Virtue we have & replace it with Luxury & Debauchery." [41]

To counteract these stumbling blocks inimical to an

---

[39] William B. Sprague, *Annals of the American Pulpit*, Vol. VIII, p. 26.
[40] Bernard Faÿ, *op. cit.*, p. 36.
[41] Simeon E. Baldwin, *Life and Letters of Simeon Baldwin* (New
Haven, [1919]), pp. 60-62.

effective spiritual as well as military alliance, Gerard and later La Luzerne, French ministers to the revolting colonies, made a deliberate attempt to overcome American prejudices against the French. They furnished articles to the newspapers and employed skilled writers and speakers to influence public opinion.

Among these was Thomas Paine. While Secretary of the Committee on Foreign Affairs, Paine accused Silas Deane, American commissioner to France, of attempt to defraud the United States. This alarmed the French minister in America and made it necessary for Paine to resign his position. Fearing that Paine would seek to avenge himself for the loss of his office, Gerard planned an antidote. Writing to Vergennes, January 17, 1779, he said in part, "The only remedy, my lord, I could imagine to prevent these inconveniences, and even to profit by the circumstances, was to have Payne offered a salary in the King's name, in place of that he had lost. He called to thank me, and I stipulated that he should publish nothing on political affairs, nor about Congress, without advising with me, and should employ his pen mainly in impressing on the people favorable sentiments towards France and the Alliance, of the kind fittest to foster hatred and defiance towards England. He appeared to accept the task with pleasure. I promised him a thousand dollars per annum, to begin from the time of his dismission by Congress." [42]

A few months later, May 29, 1779, Gerard informed Vergennes that the arrangement with Thomas Paine did not work. Paine was not the kind of man who could be

[42] Quoted in Moncure D. Conway, *The Life of Thomas Paine* (New York, 1892), Vol. I, p. 134.

bought and told what to do, as Gerard's statement seems
to indicate, "He gives me marks of friendship, but that
does not contribute to the success of my exhortations." [43]
Paine's version of the story is that he replied to Gerard's
offer in these words: "Any service I can render to either of
the countries in alliance, or to both, I ever have done and
shall readily do, and Mr. Gerard's *esteem* will be the only
compensation I shall desire." [44]

There were others, however, with whom the French
were more successful. The Rev. Samuel Cooper of
Boston, influential and prominent pastor of the Brattle
Street Church for forty years, was engaged on the terms
which had been offered to Thomas Paine. [45]   He had long
been known for his republican principles, but his Dudleian
lecture of 1774, "The Man of Sin," a diatribe against the
Papacy, makes his employment by Louis XVI peculiarly
ironical.   His sermons made New England churches ring
with the name of the King of France and Puritan congregations prayed for His Very Christian Majesty. [46]   It is
somewhat naïvely asserted that Cooper allowed his political activities to interfere with his pastoral duties and that
because of his neglect of his sermon preparation he became
notorious in clerical circles for his frequent pulpit ex-
changes. [47]   His interest in the French alliance may help
to explain the *raison d'être* of these pulpit wanderings.

[43] Moncure D. Conway, *op. cit.*, Vol. I, p. 135.
[44] *Ibid.*, Vol. I, p. 136.   M. Faÿ's (*op. cit.*, p. 133) version of this incident is that Paine accepted employment by the French on the terms mentioned.
[45] Alice M. Baldwin, *op. cit.*, pp. 93-94, 156-157.
[46] Bernard Faÿ, *op. cit.*, pp. 133-134.
[47] *Dictionary of American Biography*, edited by Allen Johnson and
Dumas Malone (New York, 1930), Vol. IV, pp. 410-411; *Cf.*, William B.
Sprague, *op. cit.*, Vol. I, p. 443.

These French influences did not, of course, result in making a Gallic nation out of the predominantly British colonies, but it need scarcely be suggested that the French alliance was not without influence on American religious thought. The mingling of American and French officers and soldiers was even more pernicious than that of the English had been in the French and Indian War. Denying where the English doubted, says Dr. Purcell, our French brothers-in-arms "were aggressively destructive rather than apologetic. As men of some learning and of an insinuating polished address, they were skillful proselytizers, answering arguments with a sneering smile or effective shrug. Thus, American officers imbibed the ideas of the continental philosophers without necessarily intimately knowing at first hand their writings." [48] Thomas Pickering is an example. "According to his own story, doubt had first come into his mind during the Revolutionary War one day when he heard General von Steuben express the deist ideas that he had received in France and say that he would believe more easily in an absurdity than in the Trinity." [49] Even at such a stronghold of Calvinism as Yale College, where the Corporation had not permitted the study of the French language,[50] President Stiles recorded subjects for senior debates which would scarcely have been debatable two decades previously. "Whether the Immortality of the Soul can be proved by Reason? The Seniors disputed it excellently & learnedly." [51]

[48] Richard J. Purcell, *op. cit.*, p. 9. *Cf.*, Robert E. Thompson, *A History of the Presbyterian Churches in the United States*, Vol. VI in *The American Church History Series* (New York, 1895), p. 58.

[49] Bernard Faÿ, *op. cit.*, p. 470.

[50] Ezra Stiles, *Literary Diary*, Vol. II, pp. 296-297; William L. Kingsley, *Yale College* (New York, 1879), Vol. I, p. 107.

[51] Ezra Stiles, *Literary Diary*, February 20, 1781, Vol. II, p. 512.

"Whether the historical parts of the Bible are of divine Inspiration?" [52] "Whether Virtue [is] founded in Opinion & human Law, or in eternal Fitness & immutable natural Law?" [53] "Whether Infidels & Libertines in Morals ought to be admitted into civil Magistracy?" [54] "Whether any Thing contradictory to Reason is to be found in the Scriptures?" [55]

The practical application of the tolerance implied in these discussions found particular expression in the newer status of Catholicism. M. Gerard, Ministre Plenipotentiaire de France, the first ambassador to the new republic, was of course a Catholic, and when Spain declared war against England in 1779, she too sent a representative to the American Congress, Señor Don Juan de Miralles. "Thus the first diplomatic circle at the American seat of government was Catholic, and openly so, for these envoys celebrated great events either in their own countries or in the United States, by the solemn services of the Catholic Church, to which we find them inviting the members of the Continental Congress and the high officers of the Republic." [56]

[52] Ezra Stiles, *op. cit.*, June 1, 1784, Vol. III, p. 123.
[53] *Ibid.*, June 28, 1785, Vol. III, p. 167.
[54] *Ibid.*, July 11, 1785, Vol. III, p. 167.
[55] *Ibid.*, June 11, 1787, Vol. III, p. 267.
[56] John G. Shea, *Life and Times of the Most Rev. John Carroll, . . . embracing the History of the Catholic Church in the United States, 1763-1815* (New York, 1888), pp. 165-166. The following invitation, for example, was extended by M. Gerard to the President and members of the Continental Congress:

M.
    Vous êtes prié de la part du Ministre Plenipotentiaire de France, d'assister au TE DEUM, qu'il fera chanter Dimanche 4 de ce Mois, à midi dans la Chapelle Catholique neuve pour celebrer l'Anniversaire de l'Independance des Etats Unis de l'Amerique.

A Philadelphie, le 2 Juillet, 1779.　　—John G. Shea, *op. cit.*, p. 171.

When the Spanish envoy, Señor Miralles, died in April 1780, the French minister, M. de La Luzerne, arranged a solemn requiem for the repose of his soul at St. Joseph's Church, Philadelphia, May 4, 1780. In a letter to Dr. Jeremy Belknap, dated June 27, 1780, Ebenezer Hazard describes this service as "the most striking instance of Catholicism I ever saw. . . . upon going into the church, I found there not only Papists, but Presbyterians, Episcopalians, Quakers, &c. The two chaplains to Congress (one a Presbyterian and the other a Churchman) were amongst the rest. I confess I was pleased to find the minds of people so unfettered with the shackles of bigotry." [57]

The same spirit expressed itself in Boston when a French priest in 1788 not only founded a Catholic church but asked for Protestant help to finish paying for it.[58] Both indignation and enthusiasm were aroused. Said *The Massachusetts Sentinel* for June 21, 1788: "Most of these happy results may be attributed to our independence and our alliance with our great and good ally, Louis of France, the protector of the rights of humanity against tyranny." [59] And this from Boston whose inhabitants had been so indignant in 1774 over the provisions of the Quebec Act! [60]

---

[57] Belknap Papers, *Collections of the Massachusetts Historical Society* (Boston, 1877), Fifth Series, Vol. II, pp. 61-62.

[58] The building had originally belonged to the French Huguenots. By 1748 their members had been Anglicized and assimilated by other churches, as Trinity and King's Chapel, and the building was sold with the proviso that it "be preserved for the sole use of a Protestant sanctuary forever. How little human provisions can control is shown by the fact that, in spite of the condition of sale, forty years later the Huguenot 'temple' was sold to the Roman Catholics, and mass was said within its walls by a Romish priest November 2, 1788."—Lucian J. Fosdick, *The French Blood in America* (New York, 1911), p. 167.

[59] Quoted in Bernard Faÿ, *op. cit.*, p. 220.

[60] *Vide*, John G. Shea, *op. cit.*, Ch. III, "The Quebec Act and its Influence on the English Colonies."

That the fathers who instituted the movement for political independence from Great Britain could have foreseen its social and religious consequences was of course out of the question. It may well be argued that the changes in American religious life of the second half of the eighteenth century would in the nature of things have come about, revolution or no revolution. But the student may more profitably concern himself with the problem of understanding the forces, conditions, and thought that actually existed and certain it is that in post-revolutionary America, the religious life was colored and variegated as never before. Nor is there any one simple explanation or causal factor. There was the natural disintegration or at least variation of the theocratic régime in New England, crumbling under the weight of its own worldly success. The seminaries of learning from Virginia to the North, intended for the training of pious youths for the sacred calling, were themselves insidiously corrupted with at least a mild and humanizing deism. Evangelical enthusiasm of the Great Awakening brought with it a democracy in religion disastrous to a learned and dignified clergy of whatever denomination. Association with European comrades-in-arms, first the British and then the French, impregnated the minds of American militiamen with principles sadly alien to the spiritual life. The rivalries and conflicting claims of divergent Protestant denominations made the supremacy and authority of any one of them less tenable or even impossible, as in the case of the Anglican Church. With loss of authority the enforcement of such quasi-political principles as Sabbath observance was relaxed. Diversity of sects all on an equal political footing, or striving to be so, made toleration necessary for political reasons—and toleration is at least a cousin of indifference. The idea of the equality of religions, if recognized as such, is fatal to fanaticism. With such forces as these abroad in the land, it is scarcely surprising that the starkest atheism was feared even if it did not exist.

CHAPTER I

ETHAN ALLEN, FREETHINKING REVOLUTIONIST

THE divers influences of the period from 1740 to 1780 on the religious life of the country and the interrelation of politics and religion are remarkably illustrated in the life and thought of "a full blooded Yankee," as Colonel Ethan Allen called himself.[1] He was born in Litchfield, Connecticut, on January 10, 1737, of typically restless, energetic, and ever-hopeful New England pioneers. Less than two years later, the family moved to the new town of Cornwall on the Housatonic River, about twenty miles northwest of Litchfield, where his childhood was spent in a log cabin.

Because of his intellectual tendencies, his father decided to send Ethan to college and arranged that he should prepare for college with the Rev. Jonathan Lee in the neighbouring town of Salisbury. The death of his father, however, unfortunately made the education of Ethan, the eldest son, impossible. At seventeen it became his duty to look after his mother, five brothers, and two sisters.

He remained ever conscious of his deficiency in formal training, and pursued his academic interests as best he could. "In my youth I was much disposed to contemplation," he tells us, "and at my commencement in manhood, I committed to manuscript such sentiments or arguments, as appeared most consonant to reason, least through

[1] Ethan Allen, *A Narrative of Col. Ethan Allen's Captivity* (Burlington, 1846), p. 48; first published in 1779.

the debility of memory my improvement should have been less gradual: This method of scribbling I practised for many years, from which I experienced great advantages in the progression of learning and knowledge, the more so as I was deficient in education, and had to acquire the knowledge of grammar and language, as well as the art of reasoning, principally from a studious application to it, which after all I am sensible, lays me under disadvantages, particularly in matters of composition. . . ." [2]

Ethan's boyhood fell in the period of the Great Awakening and it is not surprising therefore that he "was educated in what is commonly called the Armenian [sic] principles." Even at this early age, however, he rejected the doctrine of original sin,[3] although he still believed in "the infallibility of revelation." [4] While preparing for college in Salisbury, he came under the more radical influence of a deistical itinerant physician by the name of Thomas Young through whom he became acquainted with English freethought. By the time his father died, Ethan had become quite radical in his religious thinking. The story is told that he stood beside his father's grave and prayed that he would reveal to him whether there was a future life.[5]

His philosophical interests continued as the years passed. His constant questioning and complete lack of respect for ecclesiastical authority was characteristic of the bold and

[2] Ethan Allen, *Reason the Only Oracle of Man* (Bennington, 1784), Preface.

[3] *Ibid.*, p. 386.

[4] *Ibid.*, p. 387.

[5] John Pell, *Ethan Allen* (Boston, 1929), p. 7.

Mr. Pell says that Young was educated at Yale, "at a time when Locke and the Deists were all the rage among the youthful intellectuals there" (p. 14), but Young seems not to be mentioned in Franklin B. Dexter, *Biographical Sketches of the Graduates of Yale College with Annals of the College History, 1701-1815* (New York, 1885-1912), 6 vols.

venturesome frontier life. In the democratic atmosphere
of the frontier, not only is one man as good as another,
but his opinions are as valid as those of any other. In
such a real democracy there can be no distinction between
a man and his "betters"; no obeisance to learning or spe-
cialization in a community where everyone is a Jack-of-all-
trades. Allen's "presumptious way of reasoning upon all
subjects" is ascribed by President Sparks of Harvard
to "the habits acquired by his pursuits in a rude and uncultivated state of society." [6]

To the Arminian influences of the Great Awakening,
the British deism of Thomas Young, and the reaction of
dissatisfied frontiersmen against the Calvinism of their
betters, the Revolution added the influences resulting
from the French alliance. "My affections are French-
ified," wrote Ethan Allen joyously in 1779. "I glory in
Louis the sixteenth, the generous and powerful ally of
these states; am fond of a connection with so enterprising, learned, polite, courteous and commercial a nation,
and am sure that I express the sentiments and feelings of
all the friends to the present revolution. I begin to learn
the French tongue, and recommend it to my countrymen
before Hebrew, Greek or Latin, (provided but one of
them only are to be attended to) for the trade and commerce of these states in future must inevitably shift its
channel from England to France, Spain and Portugal;
and therefore the statesman, politician and merchant, need
be acquainted with their several languages, particularly
the French, which is much in vogue in most parts of Europe. Nothing could have served so effectually to illumi-

---

[6] Jared Sparks, *Life of Ethan Allen* in *The Library of American Biography* (Boston, 1834), Vol. I, p. 354.

nate, polish and enrich these states as the present revolution, as well as preserve their liberty. Mankind are naturally too national, even to a degree of bigotry, and commercial intercourse with foreign nations, has a great and necessary tendency to improve mankind, and erase the superstition of the mind by acquainting them that human nature, policy and interest, are the same in all nations, and at the same time they are bartering commodities for the conveniences and happiness of each nation, they may reciprocally exchange such part of their customs and manners as may be beneficial, and learn to extend charity and good will to the whole world of mankind." [7]

Allen's reaction to the various influences on American religious thought from Whitefield's revival through the Revolution are well illustrated in his most ambitious work, an octavo volume of 477 pages elaborately entitled, *Reason the Only Oracle of Man, or a Compenduous System of Natural Religion. Alternately Adorned with Confutations of a variety of Doctrines incompatible to it; Deduced from the most exalted Ideas which we are able to form of the Divine and Human characters, and from the Universe in General.*[8] The book is poorly written, as Allen himself well knew.[9] The long sentences lack clarity and emphasis and the repetition of his favorite ideas is tiresome, but these defects as a literary composition make it the more valuable as an exposition of the development of his thought. It is a collection of manuscripts which he had gradually compiled since his youth. He does not mention Thomas Young, but Mr. Pell believes that the book had originally been planned as a joint undertaking

[7] *Narrative*, pp. 116-117.
[8] Printed by Haswell & Russell, Bennington, 1784.
[9] *Oracles*, Preface.

designed to "shatter the smug platitudes of the Calvinists," [10] and that Allen had inherited Young's notes. [11] Henry Hall, an earlier biographer, explains that they had agreed that the one who outlived the other should publish the book. [12]

Ethan Allen, as we have already seen, belonged to a family which was not satisfied with the maintenance of the *status quo*. The established order in Connecticut was represented by the Congregational Church whose undemocratic principles were naturally repugnant to him. The doctrine "that the eternal damnation of a part of mankind greatly augments the happiness of the elect, who are represented as being vastly the less numerous," is evidence of "a diabolical temper of mind in the elect" besides involving an ignoble conception of God. "Who would imagine," he asks indignantly, "that the Deity conducts his providence similar to the detestable despots of the world? O *horrible* most *horrible impeachment* of Divine Goodness!" [13] If God has to save mankind from sin, it is not consistent with the perfections of God to assume that He will save some and not others, "whose circumstances may be supposed to be similar to, or more deserving than theirs, for equal justice cannot fail to apply in all cases in which equal justice demands it." [14]

As a practical military man, he saw advantages in the doctrine of fate to induce soldiers to face danger, "but that it should be introduced into peacable and civil life, and be patronized by any teachers of religion, is quite

[10] John Pell, *op. cit.*, p. 16.
[11] *Ibid.*, p. 226.
[12] Henry Hall, *Ethan Allen, the Robin Hood of Vermont* (New York, 1892), p. 21.
[13] *Oracles*, pp. 118-119.
[14] *Ibid.*, p. 470.

strange, as it subverts religion in general, and renders the teaching of it unnecessary: except among other necessary events it may be premised, that it is necessary that they teach that doctrine, and that I oppose it from the influence of the same law of fate, upon which thesis we are all disputing and acting in certain necessary circles, and if so, I make another necessary movement, which is, to discharge the public teachers of this doctrine, and expend their salaries in an oeconomical manner, which might better answer the purposes of our happiness, or lay it out in good wine or old spirits to make the heart glad, and laugh at the stupidity or cunning of those who would have made us mere machines." [15]

As a rule, his anti-clericalism is bounded by his dislike for the Calvinists and he is relatively kindly disposed toward Arminian clergymen, but there are occasional references to "priests" and "priestcraft" with a decided French flavor. Speaking of the depravity of human reason, for example, he says that "it is whispered about, that the first insinuation of it was from the Priests; (though the Arminian Clergymen in the circle of my acquaintance have exploded the doctrine). Should we admit the depravity of reason, it would equally affect the priesthood, or any other teachers of that doctrine, with the rest of mankind; but for depraved creatures to receive and give credit to a depraved doctrine, started and taught by depraved creatures, is the greatest weakness and folly imaginable, and comes nearer a proof of the doctrine of total depravity, than any arguments which have ever been advanced in support of it." [16] Such impositions, however, are to be

[15] *Ibid.*, pp. 96-97.　　　　[16] *Ibid.*, p. 185. *Cf.*, p. 340.

expected for "while we are under the tyranny of Priests, . . . it ever will be their interest, to invalidate the law of nature and reason, in order to establish systems incompatible therewith." [17]

Opposed as he thus was to Calvinistic determinism, Allen succeeds but imperfectly in establishing man's moral freedom. "All possible moral evil," he says, "that ever did or can take place in the infinitude of the creation of God, is neither more nor less than the deviation of moral agents from moral rectitude; and such deviations take place in consequence of a wrong and vicious use of liberty." [18] Does this imply a sinful nature in man, that, given the choice of good and evil, he chooses the latter and abuses his freedom? If so, it is more than faintly reminiscent of the book of Genesis. The explanation that men choose the evil "in consequence of an imperfect nature" [19] smacks even more of fatalism, since the individual's physical inheritance influences his moral nature and free will is operative only to the extent that he can control his inheritance. In general, however, Allen firmly believed in man's moral freedom. Man is free to choose between good and evil, but the religious man will choose the former for "conformity to moral rectitude, which is morality in the abstract, is the sum of all religion, that ever was or can be in the universe; as there can be no religion in that in which there is no moral obligation." [20]

---

[17] *Oracles*, p. 457.

[18] *Ibid.*, p. 380.

[19] *Ibid.*, p. 132. "When I was a boy, by one means or other, I had conceived a very bad opinion of Pharoah, . . . but after a few years of maturity, and examination of the history of that monarch, given by Moses, . . . I conceived a more favorable opinion of him, inasmuch as we are told that God raised him up, and hardened his heart, and predestinated his reign, his wickedness and overthrow."—*Ibid.*, pp. 104-105.

[20] *Ibid.*, pp. 468-469.

In addition to moral evil, which is at least partially subject to man's will, there are natural evils in a physical
world governed by immutable natural laws. These are
unavoidable. "The period of life is very uncertain," he
says sadly, "and at the longest is but short: a few years
bring us from infancy to manhood, a few more to dissolution; pain, sickness and death are the necessary consequences of animal life. Through life we struggle with
physical evils, which eventually are certain to destroy our
earthly composition. . . ." [21]

Speculations of this kind can scarcely fail to lead to
other theological difficulties. Through Thomas Young,
Allen had a second-hand acquaintance with Charles
Blount, the English deist (1654-1693), and such problems
of higher criticism as how Eve found thread to stitch her
fig leaves and how the serpent learned to talk.[22] But
Allen followed this line of thought more seriously.

It must be remembered, of course, that his scepticism
was provoked by an unmitigatedly literal interpretation of
the Bible, with the result that his first reaction took the
form of the usual satirical gibes at the Old Testament.
Moses especially fared badly at the higher criticism of this
frontiersman.[23] Not only is he sceptical of him as "the

---

[21] *Ibid.*, p. 472. *Cf.*, p. 140.

[22] Charles Blount, *The Oracles of Reason* (London, 1693), pp. 38-39,
44. ". . . what more perplexes me is, how out of only one Rib the whole
Mass of a Womans Body could be built?"—Charles Blount, *op. cit.*, p. 33.

[23] Unlike the freethinkers of the nineteenth century, Allen seems to have
overlooked David, but Solomon seems to have interested him. "His Song
of Songs appears to be rather of the amorous kind, and is supposed to have
been written at the time he was making love to the daughter of Pharaoh
king of Egypt, who is said to have been a princess of exquisite beauty and
exceeding coy, and so captivated his affections that it made him light
headed, and sing about the '*joints of her thighs*' and '*her belly.*' "—*Oracles*,
p. 314.

only historian in the circle of my reading, who has ever given the public a particular account of his own death," [24] but he accuses him of ingratiating himself into the esteem of the Israelites "by the stratagem of prayer, and pretended intimacy with God; he acquaints us, that he was once admitted to a sight of his Back Parts. . . ." Moses' story of the fall of man gives an ignoble conception of God. "To suppose that the craft of Hell, by the interposition of its infernals, should have been permitted by divine providence to have been exerted against a premised new made couple, is inadmissable. It appears from Moses, that they were destitute of learning or instruction, having been formed at full size, in the space of one day, and consequently void of experience; from hence we may with propriety infer, that they would have been but poorly able to cope with the wiles of the Devil who in this progressive age of the world is allowed to be more than a match for any one man (especially if in connection with a woman)." [25]

However, he shows some real insight into the significance of these stories. The stories of how "God waxed wroth with Israel, and how Moses prayed for them" to appease God's wrath, Allen interprets as "footsteps by which we may trace sacerdotal dominion to its source and

---

[24] *Oracles*, pp. 301-302.

[25] *Ibid.*, p. 376. *Cf.*, Charles Blount, *op. cit.*, pp. 40-41: ". . . if you say, that all this proceded from the ignorance and weakness of a Woman, 'twould on the other side, have been but just, that some good Angels should have succoured a poor Ignorant weak Woman, those Just Guardians of human affairs would not have permitted so unequal a conflict; for what if an Evil Spirit, crafty and knowing in business, had by his subtlety overreached a poor silly Woman, who had not as yet seen the Sun either rise or set, who was but newly come of the Mould, and wholly unexperienced in all things? Certainly a Person who had so great a price set on her head, as the Salvation of all Mankind might well have deserved a Guard of Angels."

explore its progress in the world." [26] "It seems," he adds
with fine irony, "that God had the power, but Moses had
the dictation of it. . . ." [27]

More significant than either his satiric attack on the
Old Testament or his insight into the meaning of its
stories is his exposition of the relation of the Decalogue
to the law of nature. Those of the commandments associated with Moses which are in harmony with the laws of
nature are moral and good and their violation is detri-
mental to the best interests of men, as all violations of the
rules of nature are. In so far as the laws of Moses are
worth while, however, Allen thinks that such moral precepts "were previously known to every nation under
heaven, and in all probability by them as much practised
as by the tribes of Israel. Their keeping the seventh day
of the week as a sabbath, was an arbitrary imposition of
Moses (as many other of his edicts were) and not included
in the law of nature." [28] The knowledge of the law of
nature is acquired through reason, and in so far as men
are correctly guided by reason their conduct is moral—
Moses or the Ten Commandments notwithstanding.

These imperfections in the Bible and the fact that "the
Pagan, Jewish, Christian and Mahometan countries of
the world have been overwhelmed with a multiplicity of
revelations diverse from each other, and which, by their
respective promulgators, are said to have been immediately
inspired into their souls, by the spirit of God, . . . and

[26] *Oracles*, p. 278.
[27] *Ibid.*, p. 279.
[28] *Ibid.*, pp. 191-192.
"It was unfortunate for the Israelite who was accused of gathering
sticks on the Israelitish Sabbath, that he was convicted of it; for though
by the law of his people he must have died, yet the act for which he suffered was no breach of the law of nature."—*Ibid.*, p. 309.

which, in doctrine and discipline, are in most respects repugnant to each other, it fully evinces their imposture, and authorizes us, without a lengthy course of arguing, to determine with certainty, that not more than one if any one of them, had their original from God; as they clash with each other; which is ground of high probability against the authenticity of each of them." [29]

This, he thinks, is borne out by "every commentary and annotation on the Bible." "What an idle phantom is it for mortals to assay to illustrate and explain to mankind, that which God may be supposed to have undertaken to do, by the immediate inspiration of his spirit? Do they understand how to define or explain it better than God may be supposed to have done? This is not supposable; upon what ground then do these multiplicity of comments arise, except it be pre-supposed that the present translations of the Bible have, by some means or other, become fallible and imperfect, and therefore need to be rectified and explained? and if so, it has lost the stamp of divine authority; provided in its original composition it may be supposed to have possessed it." [30]

If it is objected in favor of revelation that parts of the Bible have been preserved in its original inspiration, "who but God can tell us, which part it is?" [31] "For the scriptures must be considered as being either fallible or infallible, since there is no third way or mean between these two; for that which is not absolutely infallible and perfect, is fallible and imperfect; and since the present translation of the Bible is manifestly of the latter of these characters, it

---

[29] *Oracles*, pp. 473-474.
[30] *Ibid.*, pp. 445-446.
[31] *Ibid.*, pp. 437-438.

is not authorized to control human reason; but on the other hand, reason ought to control the Bible, in those particulars in which it may be supposed to deviate from reason." [32] Or as he expressed it on another occasion more forcibly, if more crudely, "Was it not that we were rational creatures, it would have been as ridiculous to have pretended to have given us a Bible, for our instruction in matters of religion or morality, as it would to a stable of horses." [33]

This applies to the New as well as to the Old Testament: "As chimerical as Moses's representation of the apostacy of man manifestly appears to be, yet it is the very basis, on which christianity is founded, and is announced in the New Testament to be the very cause why Jesus Christ came into the world, '*that he might destroy the works of the Devil,*' and redeem fallen man, *alias,* the elect, from the condemnation of the apostacy. . . ." [34] "We cannot be miserable for the sin of Adam, or happy in the righteousness of Christ, in which transactions we were no ways accessory or assisting as accomplices, or otherwise concerned; and are not at all conscious of those antient matters. . . . What have those old and obsolete matters to do with our virtues or vices, or with our consciousness of righteousness or wickedness, happiness or misery, reward or blame?" [35] We are sharers neither of the sin of Adam nor in salvation by the blood of the Lamb but "must finally adopt the old proverb, *viz.* every tub stands upon its own bottom." [36] The Christian epic, therefore, is no more sacred to Allen than the Hebraic tradition. "That

[32] *Ibid.,* p. 440.
[33] *Ibid.,* p. 196.
[34] *Ibid.,* pp. 383-384.
[35] *Ibid.,* pp. 397-398.
[36] *Ibid.,* p. 390.

Jesus Christ was not God is evident from his own words," [37] besides being "impossible and contradictory . . . for God and man are not and cannot be one and the same. . . ." [38] "The doctrine of the Trinity is destitute of foundation, and tends manifestly to superstition and idolatry." [39] "The doctrine of the *incarnation* itself, and the *virgin mother*, does not merit a serious confutation and therefore is passed in silence, except the mere mention of it." [40] Regarding the atonement, he says, ". . . there could be no justice or goodness in one being's suffering for another, nor is it at all compatible with reason to suppose, that God was the contriver of such a propitiation." [41]

The Bible, in short, is neither infallible nor a miraculous revelation of the will of God. But Allen does not wish to be too severe a critic and remarks that, "it must be acknowledged, that those ancient writers laboured under great difficulties in writing to posterity merely from the consideration of the infant state of learning and knowledge, then in the world, and consequently we should not act the part of severe critics with their writings, any further than to prevent their obtrusion on the world as being infallible." [42]

Naturally enough, Ethan Allen's philosophical career began with the negation of the religious beliefs of Calvinism and his own principles were a later development. He was, as he says, generally "denominated a Deist, the reality of which I never disputed, being conscious I am no Christian, except mere infant baptism makes me one; and as to being a Deist, I know not strictly speaking, whether I am one or not, for I have never read their writ-

---

[37] *Oracles,* p. 352.
[38] *Ibid.,* p. 418.
[39] *Ibid.,* p. 352.

[40] *Ibid.,* p. 356.
[41] *Ibid.,* p. 413.
[42] *Ibid.,* pp. 74-75. *Cf.,* pp. 197, 199.

ings. . . ." [48] If a deist is by definition a believer in God, the appellation is appropriate to Allen. Interestingly enough, however, this belief had to be accepted on faith rather than on reason. Reason, for Allen, is the correct interpretation of sense impressions. However, since "the eternal cause of all things is not corporeal, and therefore cannot come within the notice of our senses," [44] Allen is driven to an *a posteriori* concept of God. [45] God, he says, is disclosed to our minds through a sense of dependency, and he then proceeds to explain that the nature of God is revealed to man through reason and the "ratiocination on the succession of causes and events." [46] The finite mind of man, in other words, cannot comprehend the infinite, but aspects of God are revealed to man as man correctly interprets the order of nature. "As far as we understand nature, we are become acquainted with the character of God; [47] for the knowledge of nature is the revelation of God. If we form in our imagination a compenduous idea of the harmony of the universe, it is the same as calling God by the name of harmony, for there could be no har-

[43] *Ibid.*, Preface.

Mr. Alexander Kadison takes Professor Riley to task for representing Allen as saying, "I am no Calvinist" instead of, as it should be, "I am no Christian."—*Cf.*, I. Woodbridge Riley, *American Philosophy, the Early Schools*, p. 46; Alexander Kadison, "An Unfamiliar Figure in American Rationalism" in *The Rationalist Press Association Annual for the Year 1926* (London), p. 79.

[44] *Oracles*, p. 156.

[45] "God . . . could never have been known but by reasoning from effects to their cause."—*Oracles*, p. 156.

[46] *Ibid.*, p. 28. *Cf.*, p. 45.

[47] His concept of God can perhaps be best described in an anecdote told of his second marriage. When Judge Moses Robinson, who performed the ceremony, asked him whether he promised to live with Fanny "agreeable to the laws of God," Ethan hesitated, looked out of the window, and exclaimed, "The law of God as written in the great book of nature? Yes. Go on."—Quoted in John Pell, *op. cit.*, p. 245.

mony without regulation, and no regulation without a regulator, which is expressive of the idea of God." [48]   In so
far as man is correctly informed regarding the world of
nature, the human mind resembles the divine. "To know
a thing is the same as to have right ideas of it, or ideas
according to truth, and truth is uniform in all rational
minds, the divine mind not excepted." [49]

Like Allen's belief in God, his faith in immortality reveals even more forcibly his willingness to assume its
rationality.   Immortality obviously cannot be verified by
the senses nor explained by a cause and effect relationship.
But his optimism was greater than his insistence on reason.
"The providence of God," he says, "has been abundantly
and conspicuously displayed towards us in this life, on
which we may with great assurance, predicate our darling
and important hope of immortality. Ungrateful and foolish it must be for rational beings in the possession of
existence, and surrounded with a kind and almighty providence, to distrust the author thereof concerning their
futurity, because they cannot comprehend the mode or
manner of their succeeding and progressive existence." [50]
"When we consider the eternity and infinity of God, and
of his creation and providence, and that his ultimate design in the whole, must have been to exalt and happify
the moral world, that human life is but a presage and
pre-requisite existence for an introduction into another
more dignified in the order of being: those vain and idle
distrusts of our immortality will vanish, and our minds
will be established in a firm reliance on God, that in the
order of nature and course of his providence, (however

[48] *Oracles*, p. 30.   [50] *Ibid.*, p. 158.
[49] *Ibid.*, p. 36.

inconceivable to us) he has secured our immortality." [51]

This expression of faith would do justice to a more conventional religious devotee than Ethan Allen whom even the relatively tolerant Ezra Stiles described as a "profane & impious Deist." [52] But it also shows that Allen was less skeptical of his own revelations than of others whom he had in mind when he said, "we must be able to analyse, distinguish, and distinctly seperate the premised divine reflections, illuminations, or inspiration, from our own natural cogitations, for otherwise we should be liable to mistake our reflections and reasonings for God's inspiration, as is the case with enthusiasts, or fanatics, and thus impose on ourselves, and obtrude our romantic notions on mankind, as God's revelation." [53]

Deducing from the goodness of God the pleasing prospect of immortality, he naturally provokes the question as to the relation of our mundane existence to the life hereafter. Are we responsible for the evil that we do? Allen says, yes, for "moral evil [unlike natural evil] may be prevented or remedied by the exercise of virtue. Morality is therefore of more importance to us than any or all other attainments; as it is a habit of mind, which, from

[51] *Ibid.*, pp. 158-159.
[52] Ezra Stiles, *Literary Diary*, February 27, 1789, Vol. III, p. 345. Allen had expected this kind of criticism. "Such of mankind," he said, "as break the fetters of their education, remove such other obstacles as are in their way, and have the confidence publicly to talk rational, exalt reason to its just supremacy, and vindicate truth and the ways of God's providence to men; are sure to be stamped with the epithet of irreligious, infidel, prophane, and the like. . . . So that all the satisfaction the honest man can have while the superstitious are squibbing hell fire at him, is to retort back upon them that they are priest ridden."—*Oracles*, p. 468.
"I ask no favours at the hands of philosophers, divines or Critics, but hope and expect they will severely chastise me for my errors and mistakes, least they may have a share in perverting the truth, which is very far from my intention."—*Ibid.*, Preface.
[53] *Oracles*, p. 221.

a retrospective consciousness of our agency in this life, we should carry with us into our succeeding state of existence, as an acquired appendage to our rational nature, and as the necessary means of our mental happiness." [54]   As virtue leads to happiness, so moral evil has the opposite effect.   ". . . the vicious, who have violated the laws of reason and morality, lived a life of sin and wickedness, and are at as great a remove from a rational happiness as from moral rectitude; such incorigible sinners, at their commencing existence in the world of spirits, will undoubtedly have opened to them a tremendous scene of horror, self-condemnation and guilt, with anguish of mind; the more so, as no sensual delights can there (as in this world) divert the mind from its conscious guilt; the clear sense of which will be the more pungent, as the mind in that state will be greatly enlarged, and consequently more capaciously susceptible of sorrow, grief and conscious woe, from a retrospective reflection of a wicked life. . . ." [55]

At this point, Allen's optimism and democracy come to the rescue to save the sinner from this intellectual hell by making it a sort of temporary purgatory.   He says, "we have reason to hope and believe, through the wisdom of divine government, they may in some limited period of duration have a contrition for and detestation of sin and vanity, the procuring cause of their punishment, and be reclaimed from viciousness and restored to virtue and happiness." [56]   After all, however, the insufficiency of human understanding is such that we can know very little about future "rewards and punishments, or of the extent of them, except that they cannot be perpetual or eternal." [57]   "To suppose that our eternal circumstances

---

[54] *Oracles*, pp. 472-473.
[55] *Ibid.*, p. 132.
[56] *Ibid.*, p. 132.
[57] *Ibid.*, p. 133.

will be unalterably fixed in happiness or misery, in consequence of the agency or transactions of this temporary
life, is inconsistent with the moral government of God,
and the progressive and retrospective knowledge of the
human mind. God has not put it into our power to plunge
ourselves into eternal woe and perdition; human liberty
is not so extensive. . . ." [58] As Universalism, this religion of optimism was just beginning to become popular
at this time on New England's frontier.

Apparently having in mind some individuals for whom
the milder tenets of Universalism offer too kind a fate, he
postulates that the corrupt soul may continue to sin even
in the hereafter, "in consequence of an imperfect nature,"
and thus be "eternally subjected to agency and trial, and
consequently to alternate happiness and misery. . . ." [59]
His was a doctrine as romantic as that of some of his fellow
New Englanders who concluded that eternal punishment
in Calvin's hell of fire and brimstone was merited by the
everlasting sinning of the damned. [60] As a matter of fact,
Allen's characteristic enthusiasm at times betrayed him into
actually gloating over the reality of the old-fashioned Calvinistic hell to which he delighted to consign his Tory
enemies. In his *Narrative* he speaks of "one Joshua Loring, an infamous tory, who was commissary of prisoners. . . . This Loring is a monster!—There is not his like
in human shape. . . . He is the most mean spirited, cow-

[58] *Ibid.*, p. 130.
[59] *Ibid.*, p. 132.
[60] Herbert W. Schneider, *The Puritan Mind* (New York, 1930), p. 233.
"The course of Sin, begun here, may continue forever. . . . The misery,
produced here by Sin, may be unceasingly generated by the same wretched
cause, through ages which cannot end."—Timothy Dwight, *The Nature
and Danger, of Infidel Philosophy, exhibited in Two Discourses, addressed
to the Candidates for the Baccalaureate, in Yale College, September 9th,
1797* (New-Haven, 1798), pp. 92-93.

ardly, deceitful, and destructive animal in God's creation below, and legions of infernal devils, with all their tremendous horrors, are impatiently ready to receive Howe and him, with all their detestable accomplices, into the most exquisite agonies of the hottest region of hell fire." [61]

These seemingly incompatible views make it difficult to classify neatly Allen's views of immortality. Morality implied for him the freedom of man to choose between good and evil, right and wrong, and man was responsible for his choice. The responsibility for choosing evil, however, did not extend to the hereafter; at least not in the Calvinistic sense of the everlasting misery of the damned, although his emotionalism at times betrayed him to consign his enemies to even that extreme. Cold, logical reasoning, the ideal of his religion, successfully eluded Allen's grasp all too frequently.

These intellectual traits indicate that Allen's thinking was keener in detecting the weaknesses of the established New England religion than in establishing the positive side of his own belief. His *Compenduous System of Natural Religion* is not to be mistaken for a philosophical system,[62] but it is significant as a reflection of the influences brought to bear on the religious thought of New England. Beginning with Arminianism which was itself more democratic than Calvinism in widening the opportunities for

---

[61] *Narrative,* p. 105.

When Universalism was first introduced into Vermont shortly after the Revolution, "John Norton, the Westminster tavernkeeper, said to Ethan Allen: 'That religion will suit you, will it not, General Allen?' Allen, who knew Norton to be a secret tory, replied in utter scorn: 'No! no! for there must be a hell in the other world for the punishment of tories.' "—Henry Hall, *op. cit.,* pp. 203-204.

[62] Mr. Kadison's statement that it is, "in its way, a masterpiece of clear and direct reasoning," would probably be regarded as an overstatement by most readers.—Alexander Kadison, *op. cit.,* p. 77.

salvation, he was soon led under the tutelage of Thomas Young to the rejection of the Bible itself. Perhaps even the modern reader will concur in Allen's own estimate of himself when he said he was conscious "I am no Christian." [63] His devotion to reason, however, was religious rather than philosophical. "The knowledge of the being, perfections, creation and providence of God, and of the immortality of our souls, is the foundation of religion." [64] These are the principles of the Deist faith, and to-day they might be sufficient to stamp Allen a Christian; they are certainly not the conclusions of a reasoned philosophical system.

It is difficult to estimate the extent of the influence of the *Oracles* on the thought of the time. Dr. Purcell is inclined to believe that because of "Allen's popularity in Vermont, his Revolutionary services, and his Litchfield birth," the book was read throughout New England and that the very fact of its publication alone would incline one to doubt that there was a genuine general aversion to deism.[65] Mr. Pell tells us that, "A copy reached Goshen and created so much interest in that town that a group of people delegated Ephraim Starr to write to Ethan and find out if he would send them a few copies in return for goods from Ephraim's store, as they had no cash." [66]

The largest factor restricting its circulation was undoubtedly the fire in Haswell's (the printer's) garret which Mr. Evans estimates to have destroyed the entire edition with the exception of about thirty copies.[67] This is

---

[63] *Oracles*, Preface.

[64] *Ibid.*, p. 473.

[65] Richard J. Purcell, *op. cit.*, pp. 13-14.

[66] John Pell, *op. cit.*, p. 253.

[67] Charles Evans, *American Bibliography* (Chicago, 1910), Vol. VI, p. 266.

possibly an overstatement of the loss,[68] but certainly the
book is excessively rare to-day. An abridged edition was
published in New York in 1836 and another in Boston in
1854, but it has never been reprinted in its entirety. The
fire also of course lent itself to the interpretation by the
orthodox as a judgment from Heaven and gave color to
clerical opposition.[69] Tradition has it, according to the
introduction to the edition of 1836, that Haswell himself
consigned what remained of the edition to the flames and
joined the Methodists. Mr. Gilman characterizes the
story as a romance,[70] but it is true in spirit if not in fact.
The victory over Allen's infidelity was not to be won by
the Calvinism which had provoked his work, but by those
more democratic and emotional denominations whose
promises the unlettered frontiersmen could comprehend
more readily than Allen's quasi-philosophy. Allen himself was an extremely vigorous and powerful personality
and his lack of education was probably an advantage in his
association with pioneers in a wilderness where bears were
a great deal more numerous than college graduates. It
may have made his leadership more easy.[71] His learned
contemporary, the Rev. Samuel Williams, LL.D., de-

---

[68] *Cf.*, John Pell, *op. cit.*, p. 314.

[69] The clergy and church people did not like Allen very much. "He
dearly loved to shock their opinions, and heckle their most hallowed asso-
ciations. Riding one cold, frosty morning on his great horse, from Sunder-
land into the street of Manchester and meeting his friend, Deacon Isaac
Burton, he exclaimed: 'Good morning, Deacon! we need a little of your
brisk hell-fire about our ears this morning.' He doubtless enjoyed it infinitely, but the deacon did not."—Edward S. Isham, *Ethan Allen, A Study
of Civic Authority* in *Proceedings of the Vermont Historical Society*, 1898,
p. 66.

[70] M. D. Gilman, *The Bibliography of Vermont* (Burlington, 1897),
p. 6.

[71] Robert D. Benedict, *Ethan Allen's Use of Language* in *Proceedings
of the Vermont Historical Society*, 1901-1902, p. 71.

scribes him as, "bold, enterprising, ambitious, with great confidence in his own abilities," and explains that "the uncultivated roughness of his own temper and manners" was well adapted to his environment "where all was a scene of violence and abuse." [72] His writings reflect the strength as well as the crudeness of the frontier. His best passages are his unphilosophical but vigorous denunciations of those "disgustingly absurd" principles of Calvinism which would punish or reward men for their destined actions,[73] or his abhorrence of "the tricks and imposture of Priests" who since the "non-age" of the world have selfishly worked "to invalidate the law of nature and reason, in order to establish systems incompatible therewith." [74]

To understand this speculative frontiersman and his extraordinary career in "mining, manufacturing, real estate, fighting, imprisonment, statesmanship, diplomacy, farming and philosophy," [75] it must always be remembered that he was first and foremost a fighter for freedom. He is an example, extreme to be sure, of what "the free air of the wilderness" was finally to do to the religious principles which his Puritan ancestors had brought with them long ago. Not that he officiated at the death of the last vestige of Calvinism, but he stands as a symbol of revolt against Old World domination in religion as well as

[72] Samuel Williams, *The Natural and Civil History of Vermont* (Walpole, N. H., 1794), p. 219.

[73] *Oracles,* p. 91; cf., supra, p. 32.

[74] *Ibid.,* pp. 456-457.

[75] Ethan Allen, *A Narrative . . . with An Introductory Note by John Pell, Esq.* (New York, 1930), p. xv.

The English comedian, John Bernard, seems to have caught the spirit of the man when he describes Allen as "a graft of the old Cromwellian, psalm-singing, cut-and-thruster upon the free-and-easy, bibacious cavalier; alternately swearing and praying; singing hymns and anacrontics; sending people upwards and downwards."—John Bernard, *Retrospections of America, 1797-1811* (New York, 1887), p. 114.

in politics. "His abandonment of accepted dogma," says his latest biographer, "belongs in the same category as his abandonment of the Crown. If there was any dominant factor in his philosophy of life, it was the love of liberty. He was the slave of Freedom." [76] His substitution of Deism for Calvinism was destined to fail, but the political and religious emancipation from the Old World in politics and religion in the era of the American Revolution prepared the soil for the growth and finally the dominance during the nineteenth century of those peculiarly American religious societies which, as Professor Rusk puts it, were to succeed on America's vast frontier "in inverse ratio to their intellectual attainments, and in direct ratio to their emotional appeal." [77]

To this day the catalogue of the Library of Congress describes the *Oracles* in the words of President Dwight of Yale as "the first formal publication, in the United States, openly directed against the Christian religion." [78] But to a careful and more objective reader, with the advantage of over a century's perspective, "Ethan Allen's Bible" [79] is no longer as un-Christian as it once was and its professedly reasonable faith is smugly professed by respectable Christians, who at the same time gloat over the collapse of infidelity.

[76] John Pell, *op. cit.*, p. 228.

[77] Ralph L. Rusk, *The Literature of the Middle Western Frontier* (New York, 1925), Vol. I, p. 46.

[78] Timothy Dwight, *Travels in New-England and New-York* (London, 1823), Vol. II, p. 388.

[79] It was also known as the "Rhode Island Bible," an appellation incidentally indicative of that state's religious reputation.

CHAPTER II

ELIHU PALMER, MILITANT DEIST

PERHAPS the most distinguishing characteristic of the American Revolution was its conservatism. It had, to be sure, its social implications, particularly in the extension of religious toleration, but it was obviously not a class struggle. It achieved independence from a reigning monarch, but unlike the French Revolution, it was not fought over the principle of monarchism. Radical as he was, Ethan Allen wrote of Louis XVI in 1779, as "His Most Christian Majesty, who in Europe shines with a superior lustre in goodness, policy and arms, . . . the illustrious potentate, auspiciously influenced by Heaven to promote the reciprocal interest and happiness of the ancient kingdom of France, and the new and rising states of America." [1]

Our allies, the French, however, under the influence of their philosophers, astoundingly idealized the issues between England and her American colonies. With the aid of Rousseau's ideas of the simple life, the state of nature, and the social contract, reinforced by the general absence of facts of American affairs, they envisaged a struggle of a simple, agrarian people for freedom from the chains of a perverse, Old World monarchy. "Heroic country," wrote the Abbé Raynal, "my advanced age permits me not to visit thee. Never shall I see myself amongst the respect-

[1] Ethan Allen, *Narrative*, pp. 114-115.

able personages of thy Areopagus; never shall I be present
at the deliberations of thy congress. I shall die without
having seen the retreat of toleration, of manners, of laws,
of virtue, and of freedom. My ashes will not be covered
by a free and holy earth: but I shall have desired it; and
my last breath shall bear to heaven an ejaculation for thy
prosperity." [2]

Washington became the Fabius of the New World,
brave, calm, enlightened, and modest, working the will of
the American people. "Along with Washington went the
image of William Penn and the legend of the Quakers,
a people so pious without priests or churches, so virtuous
without dogmas. This legend already existed for a group
of intellectuals and philosophers, but it became popular
especially through Franklin, whose simple manners and
modest dignity were taken for Quakerisms. Franklin was
the prototype in accord with which all other images were
formed. People saw in him and Penn the deist sage, and
in Washington the prudent and heroic patriot." [3]

This flattering interpretation of the American Revolution found a ready acceptance as it filtered to the New
World during the 1780's. Americans naturally enough

---

[2] Abbé Raynal, *The Revolution of America* (London, 1781), p. 92.
The same idealized interpretation of America is expressed by M. de Warville. J. P. Brissot de Warville, *New Travels in the United States of
America. Performed in 1788* (Boston, 1797). For a full discussion and
bibliography of contemporary French literature about the United States,
see Bernard Faÿ, *The Revolutionary Spirit in France and America, passim.*

[3] Bernard Faÿ, *op. cit.*, pp. 144-145. *Cf.*, Bernard Faÿ, *Franklin, the
Apostle of Modern Times* (Boston, 1929), pp. 436-440, 495.

"So schafft das vorrevolutionäre und revolutionäre Frankreich ein Bild
Amerikas nach dem eigenen Ebenbilde und Idealbilde. Es wiederholt die
Aufgabe, die es ein Menschenalter zuvor England gegenüber erfüllt hatte.
Damals hatten die Franzosen auf der Suche nach Reform der heimischen
Missstände unter Montesquieus Führung die englische Verfassung ent-
deckt, rationalisiert, idealisiert und zum allgemeingültigen Vorbild erhoben.

were willing to rationalize and idealize their emancipation, particularly in view of the fact that the aftermath of the war was very disappointing indeed.[4] Unfortunate economic conditions tended to emphasize the division between conservatives and radicals. For men like John Adams and Alexander Hamilton revolutionary activity ended with the peace. The French influence, on the other hand, made an ideal of democracy itself which went beyond political independence from Great Britain. When Thomas Jefferson succeeded Dr. Franklin in Paris in 1784, "he learned to hate the power of the aristocracy and clergy, which till then he had opposed without any irritation; it was in Paris that, swept along by the philosophical torrent of the eighteenth century, this naturally adventurous intelligence became audacious to a degree bordering on madness."[5]

It remained for the French Revolution, however, to give emotional stimulus to American political demarcation, to lift the principles of democracy from the realm of the prosaic, the mundane, and even the practical to the heights of philosophic idealism. It was to be expressed in poetry and song, in banquets and parades, and to inspire or dismay the hearts of the American people beyond description. As DeTocqueville says in one of the famous chapters of

Die nächste Generation, noch unbefriedigter und glaubensdurstiger 'entdeckt' die Amerikanische Revolution und ihre Verfassungen, rationalisiert, ethisiert und idealisiert sie. Frankreich erst macht die Amerikanische Revolution zu einer Revolution auch auf geistigem Gebiete und von universaler Bedeutung und stellt die Neue Welt mit einer vollendeten Ideologie an die Spitze der Menschheit."—Otto Vossler, *Die Amerikanischen Revolutionsideale in Ihrem Verhältnis zu den Europäischen untersucht an Thomas Jefferson* (München und Berlin, 1929), pp. 64-65.

[4] *Cf.*, Edward Channing, *A History of the United States* (New York, 1912), Vol. III, Ch. XIII.

[5] Cornélis de Witt, *Jefferson and the American Democracy*, translated by R. S. H. Church (London, 1862), p. 124. *Cf.*, George H. McKee, *Th. Jefferson, Ami de la Révolution Française* (Lorient, 1928), p. 301.

his famous book, "It united and divided men, in spite of law, traditions, characters, language; converted enemies into fellow-countrymen, and brothers into foes; or, rather, to speak more precisely, it created, far above particular nationalities, an intellectual country that was common to all, and in which every human creature could obtain rights of citizenship." [6] It converted the whole American people into violent partisans wrote Col. John Trumbull. "To such a degree did this insanity prevail, that the whole country seemed to be changed into one vast arena, on which the two parties, forgetting their national character, were wasting their time, their thoughts, their energy, on this foreign quarrel. The calm splendor of our own Revolution, comparatively rational and beneficial as it had been, was eclipsed in the meteoric glare and horrible blaze of glory of republican France; and we, who in our own case, had scarcely stained the sacred robe of rational liberty with a single drop of blood unnecessarily shed, learned to admire that hideous frenzy which made the very streets of Paris flow with blood." [7]

Americans were touched as they never had been during their own revolution. Now at last after a decade they understood what it all had been about. Mere facts were as irrelevant as they were forgotten. With its glorious example of freedom America had inspired the world. Despotism had been banished and democracy was enthroned. "Among all the events recorded in history," said Elihu Palmer in his eloquent Fourth of July oration in 1797, "the most important is that of the American Revolu-

---

[6] Alexis DeTocqueville, *The Old Régime and the Revolution*, translated by John Bonner (New York, 1856), p. 24.

[7] John Trumbull, *Autobiography, Reminiscences and Letters of John Trumbull, from 1756 to 1841* (New Haven, 1841), pp. 168-169.

tion. . . . we already behold some of the effects which have flowed from this political contest. We behold them in the operations of the human mind—in the energy which has been displayed by the intellectual powers of man, and the consequent gradual decay of superstition and fanaticism—in progressive and extensive improvements exhibited in the American country—in the cultivation of science, the discovery and application of principles, the more general diffusion of knowledge, and the melioration of that unfortunate condition to which man by the tyrants of the earth has been devoted—in the French Revolution, an event of the most astonishing nature, and extremely dissimilar to any thing recorded on the page of ancient history, but which presents to afflicted humanity the consoling hope of sufferings alleviated or wholly destroyed." [8]

"While tyrants viewed with astonishment the struggles of the new world, for the establishment of liberty, and while they perceived in this event nothing more than some immediate political consequences, the discerning philosopher made his calculation of effects upon a more extensive and comprehensive view of the subject—he discovered the inevitable ruin and universal destruction of those unnatural institutions and corrupt principles which have so long disgraced the character of man, and robbed him of his highest happiness. It was these corrupt institutions, which made a renovation in the moral condition of man ex-

[8] Elihu Palmer, *An Enquiry Relative to the Moral and Political Improvement of the Human Species. An Oration, Delivered in the City of New-York, on the Fourth of July, being the Twenty-first Anniversary of American Independence* (London, 1826), pp. 37-38. This oration was first published in New York in 1797. It is an elaboration of the principles which he had expressed four years previously: *Extracts from an Oration, delivered at Federal Point, near Philadelphia, on the Fourth of July, 1793, by Elihu Palmer, citizen of Pennsylvania; and published by request of those who heard it* (New York, 1793).

tremely necessary. The ignorance, the deception, and the crimes of priests had corrupted and brutalized all human nature; and in order the more effectually to accomplish their wicked designs, they pretended to hold a high and social intercourse with celestial powers, and to receive immediately from them the mandates by which man was to be directed in his conduct. These mandates were frequently inconsistent with social and natural morality! The consequence was that when these religious impostors had effectually established the supernatural scheme with dogmas and principles of a very extraordinary and awful nature, human virtue was considered of but little consequence, and the moral condition of man became truly deplorable." [9]

However, "It is not to be presumed, that men will long remain ignorant of their moral condition in nature, after being instructed in the principles of civil science. The moral condition of man will be as essentially renovated by the American revolution as his civil condition . . . awakened by the energy of thought, inspired by the American revolution, man will find it consistent with his inclination and his interest to examine all the moral relations of his nature, to calculate with accuracy the effects of his own moral energies; and to relinquish with elevated satisfaction, those supernatural schemes of superstition which have circumscribed the sphere of beneficial activity, for which Nature designed him." [10]

This rationalization of the American Revolution in the light of the French Revolution was not confined to any particular individual or isolated group, but in no American did the ideals of the 1790's find more complete expression

[9] Elihu Palmer, *op. cit.*, p. 45.   [10] *Ibid.*, pp. 45-46.

in word and deed than in Elihu Palmer. Just as New England, even Connecticut, had given the country its most radical philosopher of the revolutionary era, another son of "the land of steady habits" arose to usher in the millennium of the Age of Reason.

Elihu Palmer was born August 7, 1764, the eighth child of Elihu and Lois (Foster) Palmer, on his father's farm at Canterbury, Connecticut.[11] His youth was spent in the turbulent years of the Revolution which together with the size and impecuniousness of the family probably accounts for his belated education. He went to Dartmouth College somewhat more mature than the average student and graduated in 1787. In college he enjoyed a good reputation for integrity and literary proficiency and was elected to Phi Beta Kappa.[12] During vacations, he taught school, and these meager earnings were supplemented by aid from the College's charity fund, which had been established ostensibly for the purpose of educating and converting the aborigines to become missionaries to their people.[13] It is an example of the ironical in life so typical of higher education in which the money of the pious has in every generation made possible the development and training of infidels.

He studied divinity a short time with the Rev. John Foster while he was preaching at Pittsfield, Massachusetts, shortly after graduating from college. After a few months at Pittsfield, Palmer received a call to Newtown, in Queens County, Long Island. On his way, he preached a Thanks-

[11] Emily W. Leavitt, *Groups of Palmer Families* (Boston, 1901), p. 115.
[12] Charles F. Emerson, *General Catalogue of Dartmouth College* (Hanover, N. H., 1911), p. 195.
[13] John Fellows, "A Memoir of Mr. Palmer" prefaced to *Posthumous Pieces* by Elihu Palmer (London, 1826), p. 4.

giving Day sermon at Sheffield, Massachusetts, and there, as far as we know, began his heretical career. "Instead of expatiating upon the horrid and awful condition of mankind in consequence of the lapse of Adam and his wife," wrote his friend, John Fellows, many years later to Richard Carlile, "he exhorted his hearers to spend the day joyfully in innocent festivity, and to render themselves as happy as possible." [14]   Before arriving at his destination, he also preached for Dr. Rogers, a respectable old Presbyterian clergyman in New York, who did not approve of the young man's liberalism.   All of which indicates, as Mr. Fellows says, "that he was but ill adapted for a Presbyterian pulpit," nor did the fates decree a change of heart for him at Newtown.   He became acquainted with a Dr. Ledyard, "a physician of that place, a man of talents and a freethinker; who used to amuse himself by attacking Mr. Palmer on doctrinal points of religion; which he found very irksome, as he could not conscientiously defend them. And having ascertained that the Doctor was trustworthy, he begged a truce with him, stating that there was no disagreement in their opinion." [15]   Mr. Riker, in his *Annals of Newtown*, confirms Palmer's heterodoxy in an anecdote: "While staying a short time at the house of Dr. Riker, during the operation for an inoculation, he was engaged one evening in study, when he repeated the lines of Dr. Watts which begin with

> Lord I am vile, conceived in sin,
> And born unholy and unclean;

setting forth the doctrine of original sin.   Then turning to Mrs. R. he declared that he did not believe a word of it,

---

[14] John Fellows, *op. cit.*, p. 5.   [15] *Ibid.*, p. 5.

no, not one word, he repeated with emphasis. Surprised at this announcement, she advised him not to give utterance to such sentiments in public, for people would not hear him." [16]

Such sentiments, however, were bound to leak out, especially since Palmer was characteristically outspoken rather than diplomatic, and it is therefore not surprising that after about six months at Newtown, 1788-1789, Palmer removed to Philadelphia. [17] Here he joined the Baptists, only to be again dispossessed of his pulpit in consequence of heretical teaching. This was in March 1791. He and a few followers who seceded with him then identified themselves with a "Universal Society" which John Fitch, the inventor of the steamboat, had recently founded. Palmer was asked to become its minister. Under the influence of this liberal association, Palmer was emboldened in the course of a sermon to deny the divinity of Christ. Openly declared Unitarianism was regarded as deliberate blasphemy and a crime. "The religious community took alarm. The right Rev. Bishop White, of the Protestant Episcopal Church, used his influence upon the owner of the building . . . and he, becoming frightened by threats of prosecution, refused permission to use it for such purposes again." [18] It not only put an end to the Universal Society, but such was the public indignation that Palmer had to flee the city to escape physical violence. [19]

[16] James Riker, *The Annals of Newtown, in Queens County, New-York* (New-York, 1852), p. 232.
[17] Wm. H. Hendrickson, *A Brief History of the First Presbyterian Church of Newtown, Long Island* (No Place, 1902), pp. 33-34; Rev. John P. Knox, *Anniversary Discourse . . . preached March 28, 1880, in the Presbyterian Church, Newtown, L. I.* (New York, 1880), pp. 11, 21.
[18] Thompson Westcott, *Life of John Fitch* (Philadelphia, 1857), p. 312. *Cf.*, J. Thomas Scharf and Thompson Westcott, *History of Philadelphia, 1609-1884* (Philadelphia, 1884), Vol. II, pp. 1404-1405, note.
[19] John Fellows, *op. cit.*, p. 6.

He sought refuge with a brother, an attorney in western Pennsylvania, and read law under his direction. In the spring of 1793 he returned to Philadelphia and was admitted to the bar. Three months later in the plague of yellow fever he lost his wife and was himself deprived of sight. "He was now left blind, and without resources to aid him to grope his way in the darkness; with little sympathy or disposition in the sectarians of any denomination to lend a helping hand to sooth his misfortune. Indeed, some did not scruple to pronounce it a judgment of God for his unbelief." [20]

With his second career closed because of this physical affliction, he went to Augusta, Georgia, and began the preaching of deism. He is said to have collected materials for Jedidiah Morse's *Geography* there,[21] but this has not been authenticated. Leaving Augusta after about a year to visit friends in Connecticut, he stopped on his way in New York and was readily prevailed upon to lecture there. It became the center of his activities as a preacher of deism and organizer of deistic societies until he died an untimely death of pleurisy on April 7, 1806, while on a speaking engagement in Philadelphia.

Like Ethan Allen's, Palmer's religious radicalism grew out of his democratic reaction to Calvinism and, as this led to his ejection from one pulpit after another and finally almost to persecution, he himself became militantly anti-Christian. When one considers the effects of the Christian system on the human mind, it is evident, he says, that it does not tend to make us happier. "By it

---

[20] John Fellows, *op. cit.*, p. 6.
[21] *Appleton's Cyclopædia of American Biography* (New York, 1888), Vol. IV, p. 637.

we are led to believe, that we are all miserable and ruined
wretches;° corrupt and exceedingly wicked from our very
birth; naturally sinful, and opposed to the will of God
in all our actions, words and thoughts; and so far from
deserving the common blessings of life, that if justice had
been done us, we should long since have been cast into
endless punishment . . . [the Deity] is supposed to be a
fierce, revengeful tyrant, delighting in cruelty, punishing
his creatures for the very sins which he causes them to
commit; and creating numberless millions of immortal
souls, that could never have offended him, for the express
purpose of tormenting them to all eternity. Thus they
are generally miserable through life, in meditating on
death and its supposed consequences." [22]

The authority of the Bible seemed to Palmer even more
doubtful than the truth of Calvinistic theology. He found
that it offered no evidence of divine authority and doubted
"that independent of the prejudices of education, and the
power of eloquence, there ever was a reasonable thinking
man, who felt a sufficient internal evidence to convince him
of the reality of the whole of its doctrines." [23]   "As a
human composition, its merits have been greatly over-
rated: it is exceeded in sentiment, invention, stile, and
every other literary qualification. The obscurity, incredi-
bility and obscenity, so conspicuous in many parts of it,
would justly condemn the works of a modern writer. It
contains a mixture of inconsistency and contradiction; to
call which the *word of God*, is the highest pitch of extravagance: it is to attribute to the Deity that which any

[22] [Elihu Palmer], *Thoughts on the Christian Religion* in *The Examiners Examined: being a Defence of the Age of Reason* (New-York,
1794), pp. 9-10.
[23] *Ibid.*, p. 7.

person of common sense would blush to confess himself the author of." [24]

The prophecies which are thought of as proofs of the divine character of the Bible are mostly irrelevant as "they are so vague and indefinite, that they cannot be applied to any specific object, person, or event." [25] ". . . when Christian theology has made mole hills into mountains, it is a duty which we owe to the cause of truth, to strip the film from off the eye, that nature may appear correct and without distortion. When prophecies are expressed in such a loose and unmeaning manner, they lose all their character and credit, and can never be cited as a proof of the divinity of that religion in which they are found." [26]

Miracles fall in the same class with prophecies. "The destruction of the cities of Sodom and Gomorrah by fire and brimstone precipitated from Heaven in the form of rain; the blowing down the walls of Jericho with rams' horns, by the triumphant march of the priesthood round the city; the marvellous and frightful story of the witch of Endor; the woeful condition of Daniel in the den of lions; the hot sultry situation of Shadrach and his two companions in the fiery furnace; together with the unnatural and hopeless abode of poor Jonah in the belly of the whale; all these are specimens of that miserable and disgusting extravagance with which this *Holy Bible* is every where replete." [27]

Instead of being satisfied with the marvellous operations of natural phenomena, says Palmer, the consistency and

---

[24] [Elihu Palmer], *op. cit.*, p. 6. *Cf.*, Elihu Palmer, *Principles of Nature; or, a Developement of the Moral Causes of Happiness and Misery among the Human Species* (London, 1823), p. 20; first published in 1801 or 1802.

[25] *Principles of Nature*, p. 76.

[26] *Ibid.*, p. 79.   [27] *Ibid.*, p. 61.

harmony of nature is violated in the interest of *"pious and holy fanaticism*. Pride and vanity have tempted man to establish religion upon a supernatural basis. The idea of associating with heaven, and holding an intercourse with celestial powers, was a circumstance of extravagant and delicious enjoyment, with a privileged order, and laid the foundation of that terrifying severity of judgment contained in the gospel declaration, *He that believeth not shall be damned*." [28]

Organized religion of whatever kind or denomination, in short, is the product of "ambitious, designing, and fanatic men" who have succeeded in becoming "leaders or influential characters among the beings who surrounded them. . . . Advantage was taken of human ignorance, and the most destructive and erroneous plans were introduced and established by length of time and the force of authority. In nations not at all, or very little improved, tradition has supplied the place of sacred writings, and they have been equally the dupes of those unprincipled chieftains who have assumed authority over them. Moses and Mahomet governed their followers with a rod of iron, and a military despotism. They were savage and ferocious men, crafty and intriguing, and they knew how to subject to their will the stupid but unfortunate followers who were devoted to their views. If Jesus was more mild, benevolent, and temperate, it was because he had less power, and because his disposition was less cruel and resentful. His followers, when clothed with power, have not paid a very high compliment to their master, for the history of their conduct evinces the most malignant design, and the earth

[28] *Ibid.*, p. 63.

has been drenched in blood to defend that system of religion, of which the meek and lowly Jesus is reputed to be the author." [29] "Moses, Mahomet, and Jesus can lay as little claim to moral merit, or to the character of the benefactors of mankind, as any three men that ever lived upon the face of the earth. They were all of them impostors; two of them notorious murderers in practice, and the other a murderer in principle: and their existence united perhaps, cost the human race more blood, and produced more substantial misery, than all the other fanatics of the world." [30]

The whole Christian scheme of salvation seemed to Palmer both absurd and contradictory. "Sophistry and folly united cannot exhibit a greater specimen of nonsense and irrationality. This story of the virgin and the ghost, to say no more of it, does not wear the appearance of much religion; and it would not, it is presumed, be difficult in any age or country, to find a sufficient number of men who would pretend to be Ghosts, if by such pretensions they could obtain similar favours, especially with the consoling reflection superadded, of becoming the progenitors of the pretended Saviour of a wicked and apostate world. How absurd and contradictory are the principles and the doctrines of this religion? In vain do its advocates attempt to cover this transaction with the machinery of ghosts and supernatural agents. The simple truth is, that their pretended Saviour is nothing more than an illegitimate Jew, and their hopes of salvation through him rest on no better foundation than that of fornication or adultery." [31] The

---

[29] *Principles of Nature*, p. 19.   [31] *Ibid.*, p. 25.
[30] *Ibid.*, pp. 166-167.

Bible is, in short, "a book, whose indecency and immorality shock all common sense and common honesty." [32]

Palmer was an inveterate champion of "enlightened reason" and republicanism against the corresponding curses of mankind, superstition and despotism. "The grand object of all civil and religious tyrants," he said in his Fourth of July oration in 1797, "those privileged impostors of the world, has been to suppress all the elevated operations of the mind, to kill the energy of thought, and through this channel to subjugate the whole earth for their own special emolument." [33] "In all the ancient world, Man, every where bending beneath the weight of a compounds despotism, seems almost to have lost the erect attitude assigned to him by the power of Nature, and to grovel upon the earth the miserable victim of ignorance and tyranny. In those regions of slavery and wretchedness, all the advantages, all the enjoyments, which would have resulted from a cultured understanding and the establishment of liberty, are concealed from the view of the human eye; and the philanthropic mind is compelled to contemplate a scene of ruin and distress capable of being exhibited only by the royal butchers and ecclesiastical impostors of the world." [34]

"The powers of man, however, in the progress of their improvement, were destined to give to the species amelioration of their unfortunate condition. It is the energy of intellect that has taken cognizance of the rights of human nature," [35] and just as his Puritan ancestors had rational-

---

[32] *Ibid.*, p. 23.
[33] *An Enquiry Relative to the Moral and Political Improvement of the Human Species*, p. 35.
[34] *Ibid.*, pp. 35-36.
[35] *Ibid.*, p. 36.

ized their settlement in New England as God's last attempt to establish His Kingdom on earth,[36] Palmer saw in the American Revolution the dawn of a new era for all mankind.

It seemed to Palmer that the evil in this world lies not in original sin or human depravity, but in the exploitation of the belief in it. The belief in "self-insufficiency" fostered by Christianity depreciates human energy and ability. "This becomes the generating cause of a thousand subsequent mischiefs; for when a man is once impressed with an idea that he is either weak or foolish, or that it is a crime to bring his faculties, small as they are, to bear upon the high sounding topics of theological doctrines, he trembles at the idea of intellectual efforts, and cries out in the language of revealed theology, *Lord, what is man!* It is a point of policy in the hierarchy to cherish this submissive temperament, and cultivate in the soul of man the divine virtue of humility. If the enemies of truth and free discussion upon religious subjects, have discovered an interest in human degradation, philosophers and philanthropists have recognized in the exaltation of human power, man restored to his true dignity and in the full possession of those moral pleasures to which his nature and his station in existence furnish so indisputable a claim. . . ."[37]

True it is, he says, that the principles governing the moral world are even more difficult of solution than those of the physical world, "but the difficulties which nature

[36] Herbert W. Schneider, *The Puritan Mind*, Ch. I, "The Holy Commonwealth."

[37] From an article entitled, "Competency of the Human Powers," by Elihu Palmer in his weekly deistic paper, *Prospect; or, View of the Moral World* (New York), December 10, 1803, p. 3.

has thrown in the way of this inquiry are much less numerous than those presented by superstition. . . . If the subtilty of thought, and the difficulty of moral discrimination, have in many cases presented to human investigation a barrier to further progress; the intentional malignant descriptions of superstition have, in almost every age and country, terrified the mind of man, and prevented the developement of substantial moral principle. Nature furnishes some difficulties, but supernatural theology exhibits many more." [88]

This is particularly well illustrated in the Hebraic and Christian tradition of the origin of moral evil. Hell had to be invented and it was then necessary "to create inhabitants suited to the nature of the climate, and the unfortunate condition in which they were to reside. The idea of a Devil was accordingly formed, and the reality of his existence rendered an indubitable truth by the reiterated assertions of superstition." [89]

In the same way, "Christianity presents us with two grand leading characters, to whom we are always referred in our inquiries upon the subject of moral evil. Adam and Jesus are these persons, and in them is said to have been concentrated the sin and righteousness of the human race. The new Testament declares that, *as in Adam all die, even so in Christ shall all be made alive.* This is a sweeping clause, in regard to the moral existence of man and flies in the face of universal experience. Facts are at war with this scriptural declaration, and it is impossible to reduce the sentiment to practice, without producing in common

[88] *Principles of Nature,* pp. 101-102.
[89] *Ibid.,* p. 102.

life the grossest violation of justice. Admitting for a moment the existence of such a man as Adam, which by the way is extremely problematical, it will not follow, that there was in him either a moral or physical death of the human race. Physically it is impossible, and morally it is unjust." [40]

To Palmer, this was almost blasphemous. He believed with Rousseau that the evil in the world lies not in man, as the Christian tradition has it, but in corrupt institutions. Man himself, therefore, is his own creator of the evil which besets him. "It is neither in the upper nor lower regions; it is not in heaven nor in hell, that the moral evil will be discovered; it is to be found only among those intelligent beings who exist upon the earth. *Man has created it, and man must destroy it.*" [41] "Every deviation from nature is the establishment of a cause which must sooner or later work ruin to his sensations, or essentially disturb the tranquility of his mind; he will find no happiness in error, and the most dreadful of all his errors is to be found in the terrible descriptions of the Divinity, that he worships; he falsely attributes to this Divinity the diversified evils which he himself has produced, and while he remains under the impression of such an opinion, he

[40] *Principles of Nature,* p. 105.
[41] *Ibid.,* p. 104.
Physical evil can be prevented only in so far as man can control and avoid the natural causes which produce them. Such is the physical nature of man, however, that it will be forever impossible wholly to prevent pain. "Look through the whole order of nature, and this solemn truth is clearly perceived, that every being possessed of feeling must eternally be exposed to a vast variety of complicated evils, painful sensation, and diversified misfortune, resulting from the constitution of the universe, and the laws by which it is governed. Earthquakes, volcanoes, lightning, inundations, are all the result of the operation of physical laws, and it is impossible to prevent the misery which they occasion, without a suspension or violation of the laws by which they were produced."—*Ibid.,* p. 118.

will be forever ignorant of the true sources of those miseries to which he is continually exposed." [42]

With moral evil thus reduced to error which in its turn results from lack of knowledge, the result seemed almost unbelievably simple to Palmer: Destroy despotism and superstition; education will do the rest. First let "Reason, righteous and immortal reason, with the argument of the printing types in one hand, and the keen argument of the sword in the other, . . . attack the thrones and the hierarchies of the world, and level them with the dust; then the emancipated slave must be raised by the power of science into the character of an enlightened citizen; thus possessing a knowledge of his rights, a knowledge of his duties will consequently follow, and he will discover the intimate and essential union between the highest interests of existence, and the practice of an exalted virtue." With superstition and prejudices out of the way "knowledge would become universal, and its progress inconceivably accelerated. It would be impossible, in such a case, that moral virtue should fail of a correspondent acceleration, and the ultimate extirpation of vice would become an inevitable consequence." [43] "Human science is extending itself into every part of the world; it has already revived the hopes of one third of the human race, and its character bears a most indubitable relation to the emancipation of the whole. The number of writers, upon subjects which include the developement of the most important moral and political principles, is constantly increasing—the number of those who think and speak with freedom, upon the most interesting topics, is every day becoming greater and

[42] *Ibid.*, pp. 123-124.   [43] *Ibid.*, p. 109.

greater; and to this source of human improvement no
limits can be assigned—it is indefinite and incalculable;
and its moral, philosophical, and political effects upon intelligent life, will one day strike with horror the oppressors
of the human race." [44] "The sun of reason has begun to
appear, dispelling the thick and almost impenetrable mists
of ignorance and superstition, illuminating the most secret
recesses of the mind, and will continue to encrease in splendor, till it shine forth in one clear, unclouded and eternal
day." [45]

Elihu Palmer was, of course, not the average American
in the year 1800, but he was nevertheless a man of his
own time. His ardent republicanism and undiscriminat-
ing anti-clericalism, his idealization of the American Revolution, his buoyant optimism and boundless faith in education, the progress of science, and, above all, in human
reason—all these are at once recognized as the fundamental antipathies, hopes, and beliefs of the Age of Enlightenment. He knew himself to be a modern man and
understood where and how his concepts of the world, of
life, and of man originated. "The ecclesiastical dissentions in Europe; the discovery of the new world; the discovery of the art of printing; the philosophical investiga-
tions of French, English, and German philanthropists;
all these, and many other powerful circumstances, were
concentred, and produced a new era in the intellectual
history of man. Newton, profiting by the errors of those
great philosophers, Descartes and Bacon; . . . developed
with clearness the physical principles and order of the

[44] Elihu Palmer, *The Political Happiness of Nations; an Oration. Delivered at the City of New-York, on the Fourth of July, Twenty-fourth
Anniversary of American Independence*, 1800, pp. 15-16.
[45] *Thoughts on the Christian Religion*, p. 17.

planetary system, and struck with everlasting death and eternal silence the theological pretension of all former ages. . . . It was not the discovery of physical truths alone that bore relation to the renovation of the human species; it was reserved for Locke, and other powerful minds, to unfold the eternal structure of the intellectual world; explain the operations of the human understanding; explore the sources of thought, and unite sensation and intellect in the same subject, and in a manner cognizable by the human faculties. Locke has, perhaps, done more than Newton, to subvert the credit of *divine Revelation;* but neither of them discovered the extent of the doctrines upon the moral interests of man. Sensation being established as the source and cause of all human ideas, a system of true and material philosophy necessarily followed. . . . Mirabaud [Holbach], Rousseau, Voltaire, Hume, and Bolingbroke, together with twenty other philosophers of France and England, combined their strength in the philanthropic cause of human improvement; they destroyed error by wholesale, and swept away the rubbish of ancient superstition, by the irresistible force of a keen and active intelligence. These moral luminaries were followed by those of more modern times, and the present age is pre-eminently distinguished by a numerous and respectable band of philanthropic philosophers, whose labours are calculated to destroy error, and elevate truth upon the ruins of every thing injurious to the peace and dignity of human society." [46]

Of his contemporaries, Palmer was an ardent admirer of Thomas Paine. "It has been the peculiarly honorable lot of Thomas Paine," he wrote in 1794, "the firm advocate

[46] *Principles of Nature*, pp. 110-112.

of truth, the undaunted champion of reason, and the reso-
lute and unconquerable enemy of tyranny, bigotry and
prejudice, to open the door to free and impartial enquiry.
He has boldly entered the field himself, and taught the
world, that no true system of principles, however sacred
they may be held in the public opinion, and however
strongly protected and enforced by the terrors of man's
vengeance here, and eternal punishment hereafter, is too
awful to be canvassed by reason, or too sublime to be comprehended by common sense." [47]   "He is one of the first
and best of writers, and probably the most useful man that
ever existed upon the face of the earth. His moral and
political writings are equally excellent and the beneficial
influence of the principles for which he contended, will
be felt through all succeeding ages." [48]

He was equally enthusiastic over Volney's, *Les Ruines,
ou Méditation sur les Révolutions des Empires* (Paris,
1791), an over-simplified study of comparative religion
explaining the common origin of all religious ideas. All
established religions are alike in that they are the means
of tyranny and oppression by which unscrupulous and designing men obtain power and wealth by priestcraft.
Translated into English by Joel Barlow, it was during the
1790's a popular companion volume to Paine's, *Age of
Reason.* To Palmer it seemed as if written by the hand
of God. "Of all the books that ever were published," he
said, "Volney's Ruins is pre-eminently entitled to the
appellation of *Holy Writ, and ought to be appointed to be
read in Churches;* not by his Majesty's special command,
but by its universal consent and approbation of all those

---

[47] *Thoughts on the Christian Religion*, p. 16.
[48] *Principles of Nature*, p. 112.

who love nature, truth, and human happiness." [49]   And
when the human mind is at last emancipated from superstition and oppression and has discovered in the constitution of nature those principles on which its real happiness
must ultimately be founded, "the writings of the philosophers and philanthropists of the present day will be found
to bear a strong relation to the progressive improvement
and real welfare of the human species; and although
superstition, from her dark and gloomy abodes, may hurl
her envenomed darts, yet the names of Paine, Volney, Barlow, Condorcet, and Godwin will be revered by posterity,
and these men will be ranked among the greatest benefactors of the human race." [50]

Though scarcely remembered to-day even by students
of American thought and religion, Elihu Palmer deserv-
edly belongs among these religious and political liberals,
his better-known contemporaries.   Strictly speaking none
of these men was an original thinker.   Their beliefs and
hopes were the expression of their age, but in America in
1800 it took an extraordinary person to make public avowal
of the new philosophy.   The learned, outside the realm
of the clergy, were for the most part equally influenced
by deism but like Voltaire lacked confidence in the lower
classes.   Palmer had boundless faith in man—in all men
—and to him the propagation of these principles to all
men was as a sacred ministry, a Gospel of liberty, reason,
and belief in human dignity and ability that was to usher
in the millennium.

[49] *Ibid.*, p. 90.
[50] *An Enquiry relative to the Moral and Political Improvement of the
Human Species*, p. 49.

CHAPTER III

ORGANIZED DEISM

THOUGH noble in its conception of the dignity, ability, and worth of man, Elihu Palmer's contribution to the life of his time is not to be evaluated primarily by the importance of his philosophical writings. He was above all a preacher and an organizer, a disseminator of the liberal thought of his day. Deism had been rather an aristocratic movement. Its principles were generally accepted privately by educated men during the last half of the eighteenth century, but they had not been formulated as a creed nor accepted in lieu of more conventional religion. In America as in England respectability called for church affiliation, and there seems to have been a feeling among gentle folk that their liberal theological views were not for the poor and lowly. They shared the old distrust of the common man. As an anonymous correspondent, signing himself "A Rich Deist," expressed it: "Very few rich men; or, at least men in the higher grades of society, and who have received a liberal education, care any thing about the Christian religion. They cast off the yoke of superstition themselves; yet, for the sake of finding obedient servants, they would continue to impose it on the poor." [1]

Palmer's faith in man, however, was not measured by economic or social position. He was nothing if not a re-

[1] Letter to the Editor, quoted in *The Temple of Reason*, Philadelphia, November 27, 1802, p. 311.

publican and in the evangelical manner set out to convert mankind. The outstanding aim of Elihu Palmer was the dissemination of deism among the lower classes by means of deistic societies and popular treatises, and it was this attempt to make infidelity a gospel for the multitudes that caused the faithful to raise the alarm. "The efforts of infidels, to diffuse the principles of infidelity among the common people," said the Rev. Robert Hall in a famous sermon, "is another alarming symptom peculiar to the present time. *Hume, Bolingbroke,* and *Gibbon* addressed themselves solely to the more polished classes of the community, and would have thought their refined speculations debased by an attempt to enlist disciples from among the populace. Infidelity has lately grown condescending: bred in the speculations of a daring philosophy, immured at first in the cloisters of the learned, and afterwards nursed in the lap of voluptuousness and of courts; having at length reached its full maturity, it boldly ventures to challenge the suffrages of the people, solicits the acquaintance of peasants and mechanics, and seeks to draw whole nations to its standard." [2]

Palmer's first opportunity came when he arrived in New York in 1794 while on his way from Georgia to visit his relatives in Connecticut. To understand the circumstances and development of the deist society which he established there, it is necessary to trace briefly its political and religious antecedents. A few years after the Peace of Paris in 1783, a democratic fraternal society called the "Tammany Society, or Columbian Order" was founded in

[2] Robert Hall, *Modern Infidelity Considered with respect to its Influence on Society* (First American, from the Third English Edition, Charlestown, Mass., 1801), pp. 44-45.

New York.   In name, in costume, and in its ceremonies it
was distinctively American.   In its earliest days, Tammany was not chiefly a political society.   Careful investigation convinced Dr. Kilroe that "the Society was instituted
primarily as a social, fraternal and benevolent organization, based on democratic principles, that its membership
was not determined by caste, but that all might mingle
on the basis of manhood rather than on that of wealth or
culture." [3]   In this respect it differed noticeably from the
Society of the Cincinnati, and as the latter with aristocratic
leanings naturally tended toward the principles associated
with the Federalist party, Tammany also became interested in politics.   This was in 1789 when the rivalry between Federalists and anti-Federalists became very bitter
in the political campaign of that year.[4]   It was then that
the Tammany Society was reorganized and began its long
political career.   In 1790, one of its leading members,
John Pintard, merchant and philanthropist, described the
society as "a political institution founded on a strong republican basis, whose democratic principles will serve in
some measure to correct the aristocracy in our city." [5]

In view of these democratic sympathies, Tammany was
of course enormously enthusiastic over the French Revolution.   When Democratic Societies were established
throughout the country following the arrival of Citizen
Genet in 1793, the New York branch, established in Feb-

[3] Edwin P. Kilroe, *Saint Tammany and the Origin of the Society of Tammany or Columbian Order in the City of New York* (Ph.D. dissertation, Columbia University, New York, 1913), p. 142.

[4] For a detailed discussion of the political campaign of 1789 in the City of New York, *vide*, Thomas E. V. Smith, *The City of New York in the Year of Washington's Inauguration, 1789* (New York, 1889), pp. 70-79.

[5] From a letter by John Pintard to Dr. Jeremy Belknap of Boston, dated October 11, 1790, quoted in Edwin P. Kilroe, *op. cit.*, p. 136.

ruary 1794, "was joined by so many members of the Tammany Society that the two bodies became almost identical in personnel." [6] The unanimity of approval of political radicalism was, however, short-lived. Genet's undiplomatic behavior and the controversy following the Whiskey Rebellion precipitated a breach in the Society. When President Washington in his sixth annual message to Congress on November 19, 1794, severely censured "certain self-created societies," the more conservative members of Tammany regretted their identification with the Democratic Societies and passed a resolution endorsing the federal administration. The radicals in turn repudiated the resolution as a minority action. The democratic element eventually prevailed in the Society, but for a time Tammany lost in prestige and importance. [7] The Hon. Judah Hammond says that almost all its members forsook it and that "at one anniversary they were reduced so low that but three persons attended its festival." [8]

When Elihu Palmer came to New York in 1794 there was thus quite a group of radicals in the Democratic Society, some of whom had followed the French example not only in politics but in religion. Mr. Fellows, a member of the Society, tells us that they immediately asked Palmer to lecture to them, "which he assented to without hesitation; and a large assembly room being obtained for the purpose, he commenced the following Sunday. A small society was formed in aid of his exertions; which assumed, without disguise, the name of Deistical Society. This

[6] *Ibid.*, p. 193.
[7] *Ibid.*, pp. 195-198.
[8] Quoted in Jabez D. Hammond, *The History of Political Parties in the State of New York* (Cooperstown, 1846), Vol. I, pp. 341-342.

appellation was advocated by Mr. Palmer, although some others were in favour of that of Theophilanthropist, as being less frightful to fanatics, not many of whom would understand the term." [9]

This was exactly the kind of thing that Palmer loved to do. He was institutionally minded and had never lost the zeal of a clergyman to spread his beliefs. Deism was for him a religion rather than a philosophy. Now with an active and militant society, he hoped to carry his beliefs into action and above all to propagate them. The hopes, beliefs, and ambitions of the new society were formulated as follows:

PRINCIPLES OF THE DEISTICAL SOCIETY OF THE STATE OF NEW YORK

Proposals for forming a society for the promotion of moral science and the religion of nature—having in view the destruction of superstition and fanaticism—tending to the developement of the principles of a genuine natural morality—the practice of a pure and uncorrupted virtue—the cultivation of science and philosophy—the resurrection of reason, and the renovation of the intelligent world.

At a time when the political despotism of the earth is disappearing, and man is about to reclaim and enjoy the liberties of which for ages he has been deprived, it would be unpardonable to neglect the important concerns of intellectual and moral nature. The slavery of the mind has been the most destructive of all slavery; and the baneful effects of a dark and gloomy superstition have suppressed all the dignified efforts of the human understanding, and essentially circumscribed the sphere of intellectual energy. It is only by returning to the laws of nature, which man has so frequently abandoned, that happiness is to be acquired. And, although the efforts of a few individuals will be inadequate to the sudden establishment of moral and mental felicity; yet, they may

[9] John Fellows, *A Memoir of Mr. Palmer*, p. 7.

lay the foundation on which a superstructure may be reared incalculably valuable to the welfare of future generations. To contribute to the accomplishment of an object so important, the members of this association do approve of the following fundamental principles:—

1. That the universe proclaims the existence of one supreme Deity, worthy the adoration of intelligent beings.

2. That man is possessed of moral and intellectual faculties sufficient for the improvement of his nature, and the acquisition of happiness.

3. That the religion of nature is the only universal religion; that it grows out of the moral relations of intelligent beings, and that it stands connected with the progressive improvement and common welfare of the human race.

4. That it is essential to the true interest of man, that he love truth and practise virtue.

5. That vice is every where ruinous and destructive to the happiness of the individual and of society.

6. That a benevolent disposition, and beneficent actions, are fundamental duties of rational beings.

7. That a religion mingled with persecution and malice cannot be of divine origin.

8. That education and science are essential to the happiness of man.

9. That civil and religious liberty is equally essential to his true interests.

10. That there can be no human authority to which man ought to be amenable for his religious opinions.

11. That science and truth, virtue and happiness, are the great objects to which the activity and energy of the human faculties ought to be directed.

Every member admitted into this association shall deem it his duty, by every suitable method in his power, to promote the cause of nature and moral truth, in opposition to all schemes of superstition and fanaticism, claiming divine origin.[10]

[10] Elihu Palmer, *Posthumous Pieces*, Principles of the Deistical Society of the State of New York, pp. 10-11.

Ambitious and even noble as some of these principles were, the society was not a success. The reason is perfectly simple: it could not attract the right people, which is to say, men of means and position. ". . . there were not many who were disposed to contribute for the support of the principles," says Mr. Fellows, "and those, for the most part, limited in means." [11] Or as a less sympathetic chronicler expressed it: ". . . it was composed of the scattered dregs of those Jacobin Infidels, who covered the democratic society with disgrace, and shed a degree of odium upon the pure doctrine of republicanism, which the efforts of the virtuous patriot, will not for years wipe away—it issued from the tomb of its fallen parent, like a foul spectre, blotted with crimes, gaping with vengeance, and eager to drag the weak and unsuspicious mind into the abyss of eternal torment.—As the graceless son of a graceless family, most frequently exerts all his ingenuity to complete the infamy of a ruined reputation, so the members of the Theistical Society meditated upon every scheme to add the last reproach to their characters, already broken and despised." [12]

The critical reader need scarcely be cautioned not to accept literally the characteristically exaggerated vituperative language of this period, but the fact remains that Palmer had to eke out a precarious and impecunious existence by "occasional excursions to other populous towns to recruit his funds," [13] and such was the popular feeling against deism that he met with opposition and frustration everywhere.

[11] John Fellows, *op. cit.*, p. 7.
[12] John Wood, *A Full Exposition of the Clintonian Faction, and the Society of the Columbian Illuminati* (Newark, 1802), pp. 27-28.
[13] John Fellows, *op. cit.*, p. 7.

The Minutes of the Common Council of the City of New York reveal an example of this antipathy: "June 26, 1797. The following petition is made to the common council: 'We the undersigned Inhabitants for ourselves and others of our fellow Citizens who are desirous of hearing a public Oration in commemoration of our National Independence delivered by Mr. Elihu Palmer on the ensuing Anniversary request that the Common Council will be pleased to consent to the large Court Room in the City hall being made use of on that occasion.' It carries ten signatures, including those of Philip Freneau, John Lamb, Jr., and Peter R. Maverick.—From the original in metal file No. 18, city clerk's record-room, endorsed 'read June 26th 1797 & rejected.' The brief entry in the minutes in reference to this petition has a marginal note, next to Palmer's name, which reads: 'An Infidel.' " [14] Palmer was to meet that kind of handicap and discouragement to his activities to the day of his death. The Fourth of July oration of 1797 had to be delivered elsewhere and fortunately it was even published. Less than a month later, William Dunlap, the playwright, confided to his *Diary*, "August 2d. [1797] read . . . Palmers oration; this oration gives me a higher idea of the man Than I had; indeed, it is energetic, philosophic & benevolent." [15]

Dunlap was a fellow liberal, but men of his position did not contribute to the *cause* of deism. Frequent references in his *Diary* show that he and his friends read Hume,

[14] I. N. Phelps Stokes, *The Iconography of Manhattan Island* (New York, 1926), Vol. V, p. 1343; *Minutes of the Common Council of the City of New York, 1784-1831* (Published by the City of New York, 1917), Vol. II, 1793-1801, p. 359.

[15] William Dunlap, *Diary*, edited by Dorothy C. Barck, *Collections of the New-York Historical Society for the Year 1929* (New York, 1930), Vol. I, p. 126.

Godwin, Voltaire, Holbach, Boulanger, *et al*. But they
were not propagandists and confined their opinions to the
exclusive circle of their intimates. Dunlap gives us a
glimpse of this: "Sept. 30th 1797 Wm Johnson drinks
tea with us & I attend club with him it being his night.
Kent, Smith, Johnson & me made the little party but it
was very pleasant. Kent remark'd that men of information were now nearly as free from vulgar superstition or
the Christian religion as they were in ye time of Cicero
from the pagan superstition—all, says he, except the literary men among the Clergy. Godwin's Enquirer lay on
the table: I read his remarks on the profession of the
priesthood. Kent was highly pleased with it, & with such
other parts of the book as he looked into." [16]

The Kent here referred to is none other than the
Honorable James Kent of Puritan ancestry and Yale training, later Chancellor of the State of New York. In religion, he was apparently as radical as Palmer at this time,
but unlike the latter he was a Federalist nor did he mix
religion with politics.[17] Elihu Hubbard Smith and William Johnson were Dunlap's most intimate friends. Like
Kent, they were both graduates of Yale, 1786 and 1788
respectively. Smith, a young physician, died a year later,
September 19, 1798, in the yellow fever plague in New
York. His parents, orthodox as became respectable folk
of Litchfield, Connecticut, anxiously inquired whether
their son died a deist, as they feared, and Dunlap tells us

---

[16] William Dunlap, *op. cit.*, Vol. I, p. 151. For the influence of
William Godwin on Dunlap, *vide*, Oral S. Coad, *William Dunlap* (Ph.D.
dissertation, Columbia University, New York, 1917), pp. 57-58.

[17] Franklin B. Dexter, *Biographical Sketches of the Graduates of Yale
College with Annals of the College History* (New York, 1907), Vol. IV,
pp. 189-194.

that the young doctor's friends were happy not to be able to answer that question, "for our beloved friend was seized so violently that he was in a stupor until death, scarcely speaking & then but when roused from his sleep to answer some question which done he slept again." [18] William Johnson was a very successful lawyer. It is interesting to note that although he undoubtedly shared the religious latitudinarianism of his friends in the Friendly Club, he conformed outwardly to religious respectability. Mr. Dexter was able to speak of him as "a devoted member of the Protestant Episcopal Church." [19]

A similarly intimate picture of the prevailing free-thought in high society comes from the pen of Col. John Trumbull, the artist. Trumbull tells of his discomfiture at a "freethinking dinner party" in 1793 at the home of Thomas Jefferson at which Senator Giles of Virginia "proceeded so far at last, as to ridicule the character, conduct and doctrines of the divine founder of our religion—Jefferson, in the mean time, smiling and nodding approbation on Mr. Giles, while the rest of the company silently left me and my defense to our fate; until at length my friend, David Franks, (first cashier of the bank of the United States,) took up the argument on my side. Thinking this a fair opportunity for evading further conversation on this subject, I turned to Mr. Jefferson and said, 'Sir, this is a strange situation in which I find myself; in a country professing Christianity, and at a table with Christians, as I

---

[18] William Dunlap, *Diary*, September 28, 1798, Vol. I, p. 343. For biographical sketches of Elihu Hubbard Smith, *vide*, Franklin B. Dexter, *Biographical Sketches of the Graduates of Yale College*, Vol. IV, p. 509; *The American Medical and Philosophical Register*, New York, January 1814, Vol. IV, pp. 391-399.

[19] Franklin B. Dexter, *Biographical Sketches of the Graduates of Yale College*, Vol. IV, p. 608.

supposed, I find my religion and myself attacked with severe and almost irresistible wit and raillery, and not a person to aid in my defense, but my friend Mr. Franks, *who is himself a Jew.*' For a moment, this attempt to parry the discussion appeared to have some effect; but Giles soon returned to the attack, with new virulence, and burst out with—'It is all miserable delusion and priestcraft; I do not believe one word of all they say about a future state of existence, and retribution for actions done here. I do not believe one word of a Supreme Being who takes cognizance of the paltry affairs of this world, and to whom we are responsible for what we do.' I had never before heard, or seen in writing, such a broad and unqualified avowal of atheism." [20]

Though not supported by such men as these, scions of respectability and means, Palmer's society gained new life and zest from the triumph of the Republican Party in the election of Thomas Jefferson in 1800. His followers must have felt that politically at least, he had anticipated correctly the order of things that was to be. With "despotism" dethroned the time was obviously propitious for courage and initiative in the fight against religious "superstition." To further its activities, therefore, the society established on November 8, 1800, a deistic weekly paper,

---

[20] John Trumbull, *Autobiography*, pp. 170-171.

There is evidence that, outside of New England, the "great" were guilty of more than usual "open neglect" of church attendance and of "the chief duties" of religion during the decade of the 1790's. The Rev. Ashbel Green, of the Second Presbyterian Church of Philadelphia and one of the chaplains of Congress for eight years from 1792, complained of the thin attendance of members of Congress at prayers. He attributed the usual absence of two-thirds of the members to the prevalence of freethinking.—Rufus W. Griswold, *The Republican Court or American Society in the Days of Washington* (New and Revised Edition, New York, 1856), pp. 433-434.

The Temple of Reason. The editor was Dennis Driscol, about whose previous activities we unfortunately know only from his enemies. He was apparently a recent immigrant from Ireland and an ex-priest. But we shall let the paper speak for itself, as it does in its first issue: "To the American Reader. The torrents of illiberal reflections and unqualified abuse poured forth every day, through the channels of bigotry and intolerance, against Deists, have provoked this publication. It is the settled maxim of the philosophical Deist, to let all men rest in peace and enjoy their speculative opinions, however absurd, without animosity or persecution: But it is, unfortunately, the settled maxim and practice of others, to abuse and revile all those who are not of their creed. This is certainly a perverse disposition, and has ever been productive of very many evils to society. In justice to what we conceive, and are convinced, to be the Truth, we can no longer remain silent. We are determined to shew to the world, the purity of our doctrines and the soundness of our principles, exposing at the same time, the corruption of those of our adversaries.

"If we were to conclude from the intemperance of overheated bigots, whose constant study is to denounce and cry down Deism in America, we must think that the inquisition had been established, with all its terrors, in the United States, and that the christian religion, in all its sects and branches, had been placed under its *holy protection*. But fortunately for the peace and prosperity of America, *Mahometism* is as much *established by law*, there, as christianity. The immortal framers of the constitution, wisely thought, that in matters of religion, all men have an equal right to private and public opinion;

and therefore, left them all on the same level— On this level we stand; and if we shew our religion to be superior to that of others, it shall be by the force of Reason, not by scurrility, deception, or persecution." [21]

To this ambitious undertaking *The Temple of Reason,* supplemented by Palmer's lectures, devoted itself with might and main. With the anonymity peculiar to the press, we are for the most part unable to identify the authorship of its contributions, but they almost invariably express the sentiments of the Paine, Volney, Godwin, Palmer school. An article by Driscol, however, entitled, "Jesus Christ a Deist and no God," is in striking contrast to Palmer's attitude toward the founder of Christianity. [22] "Let any one read what Christ is said to have spoken or preached, throughout the four gospels; and on the whole, he will find him a good Deist, recommending the practice of virtue, as the only conduct pleasing to his father. No where is he foolish or vain enough to pretend to be a God. He modestly and justly styles himself the son of man; acquiescing sometimes to be called the son of God, which has been often applied before to others. 'The sons of God went in to the daughters of men.' If men with propriety can call God their *father,* with the same propriety may they be called his *sons,* or the sons of God; yet this is the modest, meek man, whom John and Paul have dubbed a God after his death, in imitation, no doubt, of the Greeks and Romans, who used to deify men of extraordinary worth and merit even before their death!— but the blasphemy of this is obvious to every Deist, who demonstrates that there can be but one God." [23]

[21] *The Temple of Reason,* New York, Saturday, November 8, 1800, p. 1.
[22] *Supra,* pp. 63-64.
[23] *The Temple of Reason,* New York, November 15, 1800, p. 10.

An article in the issue of December 6, 1800, entitled "Man, The Author and Artificer of the Most Part of his own Evils and Misfortunes" is of course entirely in accord with Palmer's principles as well as those of Thomas Paine. Paine's pamphlet, *Agrarian Justice* (1797), dealing with this subject was suggested by a sermon published by the Bishop of Llandaff on *The Wisdom and Goodness of God in Having Made Both Rich and Poor.* This article in *The Temple of Reason* follows Paine in denying that God made rich and poor. "Poverty and riches, misery and happiness, are generally the results and consequences of good or bad governments—of wise or unwise laws—of the influence of virtue, or the prevalence of vice; and all the *natural* offsprings of human actions, not the *partial* operations of an all-just and all-wise Being." [24]

With the advent of their own publication, the activities of the society were of course strengthened. Public meetings could now be advertised and reported in some detail. The following general announcement of the scope and purpose of Palmer's lectures appeared in several issues of *The Temple of Reason:* "Mr. Palmer, still continues to deliver public discourses every Sunday evening at six o'clock, at Lovett's long room in Broadway. The object of these discourses, is to disclose and mark with discriminating precision, moral principles by which human existence ought to be governed—To develope some of the fundamental rules and laws of physical philosophy and astronomy—To prove that God is immutable, and that the working of miracles is inconsistent with the nature of his character—That a religion built upon a miraculous

[24] *The Temple of Reason,* New York, December 6, 1800, p. 33.

foundation is false—That Christian superstition has been one of the worst scourges of the human race—That the powers of men are competent for human happiness—That the triumphant reign of pure morality and sound philosophy can alone restore to the species that dignity, energy and virtue, which superstition for ages, past has destroyed."[25]

This ambitious undertaking was nothing new with Palmer, but we know more about his activities at this time because of the paper. It need scarcely be suggested that the press as a whole had not advertised deist affairs. Now they were well advertised, as for example Palmer's lecture on the "Universal Deluge": "Tomorrow evening at six o'clock, at Lovett's Long Room in Broadway, Mr. Palmer will deliver a public discourse, concerning the Deluge, or what is commonly called Noah's Flood."

MANAGEMENT OF THE SUBJECT

First—It will be shewn that the Deluge was in its nature physically impossible:

Second—That it was inconsistent with the moral perfections of God:

Third—The dimensions of the Ark, the nature and conditions of its cargo; and that it could not contain, the variety of animals, and other substances, necessary, for such a voyage:

Fourth—Observations upon the effect which such Theological Stories must produce on the moral temperament of Man.[26]

The lecture was somewhat grandiosely reviewed in the following week's issue: "Last Sunday evening, at Lovett's Hotel, Mr. Palmer delivered an able and philosophical

---

[25] *The Temple of Reason*, New York, November 8, 1800; November 22, 1800; January 3, 1801.

[26] *Ibid.*, New York, November 29, 1800, p. 31.

discourse on the Deluge, to a very numerous and respectable audience. The subject was handled in a masterly manner (as indeed, is every other) by this enlightened Deist. He proved, as we should hope, to the satisfaction of every rational mind, that this wonderful event recorded in the Bible, was physically and morally impossible—as inconsistent with the moral perfections—the goodness and wisdom of God, as with the known and established laws of nature." [27]

The positive side of the deists' faith is more interesting. Following the tradition of D'Alembert, an article is entitled, "On the Study of Astronomy, and its importance to promote the knowledge of one God and true Religion." "To form a grand idea of the Omnipotence and Wisdom of the One God, we must contemplate his works in the Heavens, by means of telescopes; and then our pride shall be humbled with the dust. One view of these stupendous works infinitely dispersed probably, through boundless space, will give us a more exalted and sublime idea of the divinity, than all the childish tricks and puny miracles recorded, or rather invented, by all the priests and impostors that ever existed! . . . To this end, we would have astronomy cultivated by all means among a free people. We would have a philosophical legislature cause observatories to be erected contiguous to every great city and town, and the people encouraged to behold the stupendous works of God, through telescopes. Of sciences, this is the most sublime and best calculated to elevate mens minds to a proper idea of the Creator and themselves." [28]

This was, of course, before the day when man became

[27] *Ibid.*, New York, December 6, 1800, p. 39.
[28] *Ibid.*, New York, November 22, 1800, p. 23.

appalled by the vastness and mechanistic disinterestedness of the universe and saw himself as a "sick fly taking a dizzy ride on a gigantic fly-wheel." Just as Ethan Allen believed in the God as revealed in Nature in general, to these later deists it seemed that God was most clearly revealed in astronomic laws. It will be recalled that the planet Uranus was discovered by Sir William Herschel in 1781. It was a period when the orthodox as well as the deists were interested in astronomy.[29] The first part of Thomas Paine's *Age of Reason* is chiefly astronomical.

With the New York society apparently flourishing in the closing weeks of 1800, organized deism was developed in Philadelphia. Since the collapse of the society founded ten years earlier by the unlucky and unhappy John Fitch,[30] the deists in the city of brotherly love had apparently contented themselves with listening to occasional lectures by the itinerant Palmer or other "enlightened" orators. With the example of both the New York and Paris societies a new attempt at organization was now made. "The Deists of Philadelphia, who are both numerous and respectable, are forming themselves, we understand, into a society, under the title of the *Theophilanthropists;* that is, the lovers of God and Man.[31] . . . We are not a little happy

[29] The Rev. President Stiles of Yale, as a student recalled, "was an ardent devotee to astronomy. It was said that he cherished the hope that in the future life he would be permitted to visit the planets, and to examine the rings of Saturn and the belts and satellites of Jupiter."—George P. Fisher, *Life of Benjamin Silliman, M.D., LL.D.* (New York, 1866), Vol. I, p. 88.

[30] *Supra*, p. 59.

[31] This society was modelled after the Church of Theophilanthropy established by Thomas Paine in Paris in January 1797. Paine emphasized that education in science was to be a principal objective of this society. ". . . we shall give scientific instruction," he said in his inaugural discourse, "to those who could not otherwise obtain it. The mechanic of every profession will there be taught the mathematical principles necessary

to see the enlightened citizens of the capital of the United States, come forward like philosophers, to avow and profess their horror and detestation of superstition and idolatry, under whatever name, and in whatever shape they may wish to exhibit themselves. Their next object, we understand, is to procure a building suitable to the purpose, and calculated, not only for religious, but scientific purposes; their Temple must be a temple of *information* and *instruction*, where their youth will receive those early notions of one God and pure religion, professed by their fathers: It is an injustice to children to allow them to be corrupted by priests, or contaminated by superstition, when the parents are enlightened themselves, and possess the means of giving sound and wholesome instruction to their offspring. Such an establishment as we here speak of, must be of singular advantage, when dedicated to pure religion, moral philosophy and science in general. · We wish our friends in Philadelphia every success their undertaking merits, and we may venture to assert, that their laudable example will be soon followed, not only in New-York, but in several other cities and towns of America—and surely, it is high time!" [32]

Two weeks later, the editor urges more specifically the erection of a similar "Temple of Instruction" in New York.[33] In the first issue of the new year he writes a pæan of praise: "The close of the last century bears witness to the *resurrection* of Republicanism and the triumph

to render him proficient in his art. The cultivator will there see developed the principles of vegetation; while, at the same time, they will be led to see the hand of God in all these things."—Moncure D. Conway, *The Life of Thomas Paine*, Vol. II, p. 255.

[32] *The Temple of Reason*, New York, December 13, 1800, pp. 46-47.

[33] *Ibid.*, New York, December 27, 1800, p. 63.

of Liberty, in the United States. By an effort worthy of
men, who had once established the rights of their species
in a new world, they rose in mass, and defeated the proj-
ects of their foreign and domestic enemies. . . . At the
time the champions of freedom and civil liberty, have been
thus active and successful, the Apostles of Deism and religious liberty, have not been idle. The publications in
Europe and America, have stemmed the torrent of superstition, and checked the progress and audacity of Priests
—Clamorous and insulting, *without opposition,* they now
remain silent as the grave. Such is the progress, and such
the triumphs of Liberty and Philosophy, during the year,
One Thousand Eight Hundred." [34]

But the triumph of philosophy of which Mr. Driscol
sang exultantly is not necessarily the same thing as practical success. After all, what is an editor to do with subscribers, enlightened though they may be, who do not even
"pay the Postage of their Letters, when they order the
Paper," [35] let alone paying for the paper? The following notice accordingly was the swan-song of the New York
edition of the paper. It is not only interesting as revealing the extent of the circulation, but is typical of the fate
of its successors.

TO THE SUBSCRIBERS OF THE TEMPLE OF
REASON

We beg leave to inform these Gentlemen, that the publication
of this Paper must be suspended, probably for a few days only.
It is now three months since its first appearance, and in that time
we are proud in acknowledging the countenance of a respectable
number of subscribers in all parts of the Union, especially in New-

---

[34] *The Temple of Reason,* New York, January 3, 1801, p. 71.
[35] *Ibid.,* New York, January 10, 1801, p. 79.

York and Philadelphia. Yet this increasing number is not alone sufficient to support a new paper, unbacked by capital, and unaided by any of those means, that usually flow in to publications of another kind; it is for these reasons, and to remove these difficulties, that we are under the necessity of suspending the publication for a moment. . . .

To obviate the difficulties and remove the embarrassments we speak of, it is expected those indebted to the paper will immediately come forward and pay what they owe. Those in Philadelphia and to the southward, will please to send to the Aurora Office and our friends to the eastward, and in New-York, will be so good as to call at No. 56 Beaver-Street; where complete sets of the numbers already published, may be had.[36]

This explanation of the suspension of the paper seems to be based on the facts, but it is interesting to see what vituperation can do: "After the temple of reason was set on foot, and had the appearance of being in a flourishing condition, the Illuminati [members of the Deistical Society], began to be jealous, that all the profits of the work would be monopolised by Driscoll.—They remonstrated with the apostate Priest, on the reasonable propriety of allowing the funds of the society, at least one half of the profits—They reminded him, that he was taken into their service, with scarcely a shirt to his back; that they clothed him in a decent garb, and placed him in a most respectable situation; that without their assistance, he probably would have been reduced to the necessity of again humming mass to a few superstitious Irish maids.—But Driscoll was too long a Jesuit not to have a more powerful regard for personal emolument, than the enriching of any society under the sun.—He discovered that the number of deists who were not Illuminati were more numerous than those who

[36] Ibid., New York, February 7, 1801, p. 111.

were; and although, perhaps, the opposition which he would meet from the Theistical society, would prevent his succeeding in New York, yet there were other towns in America which contained deists also.—He accordingly repaired to Philadelphia, and established his temple of reason in that city, under the auspices of the friends of Mr. *William Duane.*" [37]

The Temple of Reason was accordingly resumed in Philadelphia with the issue of April 22, 1801, which with characteristic enthusiasm describes bishops as "being a set of indolent, lazy, lounging, fawning sycophants, possessed of more lust of gold than either divinity or philanthropy." [38] With the memory of his New York experiences apparently still painfully in mind, Driscol remarks editorially: "The Temple of Reason, having neither fat benefices, snug sinecures, tythes, or thythe pigs for its support; nor having, like other prints of the day, power to draw on any national treasury, for the wages of adulation and sycophancy; things that are strangers to the Temple; it is expected the subscribers will cheerfully contribute towards its support. This is only a liberality for benefits to be received." [39] At the same time the editor called the attention of prospective advertisers to "the widely extending circulation of this Paper, and the avidity with which it is sought for and read," and announced his plans of "forming a Correspondence in the most respectable towns of the Union, where those who wish to read the Temple of Reason will have an opportunity of sub-

[37] John Wood, *A Full Exposition of the Clintonian Faction, and the Society of the Columbian Illuminati*, p. 43.
[38] *The Temple of Reason*, Philadelphia, April 22, 1801, p. 117.
[39] *Ibid.*, Philadelphia, April 22, 1801, p. 118.

scribing to it." [40] It is also pointed out that, "As this Paper combines Politics with Pure Religion, it becomes an object for the middling and industrious class of citizens, who, having neither means nor leisure to peruse the daily prints, will, at a glance, see the important news of the day compendiously summed up, and impartially recorded. Contrary to the opinion of most men, we hold, that Deism and Liberty should go hand in hand; and as mankind get enlightened, we are happy to find, that our opinion is verified. It would appear to be a contradiction in terms, to find men renounce *Kingcraft*, and still remain *enchanted* by Superstition and Priest-craft." [41]

In July 1801, an event occurred which again aroused the deists of Philadelphia to renewed activity to build a "temple" for their activities. Elihu Palmer had been given permission by some of the members to deliver a lecture on morality in the Universalists' Church. *The Temple of Reason* reports the outcome as follows: "The *novelty* of the subject (for it is rare to hear *pure* moral lectures in Christian churches, as well as the fame of the preacher, induced numbers, fond of truth and eloquence, to attend; but their mortification, if not their surprise, must have been great, when they found a written notice on the church door, informing them that Mr. Palmer would not preach there that evening, it being contrary to the wishes of the church; or words to this purpose. After service on Sunday, the question, we understand, was put to the vote; and by a majority of old women and bigots, it was determined that *no moral lecture* should be given in *their* church. . . . But as Mr. Palmer's object is Truth, and his wish to

---

[40] *Ibid.*, Philadelphia, April 22, 1801, pp. 118-119.
[41] *Ibid.*, Philadelphia, April 22, 1801, p. 119.

enlighten the people; as he desires to banish religious errors, and substitute the practice of morality and virtue, we fear he has no chance of ever having access to a *christian* pulpit. . . . It is painful to see superstition have her temples, and delusion its altars, while philosophy and truth have to wander abroad, like aliens or strangers in the land! Let us hope, however, that the friends of both are *now* convinced of the necessity of erecting a building, where they may be sheltered and protected from the persecution of ignorance and the malice of bigotry." [42]

It was of course not a new experience for Palmer to be denied the opportunity of delivering a lecture as scheduled. Not long afterwards, we read of his having "delivered an excellent moral discourse to a very respectable audience on Filbert street, opposite the Robin Hood, in this city. We understand he intends to deliver another discourse at five o'clock on Sunday evening next, in the same place. For the honor of Philadelphia, we are glad that *every* house is not shut to men who descant on philosophy, and inculcate the advantages of morality." [43]

Two weeks later, "At the invitation of the deists in Baltimore, Mr. Palmer has proceeded forward to preach the eternal gospel of Reason in that city, and after a short stay there, he is expected to re-visit Philadelphia.—What evil times we have fallen on!" [44]

This itinerant preaching seems to indicate that although they were now apparently more active than formerly, neither the New York nor the Philadelphia society was able to support Palmer as its pastor or leader. His activi-

[42] *The Temple of Reason*, Philadelphia, July 8, 1801, p. 207.
[43] *Ibid.*, Philadelphia, August 12, 1801, p. 247.
[44] *Ibid.*, Philadelphia, August 26, 1801, p. 263.

ties in Baltimore are reported in *The Temple of Reason* as follows: "The enlightened and liberal part of the citizens of Baltimore have been highly gratified, we understand, on a late occasion, at the rational and philosophical discourses delivered to them by Mr. Palmer. . . . Mr. Palmer received every mark of attention and approbation from the gentlemen in Baltimore, who taking into consideration that he had no church living or glebe lands to support him, contributed liberally to defray his expences, and engaged him to visit them soon again. Such conduct does honour to the good sense and feelings of the enlightened citizens of Baltimore." [45]

With his return to Philadelphia about the middle of September 1801, Palmer resumed his preaching there, this time in "the Ball room next door to Voltairs head in South Fourth Street." [46] Early in November he called a meeting of his friends at the office of *The Temple of Reason* apparently for the purpose of carrying into effect his long-desired building for the activities of the society.[47] Soon after, the following appeal was made:

TO THE LIBERAL-MINDED IN ALL PROFESSIONS, IN PHILADELPHIA

. . . a few benevolent men have opened a subscription to build a convenient Hall or Room, where discourses on Moral Philosophy will be delivered every Sunday. The public are to understand, that this is not a house of prayer; nor a house of any sort of ceremony; but it is to be a house of Reason, and the one God is to be the sole object of mental worship and veneration in it.

Though this may be considered a motive sufficiently powerful

[45] *Ibid.*, Philadelphia, September 9, 1801, pp. 278-279.
[46] *Ibid.*, Philadelphia, September 9, 1801, p. 278.
[47] *Ibid.*, Philadelphia, October 21, 1801, p. 327.

to interest the free thinking part of society in the erection of the proposed Hall, yet the citizens above alluded to, have carried their liberal and benevolent views still farther, and intend that this building should be dedicated to the instruction of Youth in the week days. The children of subscribers will have a peculiar claim of favor and attention on this new establishment, and receive an education founded on the principles of Reason and sound philosophy. As the knowledge of Mathematics and the living languages, is of such vast importance in a rising and commercial nation, these will form the primary objects of the School—And in addition to this, it is intended to procure a few of the best Astronomical Instruments to be mounted in an Observatory, for the instruction and amusement not only of the scholars, but of the community at large—The families of the subscribers shall have access to the Observatory *gratis,* whenever they are inclined to survey the heavens and admire the stupendous works of Creation.[48]

It was hoped that this enterprise with its typically deistic faith in reason, optimism in education, and revelation of God in astronomy could begin with the new year 1802, but nothing happened. Men of means could apparently not be induced to contribute. Deism was an understanding of life for them; for Palmer it was a religion, and throughout he seems to have remained a minister. It must be remembered, of course, that because of his blindness he had no other means of earning a livelihood.

While the Theophilanthropists of Philadelphia failed to erect their building, they seem to have given their support to *The Temple of Reason* at least to the extent of keeping it going during the year 1802. The New York society in the meantime seems to have been even less successful due to its affiliation with the tangled politics of the city. At the time of the presidential election in 1800, the

---

[48] *The Temple of Reason,* Philadelphia, November 25, 1801, p. 367.

Republicans—Burrites, Clintonians, and Livingstonians—had stood united to a man. The harmony was however short-lived and in the libellous aftermath, the Clintonians who were associated with the deistic society must have felt that it pays the politician to keep up the appearance of religious orthodoxy. No one apparently appreciated this fact more fully than De Witt Clinton, the reputed author in 1800 of an anonymous pamphlet in *Vindication of Thomas Jefferson* against the charge of infidelity.

In this study, however, the political rivalry between the Burrites and the Clintonians is significant primarily because of the information incidentally revealed regarding the activities of the deist society in New York. Since the meetings of the society, with the exception of public discourses, were secret, the only source of information on this subject is the writings of those who desired to expose the society. After due allowance is made for the most obvious calumny and exaggeration, there remains a plausible body of interesting details.

John Wood, who had in 1802 published the libellous *History of the Administration of John Adams,* in the same year published *A Full Exposition of the Clintonian Faction, and the Society of the Columbian Illuminati.* He explains the source of his information, as follows: "Societies of this nature would, probably, forever remain unknown, were all the members true to their oath of fidelity: but the propagation of deism, like that of treason, is a crime so heinous, that it generally sooner or later, awakens the consciences of some of the actors, whose hearts are not altogether hardened in the deeds of iniquity." [49] And from

---

[49] John Wood, *A Full Exposition of the Clintonian Faction, and the Society of the Columbian Illuminati,* p. 30.

these unfaithful members the "inside" story was obtained.

The society was divided into three or more grades after the example of the European Illuminati, founded in 1775 by Dr. Adam Weishaupt, professor of canon law in the University of Ingolstadt.[50] The members were in every case ignorant of any higher grade, but all grades were under the direction of "Mr. Elihu Palmer, the Weishaupt of the order."[51] The meetings "consisted principally in metaphysical discussions, and decisions of questions proposed by the President, or some of the members. These questions were, with some few exceptions, no otherwise criminal than as being opposed to the divine revelation, and calculated to throw an appearance of ridicule on every thing christian. Those questions which were of a more serious nature, and a deeper and blacker complexion were reserved to the meetings of the individual grades, which met separately at Palmer's house. . . . Palmer's Principles of Nature, was the text book to all the members; and it was put into the hands of every minerval at his first entrance."[52]

It is believed that prospective members were required to take the oath of the Illuminati: "I. N. N. hereby bind myself, by mine honor and good name, forswearing all mental reservation, never to reveal, by hint, word, writing, or in any manner whatever, even to my most trusted friend, any thing that shall now be said or done to me respecting my wished-for reception, and this whether my reception shall follow or not; I being previously assured

---

[50] John Robison, *Proofs of a Conspiracy against all the Religions and Governments of Europe, carried on in the Secret Meetings of Free Masons, Illuminati, and Reading Societies* (Fourth Edition, New-York, 1798), p. 18.

[51] John Wood, *op. cit.*, p. 31.　　　[52] *Ibid.*, p. 32.

that it shall contain nothing contrary to religion, the state, nor good manners. I promise, that I shall make no intelligible extract from any papers which shall be shewn me now or during my noviciate. All this I swear, as I am, and as I hope to continue, a Man of Honor." [53]

It need scarcely be observed that there seems to be nothing startling about these activities and that the element of secrecy was chiefly of psychological value. The human species apparently loves the flattering feeling of belonging to an exclusive coterie. Nor is the "Constitution of the Theistical Society of New York" adopted in January 1802 any more exciting. "The object of this society is to promote the cause of moral science, and general improvement, in opposition to all schemes of religious and political imposture." Members must be of good moral character and unequivocally attached to the objects of the society; at each meeting every member shall pay six cents to the treasurer; and finally, "Each member of the society shall observe order and decorum during the time of meeting, and cultivate a spirit of friendly and philosophical intercourse." [54]

With reference to this last provision, Wood relates an amusing anecdote: "The last article, ordering an observance of decorum in the society, during the time of meeting, was extremely necessary, if we consider the temper of many of the characters, of which it was composed—This article was the one, most frequently violated.—A young man, an attorney, lately promoted to a lucrative office, in New-York, by means of the Clintonian interest, and whose name I would expose, were it not for a regard to the feel-

[53] Quoted in John Robison, *op. cit.*, pp. 94-95.
[54] Quoted in John Wood, *op. cit.*, pp. 34-35.

ings of his family, was particularly riotous and obscene in
his conversations.—One evening he was the cause of entirely breaking up the meeting by a frolic he acted, which
I shall relate for no other purpose, but to shew the brutish
irregularity which sometimes was carried on among them,
notwithstanding their pretended regard for decency, and
the awe the presence of the philosophic Palmer might be
supposed to inspire. A bald headed Caledonian, once an
orator in the Edinburgh convention, though now in America, forced to stroll about, to teach wh—s to dance and
negroes to fiddle, rose with majestic gravity, in order to
argue with David Denniston, the impropriety of having a
president or superior in their society. In the depth of his
argument, an unlucky spider, like Pindar's louse, dropped
'with legs sprawling' on the infidel's head.—The young
attorney in eager anxiety to rescue his brother, from the
insect's venom, snatched the staff of authority which
Palmer held, but not being a skilful marksman, in place of
destroying the little tenant of the loom, he knocked the
fiddler down—The confusion which ensued, may be easier
conceived than described. It was in vain that the attorney protested the innocence of his intentions; it was in
vain that his friend, a meager looking watchmaker, advocated his cause. The blind President at length, descended
from his seat, cursing and groping among his noisy pupils,
and commanded David Denniston to enforce order; but
David's exertions were to no purpose; and the Illuminati,
were obliged to lay aside all moral discussion for the evening." [55]

Among the discussions of the society, the following were
said to have been included: "Wherein does the moral

[55] John Wood, *op. cit.*, pp. 38-39.

turpitude of incest consist?" "Ought the man commonly
called Jesus Christ, to be regarded a bastard or the son
of Joseph?" "Whether would the practice of going in all
weathers and seasons, bald headed and uncovered, be
more conducive to mental knowledge, than the ordinary
habit of wearing hair and hats?" [56]

De Witt Clinton's relation to the Theistical Society is
not clear, but there is little doubt that Wood was quite
right in saying that the members of the society were Clintonians in politics and that as his supporters they were
favored with his patronage. He gained a somewhat unfavorable reputation for unscrupulous self-interest in in-
stalling friends and family connections.[57] His cousin,
David Denniston, was an important member of Palmer's
society and an editor of the Clintonian paper, *The American Citizen and Watchtower.* If the anonymous pamphlet
in *Vindication of Thomas Jefferson* against the charges of
infidelity is correctly attributed to Clinton, it certainly reveals him to have been not unsympathetic with deism.
Whatever the reasons, however, he lived to become vice-
president of the American Bible Society and a leading
figure in the Presbyterian Church.[58] After his death, he
became the subject of a eulogy by the Rev. Lebbeus Armstrong,[59] than whom it would be difficult to find a more
fanatical believer in hell fire and brimstone.[60]

[56] *Ibid.,* pp. 39-40.

[57] Howard L. McBain, *De Witt Clinton and the Origin of the Spoils
System in New York* (Ph.D. dissertation, Columbia University, New York,
1907).

[58] *Dictionary of American Biography* (New York, 1930), Vol. IV,
pp. 221-225.

[59] Lebbeus Armstrong, *A Sermon, delivered . . . March 6, 1828, on
the death of Governor Clinton* (Saratoga Springs, 1828).

[60] *Ibid., passim.* Cf., Lebbeus Armstrong, *Signs of the Times, Past,
Present, and Future . . .* (Third Edition, New York, 1849).

So astute a politician as De Witt Clinton must have observed that it was wise to disassociate republicanism from deism. Palmer's cause was becoming increasingly unpopular. "Not one of the printers of New-York," complains *The Temple of Reason*, "except the editor of the Citizen, would permit an advertisement respecting the Temple of Reason, to be inserted in their papers." [61] Writing in the pious language of a later period, Dr. Francis recalls that, "Public opinion, as I have already intimated, had become somewhat doubtful as to the wisdom which marked the French revolution. Many, once seemingly secure in the light of nature alone, now felt themselves led into a delusion, the results of which threatened more than temporal inconvenience. . . . Few were so blind as not to see that infidelity, wrapt in the mantle of the sovereign rights of the people, indulged the hope of her triumphant establishment, and the downfall of the strongest pillars of the Christian faith." [62]

The cause of militant deism, in short, was not to prosper. Dennis Driscol had left *The Temple of Reason* in April 1802 and later in the year founded the *American Patriot* in Baltimore, a republican but not a deist journal. *The Temple of Reason* was continued however without the interruption of an issue and beginning April 17, 1802, was "Published for the Proprietors." Their identities are not given but, somewhat rashly it seems, they speak of themselves as "gentlemen of independent minds; and, as far as abilities are wanting to the support of such a paper, of independent fortunes too." [63]

[61] *The Temple of Reason*, Philadelphia, March 13, 1802, p. 55.
[62] John W. Francis, *Old New York* (New York, 1866), pp. 124-125.
[63] *The Temple of Reason*, Philadelphia, July 10, 1802, p. 189.

Three months later, however, financial loss proved an effective stimulus to a seemingly irrational but amusing generalization: "When we first undertook to publish the Temple of Reason, it appeared to us that the number of atheists was so small that society could be under no apprehension from that quarter. Superstition seemed the most formidable enemy.—The history of man, and the present state of Europe, fully justified that supposition. Upon a more intimate acquaintance with the people of North America, we have some reason to question our former judgment, and we now are inclined to think, that atheism is more prevalent among us than people are in general aware of. . . . Atheists of this description, may be considered like maggots bred out of the corruptions of christianity, and are much worse than the filth to which they owe their origin; because they prey, unseen, or under a specious mask, on the very vitals of society. A considerable number of such mischievous machines have become subscribers to the Temple, with a lye in their mouths and villainy in their hearts, calling themselves deists, when they were not deists, promising to fulfil the conditions of subscription, without any such intention, and of course not one of them have paid one cent towards it." [64]

And on the same page appears a crisp note,

TO THE DISTANT SUBSCRIBERS TO THE TEMPLE WHO HAVE NOT PAID THEIR SUBSCRIPTION

Gentlemen,

When you subscribed for this paper you bound yourselves to pay three dollars in advance. Why have you not done it? The proprietors, with the assistance of some punctual deists, have made a shift to send you 32 Numbers, and if you are willing you

[64] *Ibid.*, Philadelphia, October 2, 1802, p. 255.

will easily find the means of remitting the amount of a year's subscription, which will enable them to do justice to these honest men,
by publishing the remaining 20 Numbers.[65]

On November 20, 1802, another earnest plea is made
for payment of subscriptions, "as cash is very much needed
at present." [66]   And with the issue of February 19, 1803,
The Temple of Reason came to an end; this time without
a resurrection.   "This is the last number of the second
volume.—If the Subscribers had punctually paid, it would
have continued in Philadelphia.   As it is, Mr. Palmer, in
a few weeks, intends to revive it in New-York, when he
will, no doubt, be thankful for a continuance of the favours
of those who are real friends to the cause of Deism, or
advocates of the unity of the Supreme Being." [67]

Palmer, the ever-optimistic Palmer, was to carry on.
There had been some talk of continuing *The Temple of
Reason* in Baltimore,[68] possibly under the direction of
Driscol who was down there, but one has the feeling that
Driscol was not the kind of man to die a martyr to a lost
cause.   Elihu Palmer was.   Or it may be that Palmer himself had contemplated removing to Baltimore which, as he
says, was mentioned as the place of its publication when the
new paper, *Prospect, or View of the Moral World*, was
first proposed.[69]   Finding however "that by far the greatest number of subscribers" were in New York and the
adjacent country, he decided not to change his headquarters.   He was also still giving his lectures in Snow's tavern
on Broadway.

[65] *The Temple of Reason*, Philadelphia, October 2, 1802, p. 255.
[66] *Ibid.*, Philadelphia, November 20, 1802, p. 303.
[67] *Ibid.*, Philadelphia, February 19, 1803, p. 410.
[68] *Ibid.*, Philadelphia, February 5, 1803, p. 391.
[69] *Prospect*, New York, December 17, 1803, p. 15.

Details are lacking, but we know that in 1803, Palmer acquired a helpmeet in his work. "He was married," we learn from Mr. Conway, "by the Rev. Mr. Watt to a widow, Mary Powell, in New York." [70] Mrs. Powell kept a boarding house at 71 Cortlandt Street where Palmer had been living for some time.[71] Palmer succeeded in converting her to deism, and after his death she turned a few pages of an unpublished manuscript over to Palmer's friend, John Fellows, for safekeeping to avoid having them burned by a more orthodox sister. Mr. Fellows speaks of Mrs. Palmer as "a woman of good sense, and fine moral feelings, and possessed as strong an interest as her husband in promoting the cause of truth." [72]

With the aid of Mrs. Palmer, Palmer edited the new deist weekly and tardy successor to *The Temple of Reason* himself. Believing that "the period has at length arrived in which the civilized world has recognized the necessity of moral principles to regulate the conduct of intelligent beings," he explains to the public the aim of his periodical. He proposes that every theological system be judged by the purity of its moral precepts. Sincere believers certainly should have nothing to fear from such an inquiry for, "whatever is divine is true, and will pass safely the intellectual ordeal of individuals, nations, and ages. It should be presumed then that the friends of christianity would rejoice in a periodical publication of this kind. . . ." An assumption, of course, which none knew better than Palmer to be totally unfounded. "But it is not to the examination of religious subjects alone that this paper

[70] Moncure D. Conway, *op. cit.*, Vol. II, p. 363.
[71] David Longworth, *New-York Directory, 1801*, p. 253; David Longworth, *New-York Directory, 1802*, p. 285.
[72] John Fellows, *op. cit.*, p. 3.

will be confined; it opens itself also to the reception of all moral, philosophical, and literary productions, useful to society, and calculated to augment the science and happiness of human life." [73]

As these quotations of its aims indicate, the *Prospect* is primarily a restatement of the principles which its editor had formulated in his other works. They are here more concisely stated and through the medium of a weekly intended to reach a new and wider audience. The territory to be reached is indicated in the statement to subscribers: "It will be recollected by our subscribers, that one half of the annual price of this Paper was to be paid in advance: in conformity to this regulation subscribers in this city will please to make the first half year's payment to the Editor, No. 26, Chatham-Street.—Those in Orange County, and the adjacent country, to Dr. Jonathan Hedges, Newburgh.—Those in Philadelphia, to Mr. Isaac Hall, corner of Vine and Front-Street.—Those in Baltimore, to Mr. Peter Stygers.—Those in every other part of the country to any of the above named Persons to whom it may be most convenient." [74] This list of agencies was further extended on July 28, 1804, to include Mr. Rufus Spalding at Rhinebeck, New York, for subscribers in Dutchess County.

With the advent of the *Prospect*, the activities of the deists are again advertised. From the first issue, December 10, 1803, to the issue of March 10, 1804, Palmer advertised weekly that, "Public Discourses, upon Moral and Philosophical Subjects, will be delivered by the Editor every Sunday evening, at 6 o'clock, at Snow's long room,

---

[73] *Prospect*, New York, December 10, 1803, pp. 1-2.
[74] *Ibid.*, New York, December 10, 1803, p. 8.

No. 89 Broad-Way." [75] In the issues of January 28, 1804,
February 4, 1804, February 11, 1804, and February 18,
1804, the editor also announced that he would deliver "A
Political Lecture" on "Tuesday evening next, at 7 o'clock,
at Shepherd's Long-Room, Druid's grove Tavern, No. 11,
George-street." [76] Beginning March 24, 1804, the Sunday evening discourses were changed from Snow's long-
room to Shepherd's long-room, and began to be advertised in stronger language as "concerning the principles
and character of Christian superstition." These were continued to include the issue of May 5, 1804. [77] They were
then interrupted until July 14, 1804, when the editor
again advertised to speak "on the baneful effects of ancient
superstition" at Shepherd's long-room. [78] On July 28,
1804, the place of the lectures was changed to the "As-
sembly-Room, No. 68, William-street," but only two
meetings were advertised to be held there. [79]

These changes in the place of meeting give the impression that conditions were not entirely satisfactory and we
are therefore not surprised to find Elihu Palmer making
another attempt to erect a building for the activities of the
society:

TEMPLE OF NATURE

A plan is now under consideration, in this city, for the purchase of a lot, and the erection of a building intended to be used
for the worship of One God Supreme and Benevolent Creator
of the world; and for other purposes of a literary kind. To facilitate an object so important, a meeting of the friends to Natural

[75] *Ibid.*, pp. 8, 16, 24, 32, 40, 48, 56, 64, 72, 80, 88, 96, 104, 112.
[76] *Ibid.*, January 28, 1804, p. 64; February 4, 1804, p. 72; February 11,
1804, p. 80; February 18, 1804, p. 88.
[77] *Ibid.*, pp. 128, 137, 145, 152, 160, 168, 176.
[78] *Ibid.*, pp. 256, 264.   [79] *Ibid.*, pp. 272, 280.

Religion will be convened on Monday evening next, at seven o'clock, at Snow's, No. 89, Broadway; at which time and place all persons who wish to encourage this plan, are respectfully invited to attend.[80]

The following week, August 25, 1804, the meeting was reported as follows:

TEMPLE OF NATURE

On Monday evening last, there was a meeting in this city, of some of the friends to Natural Religion, the object of which was to obtain subscriptions for building a Church, and, although the meeting was not very numerous, we are happy in being able to state, that the spirit exhibited on that occasion augers well to the ultimate accomplishment of the object. Six hundred dollars were subscribed on that evening, and if the friends to the cause who were not present should exhibit an equal zeal, of which there can be no doubt, a failure of this plan will be impossible. Another meeting will be held on Monday evening next, at 8 o'clock, at the house of the Editor, No. 26, Chatham-street, for the purpose of obtaining further subscriptions, &c. While so many altars are raised to advance the cause of superstition, it will be a pity indeed if one cannot be reared in honor of the true and living God, and to promote the exalted cause of a pure and incorruptible morality![81]

Another meeting was announced in the issue of September 15, 1804:

We are requested to inform all those who hold Subscription Papers for building the Temple of Nature, that there will be a meeting of the Subscribers on Monday evening next, at seven o'clock, at Shepherd's Long-Room, No. 11, George-street.— All persons friendly to the cause of natural religion, and who wish to become share-holders in the building are invited to attend.[82]

[80] *Prospect*, August 18, 1804, p. 296.
[81] *Ibid.*, August 25, 1804, p. 304.
[82] *Ibid.*, p. 328.

But this is the last to be heard from the Temple of Nature. No more notices of discourses appeared in the *Prospect* for several months until February 23, 1805, when
the editor was scheduled to speak "every Sunday evening,
in Mustan's Long Room, No. 11, George-Street, at half
past six o'clock," and these notices were continued until the
end of the *Prospect* with the issue of March 30, 1805.[83]

The apparent failure in the undertaking to build the
Temple of Nature, the intermittent Sunday evening discourses and their removal from place to place, are all
straws indicating that the wind was not favorable to the
dissemination of Palmer's ideas. He no doubt still had
his followers who attended his Sunday evening lectures
which he delivered whenever he was in the city, but substantial financial backing continued to be sadly lacking.
This is further confirmed by notices, reminiscent of *The
Temple of Reason*, referring to the financial difficulties of
the *Prospect*. In the April 28, 1804, issue of the *Prospect*,
the following appeal appears above the editor's name:
"Those Subscribers to the Prospect, who have not made
their first half year's payment, are requested to do it as
soon as possible;—This will enable the Editor to fulfil
his contract and continue the publication without embarrassment." [84] On July 21, 1804, the delinquents, "who
have not made their second half year's payment, will
oblige the Editor by doing it as soon as possible." [85]
Finally in the issue of March 30, 1805, the editor makes
the following detailed announcement:

[83] *Ibid.*, pp. 64, 72, 80, 88, 96, 104. With the first issue in 1805, pages
were numbered as if beginning a new volume.

[84] *Ibid.*, p. 168. This notice was repeated the following week, May 5,
1804, p. 176.

[85] *Ibid.*, p. 264.

TO THE SUBSCRIBERS FOR THE PROSPECT

This number completes the first quarter of the year for eighteen hundred and five. Circumstances make it necessary to call the attention of our friends and patrons to some important facts essentially connected with the future progress of this paper. In the first place, it ought to be obvious to every intelligent mind, that a periodical publication of this sort, containing no advertisements to furnish pecuniary resources, and opposing itself constantly to the current of public opinion, must labour under peculiar disadvantages, to which other papers, pamphlets, and magazines, are not exposed. . . . The Prospect for the year eighteen hundred and four, claimed from the subscribers and its friends, a payment of one half of the sum in advance; upon trying the experiment, it was found incompetent to meet the current expenditures of the establishment. In addition to this, the year terminated with a deficiency of nearly one fourth part of the sum, which ought to have been received from the whole number of subscribers. When the Editor commenced the paper for the present year, he stated that the whole subscription should be paid in advance; but notwithstanding this precautionary arrangement, he is sorry to observe, that there has not been received one half the sum necessary to pay the expenses of the first quarter's printing, setting aside all other expenses, necessarily connected with the establishment. The Editor, therefore, informs his subscribers, that the publication of the Prospect will be suspended for four weeks, and he earnestly solicits all the subscribers to make payment during that time, by which he will be enabled to proceed with regularity, and without embarrassment.[86]

The *Prospect* never appeared again. Like his fond hopes for a Temple of Nature it, too, failed. At forty-one Palmer had grown old, weary, and tired of opposing himself "constantly to the current of public opinion." "The world is not yet so enlightened, or so liberal," he wrote sadly, "as to depart in any high degree from its in-

[86] *Prospect*, pp. 97-98.

terests and its prejudices," and "the philosophers and contemplative men, who have dared to look superstition full in the face, are, comparatively speaking, few in number." [87] The blind Palmer was both a heroic and a tragic figure. Many of the principles for which he stood have long since lost their novelty in wide acceptance, but when he died a year after the failure of the *Prospect*, it was as the champion of a cause which had brought him only poverty and opposition.

[87] *Ibid.*, March 30, 1805, pp. 97-98.

CHAPTER IV

THE SOCIETY OF ANCIENT DRUIDS

AN interesting outpost of Palmer's New York deist society was in the town of Newburgh, about sixty miles up the Hudson. This little town had been ardently patriotic during the American Revolution and "was fertile soil for Jeffersonian democracy." [1] Under the influence of the French Revolution, one kind of radicalism led to another and by the end of the 1790's, Newburgh's historian says that at no place did the anti-religious sentiments of Voltaire and Paine prevail to a greater extent. [2]

In one of the earliest extant copies of a Newburgh newspaper, *The Mirror,* appears part of a long letter from an irate and unknown layman to a clergyman who had warned and threatened him with the worst in the great hereafter. "To Jonathan Freeman, An ostensible ambassador from a court above, but perhaps more properly a renegado emissary from a well known court below." "The doctrine of passive obedience and non-resistance to clerical as well as political rules has gone into disuse and disrespect, and I hope and trust, it will never be revived as long as the least shadow of intelligence pertains to the human race— It is the loss of this dominion however, which I presume galls you more than the abundant effusion of human blood; for

[1] Dixon Ryan Fox, *The Decline of Aristocracy in the Politics of New York* (Ph.D. dissertation, Columbia University, New York, 1918), p. 48.
[2] E. M. Ruttenber, *History of the County of Orange: with a History of the Town and City of Newburgh* (Newburgh, N. Y., 1875), p. 165.

clergymen of your description fond of power, prerogative and previledges have not been the most sparing of the vital fluid.—Indeed your first invective against the French nation, seems rather to have originated from their destruction of clerical order and respect, than from the real injuries which your country has sustained. The fact is the reformation of the calender and the abolition of the Sabbath, is a bone which sticks in your throat which you are determined neither to swallow or digest. Swollen with rage and armed at all points with holy zeal, you in the language of senator Tracey, wish to arm every woman and child in America, against every woman and child in France; like father Peter waving your crucifix in your hand, and animating all America in the holy conflict, you are determined to dispossess the infidels of the holy land. . . . Had you, have pointed out the awful end and death of Ethan Allen, as a warning to me in a friendly, private manner, and had you, have proven his fate the ligitimate consequence of his infidelity, you might have been entitled to my respect and gratitude, if no credit had been given to the orthodoxy of your opinions. But when you in the language and accents of spiritual pride, haughtiness and superiority, hold it up in terrorem to frighten me into an acknowledgement of your clerical superiority, and a timid acquiescence in your religious and political opinions, I shall reject the threat as a chimera & bugbear, calculated rather to facinate and intimidate the mind, than to soften the heart and illuminate the understanding. . . . Turn your reflections sir, in upon your present state of mind, look at the inveterate fury of your peurile superstitious productions, your rancorous hatred to the progress of civil and religious liberty, contemplate the dirty lava you have emitted from the Crater of your combustible and effervercing intellect, and I fancy that if you are spiritually discerned, you can trace a more exact resemblance of a boar in combat than the death of Ethan Allen." [3]

Though far removed from the active scenes of the French Revolution, it breathes in nearly every line opposition to the privileged in church and state and shows that the spirit of Ethan Allen was still alive in this frontiersman of Orange County.

Nor was this spirit of republicanism and deism confined to Newburgh's *hoi polloi*. When a select group of its patriotic citizens met at Gardner's Coffee-room on Friday, the twenty-first of June, 1799, "for the purpose of consulting upon, and making arrangements for the celebration of the ensuing 4th of July," they solemnly resolved that the day be duly "celebrated in this town," and "that Elihu Palmer, deliver a political oration on that day at the Academy." David Denniston, with whom we are already acquainted as a leading figure in Palmer's deist society in New York, was the secretary of the committee in charge of the arrangements. [4]

The fact that it was the only Fourth of July oration delivered in Newburgh in 1799 is evidence of the religious and political liberalism of its citizens. *The Mirror* of July 9, 1799, reported fully the day's festivities:

ANNIVERSARY OF AMERICAN INDEPENDENCE—
JULY 4

This day, the birth-day of our liberty and political existence was celebrated in this place, with those republican sentiments and

[3] *The Mirror*, Newburgh, Monday, October 22, 1798.
[4] *Ibid.*, Newburgh, Tuesday, June 25, 1799.

patriotic feelings which ought ever to characterise the conduct of those who are the advocates of free constitutions, and the zealous defenders of equal liberty in every part of the world.

At twelve o'Clock a procession was formed, which moved from the house of Mr. E. Howell, to the Academy, in the following order:

> *Artillery company,*
> *Federal and Militia officers,*
> *Citizens,*
> *Light-Infantry company.*

The assembly which attended on this occasion being seated in the Court room, the declaration of Independence was read by Mr. D. Denniston; after which a political oration was delivered by Mr. Palmer, containing those genuine sentiments of republicanism, which constitutes the basis of American liberty, intermingled with remarks relative to the progressive improvement of free governments, and exhibiting a developement of those moral and mental powers the operation of which bear so strong a relation to the amelioration of the human race.

The company then returned to Mr. Howells' where they dined together in the utmost harmony—after which the following toasts were drank accompanied with a discharge from the artillery:—

1st.   The memorable 4th of July, '76—May the principles that gave birth to the day become universal among all nations.

3d.   The philosophers and philanthropists of all countries— May their labours restore the slaves of despotism to the dignity of man.

4th.   The arts and sciences—May their progress never be impeded by the destructive operation of despotism.

7th.   The *republicans* of the whole earth—May they eat the bread of their own industry and enjoy the happiness that belongs to good men—*3 cheers.*

9th.   The despotisms of the earth—May they expire at the feet of republican virtue—*3 cheers.*

10th.   The Federal constitution—May the republican virtue of America preserve it inviolate.

11th.   Unconditional slavery—May its destruction establish political consistency in America.

12th.   May the friends of political liberty never become the advocates of moral despotism—*3 cheers*.

13th.   The liberty of the Press—May the despots who would destroy it become the execration of the human race.

15th.   Republicanism to the whole earth—May its benign effects be co-extensive with the rays of the sun.

By Mr. Palmer—The energy of the human mind—May freedom of enquiry mark its operations upon all subjects and in all countries.

The celebration of the day closed with rational mirth and festivity, and each citizen seemed to recognise those genuine principles of republicanism which gave birth to the freedom and independence of the United States of America.[5]

Some of these same influential citizens of Newburgh had organized themselves into an interesting radical religious body called "The Druid Society." Like its sister organization, the Deistic Society in New York, it was a radical offshoot of an earlier and more conservative society. A Masonic lodge had been established in Newburgh in 1788,[6] and it seems, as one attempts to piece together the fragmentary facts, that as the brothers, or at least a number of them, became more and more radical in the feverish days of the French Revolution, the metamorphosis from Mason to Druid resulted. The Druids held their meetings in the room formerly occupied by the Masons and continued to use a ceremony similar to the Masonic.[7] It is interesting to note, too, that as the Druid Society died out contemporaneously with the end of

[5] *The Mirror*, Newburgh, Tuesday, July 9, 1799.
[6] E. M. Ruttenber, *op. cit.*, pp. 351-352.
[7] *Ibid.*, p. 175.

Palmer's activities in New York City, a new Masonic Lodge was instituted in Newburgh in 1806.

The question naturally arises as to why these apostate Masons chose the name of Druids. It seems that when they abandoned Christianity, with which Masonry in America had not been incompatible, they went back to the religion of the ancient Druids who were sun worshippers. It was commonly believed at that time, by the radicals of course, that both Christianity and Masonry were derived from the worship of the sun, of which Volney's chapter on "Christianisme, ou culte allégorique du Soleil" [8] is typical. The Druids thus went back to the pure worship of the great luminary, the visible agent of a great invisible first cause, and regarded Christianity as a later accretion and subversion of the true faith, a superstition, in short, developed by a designing and unscrupulous priesthood, to put it mildly in the language of the day. These Newburgh Druids thus seem to have been Masons who did not believe in Christianity. [9]

The Druids, no doubt, were responsible for Palmer's delivering the Fourth of July oration in Newburgh in 1799. In fact, on the margin of the copy of *The Mirror*

[8] M. Volney, *Les Ruines, ou Méditation sur les Révolutions des Empires*, pp. 288-301. For a discussion of French influence on Freemasonry in America, see Lucian J. Fosdick, *The French Blood in America*, Part IV, Ch. III, "The French in Freemasonry."

[9] This thesis that Masonry is descended from the religion of the Druids is developed in an interesting essay by Thomas Paine, *Origin of Freemasonry*, written in New York City in 1805. Paine mentions a society of Masons in Dublin who called themselves Druids.—*The Life and Works of Thomas Paine*, Patriots' Edition, edited by William M. Van der Weyde (Thomas Paine National Historical Association, New Rochelle, N. Y., 1925), Vol. IX, pp. 167-189.

M. Faÿ in his study of Dr. Franklin tells of the association of Masonry, Druidism, and Deism in England in the days when Franklin was a printer in London.—Bernard Faÿ, *Franklin, the Apostle of Modern Times*, pp. 90-91.

of July 9, 1799, in the Newburgh Library is written, with a cross referring to Palmer, "A Deist preacher that recides in Newburgh." The New York society was not very active just at that time and Palmer had evidently accepted an invitation to remain in Newburgh for a while.

The Newburgh Druids acquired a reputation even more evil and shocking than the Deists of New York or the Theophilanthropists of Philadelphia.[10] ". . . they met weekly," says the Rev. John Johnston, "for the purpose of ridiculing the Bible, and of confirming each other in unbelief. . . . They invited to Newburgh a blind man, of the name of Elihu Palmer, and led him to the academy, to deliver to them weekly lectures in opposition to the Bible. . . . This man was brought to Newburgh under a promise of an annual salary, to detail from Sabbath to Sabbath the opinions of Voltaire, Paine, Rousseau, Godwin, and others of the same stamp. A weekly infidel paper was also published in Newburgh. Paine's *Age of Reason*, Tyndal's *Christianity as Old as Creation*, and other books of the same kind, were reprinted, and circulated with all diligence. These, and similar books, were found in every tavern, or shop, or private house from which they were not positively excluded. These men also had rooms, where obscene prints and pictures were exhibited; and young persons, and even children, were invited and decoyed to view these drawings, which were generally intended to throw ridicule on some portion of sacred history. So bold and outrageous had these infatuated men become, that on a Sabbath after the Lord's Sup-

---

[10] Many years later, Dr. Francis still remembered having heard that at Newburgh, "the typical symbols of Christianity were sometimes outrageously profaned, and the holy sacraments prostituted to the vilest ends." —John W. Francis, *Old New York*, p. 132.

per had been administered, they collected at a spring near the place of worship, and, in mockery of what had been done in the church, gave a piece of bread and some water to a dog, using the words of our blessed Redeemer, when he instituted the holy supper. It ought to be known, that the principal actor in this impious transaction did not long survive. On the following Sabbath evening he was found in his room, with the door locked, apparently in a fit. The door was forced, and he was seen lying on the floor, convulsed with awful spasms, and he expired without being able to utter a word. Whether he had taken anything with a view to self-destruction, or whether it was the immediate act of God, without his voluntary agency, we know not. True, a good man may die suddenly, without being able to say a word to surrounding friends; but the proximity of the sudden and awful death of this man to the impious transaction of the preceding Sabbath leads the mind into fearful conjectures. This occurred in July, 1799. . . . On another occasion, a clergyman, after preaching, was attacked by a fierce dog, set on by several persons belonging to the Druid society. For a time it seemed as if these infatuated men had determined that there should not remain in Newburgh and its vicinity a vestige of Christianity; and they employed every means in their power to accomplish their object. But God, in mercy, brought to naught their wicked counsels." [11]

Although the main facts of this ominous story are generally conceded to have been as Dr. Johnston states them, Mr. Ruttenber confirms the modern reader's impression

[11] John Johnston, *The Autobiography and Ministerial Life of the Rev. John Johnston, D.D., edited and compiled by the Rev. James Carnahan, D.D., late President of the College of New Jersey* (New York, 1856), pp. 90-94.

that Dr. Johnston's account "comes to us somewhat colored perhaps by religious prejudice." [12]   James Donnelly, who had been a member of the Druid Society for a time, told Mr. Ruttenber in 1858 that "the Druids first organized as a debating society. I joined the society under the impression that it was to be conducted for the benefit and instruction of the members. The laws said that neither politics nor religion were to be discussed. I met with the society four or five times, and finding that politics were discussed, I quietly withdrew and never troubled myself about them afterwards, as I did not approve of a secret political society. Perhaps two-thirds of the members were infidels. . . . I have heard of vile acts attributed to some of the members, as well as to some who were not. A great many withdrew after I left." [13]

Another contemporary, Jacob Schultz, recollected that the interpretation of the pious of the immediate hand of God in the death of Dr. Phineas Hedges, to whose sudden death Dr. Johnston refers, was not generally believed. [14]

[12] E. M. Ruttenber, *op. cit.*, p. 166.

[13] Quoted in *ibid.*, pp. 174-175.

As time went on, reports spread of the untimely and unnatural deaths of members of the Druid Society. "It is a notorious fact," says President Carnahan of the College of New Jersey, the editor of Dr. Johnston's autobiography, "that several belonging to the Druid Society died drunkards, committed suicide, or came to their end in a horrid manner. In the grave-yard in Newburgh, there is a stone, which after giving the name of the deceased, and the date of his death, adds, 'A victim of intemperance.' This stone was erected and the inscription written by an inebriate son of the deceased. Such are the effects of infidelity—'Without natural affection.' "—John Johnston, *op. cit.*, Appendix B, pp. 203-204.

This kind of misinformed moralizing with respect to the Newburgh infidels reached its height in Abner Cunningham's, *Practical Infidelity Portrayed and the Judgments of God made manifest* (Third Edition, New-York, 1836).

[14] E. M. Ruttenber, *op. cit.*, p. 166.

Dr. Jonathan Hedges who five years later, in 1804, was agent for Palmer's *Prospect* in Newburgh was undoubtedly a member of the same Hedges family.

The Mirror, which was the official "infidel" paper in New-burgh at the time, reports that Dr. Hedges died suddenly and does not mention the cause of his death, indicating that it was not known. As the following obituary indicates, conditions in Newburgh were unlike those in New York. In Newburgh men of education, position, and respecta-bility were militant republicans and deists:

DIED suddenly in this town, on the morning of the 2d inst. *Doctor Phineas Hedges.* In justice to his memory, it ought to be observed, that he was a man possessed of a strong mind, and this mind was highly cultivated and improved by the principles of general science, and the knowledge of the philosophy of nature.— He was a man possessed of a firm principle of integrity and jus-tice, and his conduct was regulated in conformity to the theory which his mind had conceived on these subjects. In his profession as a medical man, his talents and skill were highly estimated, and his death considered in this respect is a serious misfortune to the community in which he lived. In a political point of view, Doc-tor Hedges constantly exhibited a firm attachment to the genuine principles of republicanism, which must ever constitute the essence of national happiness in America. Philosophy, integrity, a love of liberty, and a knowledge of the medical art, were the distinguish-ing features in his character, and his death will be lamented by his intimate friends, and severely felt by the community at large.[15]

Even in Newburgh in 1799, however, infidelity was not permitted to reign without opposition. In the summer of that year, "Several gentlemen of no ordinary talents have it in contemplation to enter into a course of discussion and criticism, on the fashionable doctrines in religion, gov-ernment, and ethics, which are propagated at this time, with incredible zeal. The Commercial Advertiser and Spectator are selected as the channels of communication,

[15] *The Mirror,* Newburgh, Tuesday, July 9, 1799.

on account of their extent of circulation in city and country. This plan it is expected, will commence within three or four weeks. Persons of talents, who are not engaged in this enterprize, and who may wish to figure among 'these defenders of the moral and civilized character of Man,' will find their communications well received and duly noticed by the publishers. The names of the persons engaged in this laudable undertaking cannot be made public." [16]

Whether "these defenders of the moral and civilized character of Man" succeeded in organizing themselves and refuting the Druids is not known, but with the turn of the century and the election of Mr. Jefferson, republicanism gradually dropped its association with deism. Whereas in 1799, the editor of *The Mirror* maintained that, "It is a principle founded upon the universal opinion of philosophers, that a free and liberal press is the grand palladium of civil and religious liberty," [17] in 1800 the emphasis is entirely on politics, and philosophers, who were at this time invariably deists, were forgotten. Republicanism gradually became associated with Christianity. *The Rights of Man*, which replaced *The Mirror* in 1800, proved that to be a Christian, it is necessary to be a Republican: "Can any man be justly entitled to the appellation of christian while he is evidently an immoral man? no. Can any one be justly called a moral man, while his political principles induce him to support and advocate measures destructive to the dearest rights and interests of society? no." [18] *Ergo*, only a Republican can be a Chris-

[16] *The Mirror*, Newburgh, Tuesday, July 9, 1799.
[17] *Ibid.*, Newburgh, Tuesday, July 9, 1799.
[18] *The Rights of Man*, Newburgh, April 28, 1800.

tian! This is particularly interesting in view of the fact that Elias Winfield, the publisher of *The Rights of Man*, who was also a physician and druggist, was a member of the committee which had chosen Elihu Palmer to deliver the Fourth of July oration in 1799. It seems more likely that this was part of a deliberate attempt to free republicanism from the stigma of deism in the election of 1800 than that Winfield had in the meantime deserted the "infidel" crew.

The Rights of Man was much more genteel than *The Mirror* had been. Unlike the vigorous if crude effusions of 1798 when men were still men and minced no words, in 1802, the editor, Dennis Coles, politely announced that, "Essays and Communications, divested of personal abuse and partial invectives, are solicited from gentlemen of talents and leisure; and the effusions of female genius received with peculiar delight." [19]

In 1804, the Fourth of July oration was delivered in the Presbyterian Meeting House instead of in the Academy. Newburgh was still ardently republican, if the orator of the day correctly expressed the sentiments of "a very crowded and respectable audience." "It behooves us, my fellow citizens, to cherish that ardent thirst for liberty which at present so nobly distinguishes the American character, and has proved the bulwark against which the billows of despotism have been spent in vain." The despotism referred to by the orator was of the days of Federalism when, "An Adams succeeded [Washington] and the *reign of terror* commenced—The *gew gaws* of *nobility*, the *pageantry of a court*, a *hereditary chief magistrate*, *stars*, *garters*, and *ribands* were the objects for

[19] *Ibid.*, Newburgh, April 28, 1800.

which the men in power were contending, and by which their vanity was to be gratified." [20]   But one looks in vain for any reference to the overthrow of "superstition" or to the day when freedom of enquiry will prevail upon all subjects and in all countries.   On the contrary, the editor, Thomas Wilson, expresses the pious consolation that, "To the pious and reflecting mind, it will be matter of exultation and joy, that Hamilton died in the firm belief of Christianity." [21]   And from this time on frequent accounts of revivals from Vermont to Georgia appear in the columns of the *Rights of Man* and its fellow republican paper, the *Recorder of the Times*.   A great revival is reported in Bridgeport, Vermont, with three thousand assembled, over a third of whom "have been added to the churches in the western part of Vermont." [22]   It shows how great a change had come over the state of Ethan Allen in half a decade. In the same issue of the *Rights of Man* appears an account of a great camp meeting at Wilmington, North Carolina, where "The windows of heaven were opened, and the powers of the world to come were manifested in copious showers; without respect of persons, numberless lay prostrate on the ground. . . . Others were struggling into life eternal by faith in Christ, while the prayers and intercessions of the old professors of religion were going up as a cloud of incense, perfumed with the blood of the Gracious Redeemer." [23]

The *Recorder of the Times* in an article on the influence of camp meetings in the South, which later appeared also in the *Rights of Man*, says, "Deists have become

---

[20] *The Rights of Man*, Newburgh, July 30, 1804.
[21] *Ibid.*, Newburgh, August 6, 1804.
[22] *Ibid.*, Newburgh, August 20, 1804.
[23] *Ibid.*, Newburgh, August 20, 1804.

admirers of divine revelation—Drunkards have learned
and practised the doctrines of sobriety—Profane swearers
have learned to venerate the name of God with profound
reverence—those who profaned the sabbath day now keep
it holy—Libertines are reformed—the proud humbled—
the envious, love their neighbors—the malicious, seek the
welfare of mankind—those who possess the cruel disposition of the wolf, now enjoy the meekness of the lamb—
many who were a disgrace to the human race, a reproach
to their families, and a scandal to themselves have, at these
meetings, been reformed, and become respectable hus-
bands, parents, and neighbors, citizens and Americans.—
Persons of every description have experienced the influence of these meetings; old & young, rich and poor, bond
and free, black and white, the philosopher and the rustic,
the scholar & the ignoramus, the magistrate & the private
citizen, physicians, lawyers, merchants, mechanics and
farmers, have experienced the good effects of them." [24]

Even more significant is the interpretation that these
revivals prove the calumny of the Federalists in accusing
the Republicans of infidelity: "These things have taken
place under the administration of Mr. Jefferson, the man
who has been represented to us as an Infidel; and the very
people who are averse to his administration, live in the
enjoyment of those blessings, his administration as a secondary cause procured for them. That we enjoy many
blessings under his wise and virtuous administration, cannot be denied; and as if Almighty God intended forever
to silence the calumny of his enemies, he has poured out
his spirit among the people in a manner before unknown

[24] *Recorder of the Times,* Newburgh, Wednesday, August 29, 1804.

in America." [25]   Belying the direct prophecies of Federalism four years before, Republicans now pointed proudly to the marriage of Jeffersonian democracy to evangelical Protestantism.

The revivals soon drew nearer home to Newburgh. In September, 1804, the Methodists held a three-day camp meeting in Carmel, Dutchess County (now in Putnam County), with a congregation estimated at seven thousand. "The lord was in the midst and manifested his presence— many found peace; some were convinced of sin, and others found full redemption in the blood of the Lamb.—The meeting continued night and day; the rejoicing of some, and the distress of others, made it a melting scene." [26] "The number awakened, re-awakened, converted, restored from backsliding, and sanctified at this camp meeting could not be ascertained with any degree of precision. In eternity it will be known and cause transports which never shall end." [27]

Amid this changed religious scene, the following notice of a meeting of the Druids seems like a spectral apparition of a by-gone age:

SOCIETY OF ANCIENT DRUIDS

The Members are requested to meet at their Lodge Room on Saturday, the 22nd inst. at three o'clock in the afternoon, to celebrate their anniversary festival: at which time and place an Oration will be delivered by one of the members.

ALEXANDER FALLS, Sec.[28]

Sept. 7, 1804.

[25] *Recorder of the Times*, Newburgh, Wednesday, August 29, 1804.
[26] *Rights of Man*, Newburgh, October 1, 1804.
[27] *Ibid.*, Newburgh, October 8, 1804.
[28] *Ibid.*, Newburgh, September 10, 1804.

The notice was repeated in the *Rights of Man* in the issue of September 17, 1804, and then the Druids were never heard of again. They probably had other meetings of which no records remain, but the spirit of the times was all against them. As an old member recollected many years later, "I never knew how the society broke up, but always supposed it died out with the infidel movement." [29]

[29] Quoted in E. M. Ruttenber, *op. cit.*, p. 175.

CHAPTER V

OTHER PROPHETS

ASSOCIATED more or less with Elihu Palmer, the chief organizer and expositor of deism as a religion, were several other leaders. The most important of these was Thomas Paine.

Paine naturally did not find himself comfortable in the France of Bonaparte and had been contemplating returning to America. Soon after the inauguration of Mr. Jefferson in 1801, the President wrote a very cordial letter inviting him to return on the sloop-of-war, *Maryland,* the honored guest of a grateful nation. Referring evidently to the bad feeling and misunderstanding which had prevailed between Paine and Jefferson's presidential predecessors, Jefferson wrote, "I am in hopes you will find us returned generally to sentiments worthy of former times. In these it will be your glory steadily to have laboured, and with as much effect as any man living. That you may long live to continue your useful labours, and to reap their reward in the thankfulness of nations, is my sincere prayer. Accept assurances of my high esteem and affectionate attachment." [1]

On October 30, 1802, Thomas Paine landed at Baltimore. He had left America in April, 1787, to visit his old home in England, expecting to remain abroad a year.

---

[1] Letter to Thomas Paine, March 18, 1801. *The Writings of Thomas Jefferson,* edited by Paul L. Ford (New York, 1897), Vol. VIII, p. 19.

More than fifteen years had passed amid adventures and
hardships which in fiction would seem incredible. They
had left their marks on him. He returned an old man,
seeking peace and quiet for his declining years. He was
probably surprised at the furor which his arrival in America excited. "You can have no idea," he wrote to a friend
in London, "of the agitation which my arrival occasioned."
Every paper is "filled with applause or abuse." [2]

The "infidels" hailed the event as providential. Said
The Temple of Reason exultantly: "The prayers of Christians have not been attended to—The Supreme and Wise
Ruler of the Universe was not to be diverted from his
eternal purpose, by their petitions—Thomas Paine, the
friend of liberty, and the apostle of the one only God, has
arrived at Baltimore, in good health, sound intellect, and
high spirits, agreeable to the wishes (not the prayers) of
every real friend to reason and humanity.—The christians
already tremble for their Superstition—the craft feel
themselves in danger—while the friends of moral truth,
founded on the nature of man, and the relation he stands
to his Maker, expect in him a firm supporter and advocate
of genuine unsophisticated morality; and a powerful an-
tagonist against those who have retreated to the last citadel
'the necessity of imposture.' " [3]

For the Federalists, on the other hand, the event was
equally providential. It afforded them a remarkable opportunity to exploit the rising tide of public opinion against
infidelity for political purposes. Had they not long and
vociferously predicted that Mr. Jefferson's election would

[2] Quoted in Moncure D. Conway, *The Life of Thomas Paine*, Vol. II,
p. 309.
[3] *The Temple of Reason*, Philadelphia, November 6, 1802, p. 287.

result in reducing the American people to the state of atheism? And now the author of the *Age of Reason* himself was honored by the chief executive of the nation who hoped that he "may long live to continue his useful labours"! When the *New England Palladium* of Boston heard of the President's invitation it fairly shrieked: "What! invite to the United States that lying, drunken, brutal infidel, who rejoices in the opportunity of basking and wallowing in the confusion, devastation, bloodshed, rapine, and murder, in which his soul delights?"[4] The critical Mr. Dennie, "noted among his classmates [Harvard, 1790] for his elegance and for his unusual acquaintance with polite letters,"[5] published in his weekly *Port Folio* of Philadelphia: "If during the present season of national abasement, infatuation, folly, and vice, any portent could surprise, sober men would be utterly confounded by an article current in all our newspapers, that the loathsome Thomas Paine, a drunken atheist and the scavenger of faction, is invited to return in a national ship to America by the first magistrate of a free people. A measure so enormously preposterous we cannot yet believe has been adopted, and it would demand firmer nerves than those possessed by Mr. Jefferson to hazard such an insult to the moral sense of the nation. If that rebel rascal should come to preach from his Bible to our populace, it would be time for every honest and insulted man of dignity to flee to some Zoar as from another Sodom, to shake off the very dust of his feet and to abandon America."[6]

[4] "Thomas Paine's Second Appearance in the United States," in *The Atlantic Monthly*, July 1859, Vol. IV, p. 10.

[5] *Dictionary of American Biography*, edited by Allen Johnson and Dumas Malone (New York, 1930), Vol. V, p. 235.

[6] *The Atlantic Monthly*, July 1859, Vol. IV, p. 10.

And when Paine finally arrived, the reactionary press exhausted the resources of the dictionary to express the unutterable, only to sink back at last impotent with rage. The Baltimore *Republican; or Anti-Democrat* refers to him as, "Thou lilly-livered sinical rogue, thou gibbet inheriting slave, thou are nought but the composition of a knave, beggar, coward, pander, and the son and heir of some drunken she-devil. . . ." [7] And Alexander Hamilton's supporter, William Coleman, published the following:

TO TOM PAINE

Detested reptile! wherefore hast thou come
  To add new evils to our groaning land?
To some wild desert let thy carcase roam,
  Where nought can wither by thy blasting hand.

.   .   .   .

In the dark hour that brought thee to our shore,
  The shade of Washington did awful scowl—
Hence, gloomy monster! curse mankind no more,
  Thy person filthy as thy soul is foul.

When life's electric spark shall quit thy frame,
  Myriads of devils wait to seize their prey;
With shouts and yell they loudly call thy name,
  Then bear thee to thy destin'd doom away. [8]

It appeared that President Jefferson was alarmed by the violence of public opinion and regretted his connection with Paine's return. At any rate, he failed to evidence any friendliness toward him until Paine wrote him on January 12, 1803:

[7] *Republican; or Anti-Democrat*, Baltimore, November 26, 1802.
[8] *New-York Evening Post*, December 8, 1802.
These verses and articles were copied by one paper from another all over the country.

I will be obliged to you to send back the Models, as I am packing up to set off for Philadelphia and New York. My intention in bringing them here in preference to sending them from Baltimore to Philadelphia, was to have some conversation with you on those matters and others I have not informed you of. But you have not only shown no disposition towards it, but have, in some measure, by a sort of shyness, as if you stood in fear of federal observation, precluded it. I am not the only one, who makes observations of this kind.[9]

Jefferson replied immediately, assuring Paine, "You have certainly misconceived what you deem shyness. Of that I have not had a thought towards you, but on the contrary have openly maintained in conversation the duty of showing our respect to you and of defying federal calumny in this as in other cases, by doing what is right."[10] Paine was invited to a visit in spite of the protests of the ladies of the presidential mansion to whom the President is said to have replied, in substance, " 'Mr. Paine is not, I believe, a favorite among the ladies—but he is too well entitled to the hospitality of every American, not to cheerfully receive mine.' Paine came and remained a day or two. As in their correspondence, Jefferson did not talk with him on the subject of religion. He called him out on historical, political and similar topics. Paine's discourse was weighty, his manners sober and inoffensive; and he left Mr. Jefferson's mansion the subject of lighter prejudices than he entered it."[11]

But most men of influence and position who had been

[9] Quoted in Moncure D. Conway, *op. cit.*, Vol. II, p. 315.
[10] Letter dated January 13, 1803. *The Writings of Thomas Jefferson*, edited by Paul L. Ford, Vol. VIII, p. 189.
[11] Henry S. Randall, *The Life of Thomas Jefferson* (New York, 1858), Vol. II, p. 644.

Paine's friends in "the times that tried men's souls" avoided him now. "His principles avowed in his *Age of Reason*," wrote Dr. Benjamin Rush, "were so offensive to me that I did not wish to renew my intercourse with him." [12] He returned to his home in Bordentown, New Jersey, where in the genial atmosphere of Deborah Applegate's tavern he is said to have turned several church members from their faith, "and on this account and the general feeling of the community against him for his opinions upon religious subjects he was by the mass of the people held in odium, which feeling to some extent was extended to Col. Kirkbride, who, though, was known by all to be a Christian." [13] Kirkbride remained a loyal friend. When they together visited the Colonel's brother-in-law, Samuel Rogers, who in the old days had also been a friend of Paine's, as he entered the door Rogers turned his back and refused his hand because it had written the *Age of Reason*. [14] These were trying days for a man returning home, old and tired. Mobs hooted him. In March 1803, when Col. Kirkbride sought to arrange passage for Paine on the stage from Trenton to New York, the stage owner, Capt. John Voorhis, declared, " 'he'd be damn'd if Tom Paine should go in *his* stage': and gave as his reason, that Paine was an infidel or deist!—Col. Kirkbride next went to the stage-office of Mr. John Vandegrift,

[12] Quoted in Moncure D. Conway, *op. cit.*, Vol. II, p. 318.

[13] E. M. Woodward and John F. Hageman, *History of Burlington and Mercer Counties, New Jersey* (Philadelphia, 1883), p. 471.

Col. Kirkbride was probably a nominal Christian. In a letter to Palmer, Paine wrote, "There is an intimate friend of mine, Colonel Joseph Kirkbride of Bordentown, New Jersey, to whom I would wish you to send your work [*Principles of Nature*]. He is an excellent man, and perfectly in our sentiments."—Letter dated at Paris, February 21, 1802, in Moncure D. Conway, *op. cit.*, Vol. II, p. 299.

[14] Moncure D. Conway, *op. cit.*, Vol. II, p. 325.

where he met with a like refusal, in similar language, for the same reason." [15]

So staunch a republican and old friend as Samuel Adams was estranged. In a letter dated at Boston, November 30, 1802, he wrote:

Sir,—

I have frequently with pleasure reflected on your services to *my* native and *your* adopted country. Your Common Sense, and your Crisis, unquestionably awakened the public mind, and led the people loudly to call for a declaration of our national independence. I therefore esteemed you as a warm friend to the liberty and lasting welfare of the human race. But when I heard you had turned your mind to a defence of infidelity, I felt myself much astonished and more grieved, that you had attempted a measure so injurious to the feelings and so repugnant to the true interest of so great a part of the citizens of the United States. The people of New England, if you will allow me to use a Scripture phrase, are fast returning to their first love. Will you excite among them the spirit of angry controversy at a time when they are hastening to amity and peace? I am told that some of our newspapers have announced your intention to publish an additional pamphlet upon the principles of your Age of Reason. Do you think that your pen, or the pen of any other man, can unchristianize the mass of our citizens, or have you hopes of converting a few of them to assist you in so bad a cause? We ought to think ourselves happy in the enjoyment of opinion, without the danger of persecution by civil or ecclesiastical law. Our friend, the President of the United States, has been calumniated for his liberal sentiments by men who have attributed that liberality to a latent design to promote the cause of infidelity. This, and all other slanders, have been made without the least shadow of proof. Neither religion nor liberty can long subsist in the tumult of altercation, and amidst the noise and violence of faction. *Felix qui cautus.* Adieu.[16]

[15] *American Citizen*, New York, March 19, 1803.
[16] *The Writings of Samuel Adams*, edited by Harry A. Cushing (New York, 1908), Vol. IV, pp. 412-413.

The unmistakable implication that their friendship was over must have saddened Paine. The letter also shows how eagerly respectable republicans strove to free themselves from the stigma of infidelity. Conservative in religion, although not in politics, they closed their thoughts to Jefferson's religious latitudinarianism and branded such imputations as malicious Federalist propaganda—as in fact most of it was even though not entirely devoid of truth.

"In New York Paine enjoyed the same kind of second-rate ovation as in Washington. A great number of persons called upon him, but mostly of the laboring class of emigrants . . ." [17] Prominent republicans, with few exceptions, deliberately avoided him. Of Commodore Nicholson, for example, whose house was an unofficial republican headquarters in New York, Henry Adams explains, "both Mrs. Nicholson and the Commodore were religious people, in the American sense as well as in the broader meaning of the term. They were actively as well as passively religious, and their relations with Paine, after his return to America in 1802, were those of compassion only, for his intemperate and offensive habits, as well as his avowed opinions, made intimacy impossible." [18]

Palmer's deists and other liberals were delighted with Paine's presence. They gave a large dinner for him, March 18, 1803, at the City-Hotel attended by about seventy people. Said the *American Citizen* whose editor, James Cheetham, was one of the principal promoters of this event: "On Friday last a dinner was given at the City-Hotel, in honor of the author of *Common Sense*. At 4 o'clock a numerous company of republicans sat down to

---

[17] *The Atlantic Monthly*, July 1859, Vol. IV, p. 12.
[18] Henry Adams, *The Life of Albert Gallatin* (Philadelphia, 1879), pp. 101-102.

dinner, after which the following toasts were drank, accompanied with appropriate songs and music—at ten o'clock the company retired in perfect harmony and order." Among the numerous toasts were, "Gratitude to the benefactors of our country;" "Opinion—a sacred right, acknowledged by all but tyrants;" "Reason, the sun of social existence—may its illuminating influence dispel the fogs of prejudice and error;" and "after Mr. Paine had retired—the President gave—Mr. THOMAS PAINE— He has dared when under the jaws of tyrants to vindicate the rights of Man—Shall he now be deterred by the reproaches of a forlorn remnant of aristocracy?—6 cheers;" "A new world and its liberties, and may the right of enquiry into the truth or falshood of systems of government, or systems of religion, be ever supported by the people of the United States." [19]

From this time on, Paine resided either on his farm at New Rochelle, about twenty miles from New York, or in the city itself. During the first two or three years after his return from abroad, he seems to have lived fairly happily despite the Federalists who used him as a means of discrediting the Republican party through associating deism or infidelity with republicanism. He was popular among liberal intellectuals. "He was often joined in his walks about town by some of our most enlightened citizens in social conversation . . . none could surpass him in the social circle, from the abundance of his varied knowledge and his vivid imagination." [20]

He was of course heartily in sympathy with Palmer's activities in promoting the religion of deism in New York,

[19] *American Citizen*, New York, Monday, March 21, 1803.
[20] John W. Francis, *Old New York*, pp. 139-140.

of which he had known even before returning to America. Palmer had sent him a copy of the *Principles of Nature* which he acknowledged in a letter dated at Paris, February 21, 1802, "since the Fable of Christ." He speaks of it as an "excellent work," and adds, "I see you have thought deeply on the subject, and expressed your thoughts in a strong and clear style." [21] He was now a member of the Deistic Society in New York. During the summer of 1804 when Palmer was again making plans for the building of a Temple of Nature,[22] Paine hoped that the plan would "open a way to enlarge and give establishment to the deistical church." [23] He spent the winter of 1804 to 1805 in New York and "threw himself warmly into the theistic movement." Mr. Conway thinks that no doubt he "occasionally spoke from Elihu Palmer's platform," [24] but since the *Prospect*, which was still published during that winter, does not mention any lectures by Thomas Paine it is not likely that he furthered the activities of the society in that way.

He was however an important contributor to the *Prospect*. The first of his articles was on a sermon, "Modern Infidelity," by an English Protestant minister. "The preacher of the foregoing sermon speaks a great deal about *infidelity*, but does not define what he means by it. His harangue is a general exclamation. Everything, I suppose, that is not in his creed is infidelity with him, and his creed is infidelity with me. Infidelity is believing falsely. If what christians believe is not true, it is the christians

[21] Quoted in Moncure D. Conway, *op. cit.*, Vol. II, p. 298.
[22] *Supra*, pp. 109-110.
[23] Letter to Col. John Fellows, dated at New Rochelle, July 9, 1804. Quoted in Moncure D. Conway, *op. cit.*, Vol. II, p. 340.
[24] Moncure D. Conway, *op. cit.*, Vol. II, pp. 362-363.

that are the infidels." He says that it cannot be proven that the Bible is *revealed religion* and maintains that it is a book of history and not revelation. "The obscene and vulgar stories in the bible are as repugnant to our ideas of the purity of a divine Being, as the horrid cruelties and murders it ascribes to him, are repugnant to our ideas of his justice. It is the reverence of the *Deists* for the attributes of the Deity, that causes them to reject the bible." [25]

To the reader already familiar with the movement of militant deism, this kind of harangue has lost its novelty. His other contributions are in the same vein, as their titles suggest: "Of the Word Religion, and other words of uncertain signification;" [26] a letter to the editor of the *Prospect* praising the latter's "judicious remarks . . . on the absurd story of Noah's flood," which had appeared in the issue of February 25, 1804; [27] "Of the Tower of Babel;" [28] "Of Cain and Abel;" [29] "Of the Old and New Testament;" [30] a letter written by Thomas Paine in Paris, May 12, 1797, defending his views on the Bible expressed in the *Age of Reason;* [31] "Of the Religion of Deism compared with the Christian Religion, and the superiority of the former over the latter;" [32] "Hints towards forming a

---

[25] *Prospect,* February 18, 1804, pp. 83-84.

[26] *Ibid.,* March 3, 1804, pp. 98-101.

[27] *Ibid.,* March 10, 1804, p. 108.

[28] *Ibid.,* March 24, 1804, pp. 126-127.

[29] *Ibid.,* March 31, 1804, pp. 132-133. This contribution is neither signed nor initialed, but is attributed to Paine and included in his *Works. Cf. The Life and Works of Thomas Paine,* edited by William M. Van der Weyde, Vol. IX, pp. 93-95.

[30] *Prospect,* March 31, 1804, p. 131. This article is signed, "A true Deist."

[31] *Ibid.,* May 26, 1804, pp. 195-199.

[32] *Ibid.,* June 30, 1804, pp. 235-239, and July 7, 1804, pp. 243-247.

Society for enquiring into the Truth or Falsehood of Ancient History, so far as History is connected with systems of Religion ancient and modern;"[33] "Of the Books of the New Testament. Addressed to the believers in the book called the Scriptures;"[34] "Of the Sabbath Day of Connecticut."[35]

There were also a few articles written in the same spirit but provoked by specific events of the day. One of these was an open letter "To Mr. Moore, of New-York, Commonly called Bishop Moore." It refers to the Holy Communion which the Rev. Dr. Moore had administered to Alexander Hamilton on his death bed. In a sermon on this subject Dr. Moore had said, "By reflecting on this melancholy event let the humble believer be encouraged ever to hold fast that precious faith which is the only source of true consolation in the last extremity of nature. Let the infidel be persuaded to abandon his opposition to the Gospel." Paine took exception. "Priests may dispute with priests," he said, "and sectaries with sectaries, about the meaning of what they *agree* to call scripture and end as they began; but when you engage with a Deist you must keep to fact. Now, Sir, you cannot prove a single article of your religion to be true, and we tell you so publicly. Do it, *if you can.*" On the other hand, "Deism is the only profession of religion that admits of worshipping and reverencing God in purity, and the only one on which the thoughtful mind can repose with undisturbed tranquility. God is almost forgotten in the Christian religion. Every

---

[33] *Ibid.*, July 21, 1804, pp. 259-263.

[34] *Ibid.*, September 1, 1804, pp. 307-311, and September 8, 1804, pp. 314-317. This article is signed "Detector-P."

[35] *Ibid.*, September 15, 1804, pp. 326-327. Signed, "An Enemy to Cant and Imposition."

thing, even the creation, is ascribed to the son of Mary."
Not of course that Paine hoped to be able to convince the
Bishop: "But you are a priest, you get your living by it,
and it is not your worldly interest to undeceive yourself."
It is interesting that Paine signs himself in this letter, "A
Member of the Deistical Church." It indicates that he
felt himself to be an active member of a genuinely re-
ligious organization.[36]

Shortly after, Paine contributed another letter, this time
to the Rev. John Mason, on the same subject, the death of
Alexander Hamilton. In closing it reads: "As adoration
paid to any being but God himself is idolatry, the Christian
religion by paying adoration to a man, born of a woman,
called Mary, belongs to the Idolatrous class of religions,
and consequently the consolation drawn from it is a delusion. Between you and your rival in communion ceremonies, Dr. Moore, of the Episcopal church, you have, in
order to make yourselves appear of some importance, reduced General Hamilton's character to that of a feeble-
minded man, who in going out of the world wanted a
passport from a priest. . . . The man, sir, who puts his
trust and confidence in God, that leads a just and moral
life, and endeavours to do good, does not trouble himself
about priest when his hour of departure comes, nor permit priests to trouble themselves about him. They are, in
general, mischievous Beings where character is concerned;
a consultation of priests is worse than a consultation of
physicians."[37]

In the issue of September 1, 1804, he wrote an article,

---

[36] *Prospect*, August 4, 1804, pp. 276-278.
[37] *Ibid.*, August 18, 1804, pp. 290-294. Signed, "A Member of the
Deistical Congregation."

"To the Members of the Society stiling itself the Missionary Society." It refers to an account in the *New-York Gazette* of August sixteenth on the presentation of a Bible to the chiefs of the Osage Indians. Paine, signing himself "A Friend to the Indians," feared the influence of missionaries on the Indians. "Priests, we know, are not remarkable for doing any thing gratis. They have, in general, some scheme in every thing they do, either to impose on the ignorant, or derange the operations of Government." [38]

As these titles and quotations indicate, the vigor of Paine's homely style was not abated nor his powers of invective less virulent. But his themes had become old and worn. His fellow deists had expected a third part of the *Age of Reason*,[39] but nothing startling or important came from his pen. After a decade's exposure of "Christian idolatry and superstition, of the wiles of priestcraft, and the obscenity of the Bible," Palmer's followers lost interest in these denunciations, especially since even the Christian clergy had also become somewhat indifferent to "infidelity."

With the failure of Palmer's *Prospect* in the spring of 1805,[40] the activities of organized deism in New York came to an end for the time being. Paine could not carry on Palmer's work; perhaps Palmer himself could not have continued his old activities had he lived. The times were no longer propitious for the promulgation of deism.

[38] *Ibid.*, September 1, 1804, pp. 305-307.

[39] In a letter dated at Paris, February 21, 1802, Paine had written to Palmer: "I expect to arrive in America in May next. I have a third part of the Age of Reason to publish when I arrive, which, if I mistake not, will make a stronger impression than any thing I have yet published on the subject."—Quoted in Moncure D. Conway, *op. cit.*, Vol. II, p. 299.

[40] *Supra*, p. 112.

Paine became more and more an object of public odium and contempt. Even an attempt to murder him was made.[41] Private problems, financial and personal, added to the difficulty and sadness of his old age. He wrote to Jefferson alluding to his financial difficulties and reminding the President that the State of Virginia had once proposed to give him a tract of land. He also suggested that Congress should reward his services. Both Jefferson and Madison were sympathetic, but of course nothing could be done.[42] Friends and acquaintances wisely shunned his company. A singer in the Presbyterian Church, of which the Rev. John Mason was pastor, who out of curiosity went to visit Paine was suspended.[43] It did not pay to be identified with infidelity. Isaac Hall of Philadelphia, who had been an agent for Palmer's *Prospect* in that city,[44] is said to have been refused the lease of a municipal wharf because he was "one of *Paine's* disciples."[45] At New Rochelle in 1806, Paine was not permitted to vote on the ground that he was not an American citizen![46] John Lambert, who visited in New York in this period, spoke of "the general detestation and contempt in which Paine was held by every respectable inhabitant of New York, where he resided. Not the most zealous partisan of Mr. Jefferson will notice him in public; and even those who

[41] Moncure D. Conway, *op. cit.*, Vol. II, pp. 341-342.

[42] *Ibid.*, Vol. II, pp. 358, 371.

[43] *Ibid.*, Vol. II, p. 362, note.

[44] *Supra*, p. 108.

[45] Letter to John Inskeep, Mayor of Philadelphia, from Isaac Hall, dated at Philadelphia, January 27, 1806, in *Aurora General Advertiser*, Philadelphia, Thursday, January 30, 1806; letter to the Editor of the *Aurora*, William Duane, from John Purdon, in *Aurora General Advertiser*, Philadelphia, Saturday, February 1, 1806; letter to John Inskeep, from Thomas Paine, *Aurora General Advertiser*, Philadelphia, Monday, February 10, 1806.

[46] Moncure D. Conway, *op. cit.*, Vol. II, pp. 374-375, 379-381.

are so lost as to admire his writings, are ashamed to be seen in his company." [47]   Lambert was not in sympathy with deism and his opinions should not be uncritically accepted, but it is true that the democrats had long since discovered that it was wise to be publicly, if not privately, divorced from infidelity.

And then his health failed. Except for the gout and a bad fall in the early months of 1804,[48] he had been quite well. But in August 1806, he was seized with a fit of apoplexy which, as he says, "deprived me of all sense and motion. I had neither pulse nor breathing, and the people about me supposed me dead. . . . The fit took me on the stairs, as suddenly as if I had been shot through the head; and I got so very much hurt by the fall, that I have not been able to get in and out of bed since that day. . . . I consider the scene I have passed through as an experiment on dying, and I find death has no terrors for me." [49]

The British traveller, John Melish, who visited Paine just at this time recorded: "On the 20th of August [1806], I was introduced to that celebrated character, Thomas Paine. He was confined in New York by a hurt in his leg, and lived in the house of a Mrs. Palmer, a widow of the late deistical minister in that city. The gentleman who introduced me was well acquainted with Mr. Paine, and I was politely received as his friend." [50]

From this time on the last three years of his life became

[47] John Lambert, *Travels through Canada, and the United States of North America, in the Years 1806, 1807, & 1808* (Third Edition, London, 1816), Vol. II, p. 368.

[48] Moncure D. Conway, *op. cit.*, Vol. II, p. 336.

[49] From a letter to Andrew A. Dean, to whom Paine's farm at New Rochelle was let, dated at New York, August 1806. Quoted in Moncure D. Conway, *op. cit.*, Vol. II, p. 376.

[50] John Melish, *Travels in the United States of America, in the Years 1806 & 1807, and 1809, 1810, & 1811* (Philadelphia, 1812), Vol. I, p. 64.

increasingly unhappy. He never fully recovered his health and, what was probably still worse, became involved in bitter controversies with suits of libel and slander. Impoverished, old, ill, his nerves shattered, deserted by nearly all his old friends, acquaintances, and even followers, he was obviously unable to carry on the work of militant deism. The religious issue, however, was the dominant note to the end. "When the news got abroad that the Arch-Infidel was dying, foolish old women and kindred clergymen, who 'knew no way to bring home a wandering sheep but by worrying him to death,' gathered together about his bed. Even his physician joined in the hue-and-cry. It was a scene of the Inquisition adapted to North America,—a Protestant *auto da fé*. The victim lay helpless before his persecutors; the agonies of disease supplied the place of rack and fagot." [51] He clung to his deistic faith to the end, but such was the spirit of the day that stories of his having recanted and declared that the devil had inspired the *Age of Reason* and of his crying, "Lord Jesus, have mercy upon me," were widely believed.

Besides Thomas Paine and Elihu Palmer, a Universalist preacher, John Foster, was loosely associated with the movement for a time. He was perhaps the same Foster who had taught Palmer divinity in Pittsfield back in 1787,[52] and we hear of him now as a fellow-liberal and friend of both Palmer and Paine. In 1803, Foster kept a school in Stonington, Connecticut, where Paine seems to have visited him.[53] A year later, Foster was more closely

[51] *The Atlantic Monthly*, July 1859, Vol. IV, p. 14.
[52] *Supra*, p. 57.
[53] Moncure D. Conway, *op. cit.*, Vol. II, p. 328.

identified with the deistic movement. In a letter to Col.
Fellows, dated July 31, 1804, Paine wrote, "I am glad
that Palmer and Foster have got together. It will greatly
help the cause on. . . . We have already silenced the
clamor of the priests. They act now as if they would say,
let us alone and we will let you alone." [54] This was when
the *Prospect* and the movement for the "Temple of Nature" was at its height. Dr. Francis says of the relationship between Palmer and Foster, "During the later years
of his pastoral functions, as he called them, he [Palmer]
was aided by a colaborer in another part of the city, of
physical proportions even more stately, of still more daring speech, whose voice was as the surge of mighty billows, whose jacobinism was, if possible, still fiercer; I
allude to John Foster: I have heard many speakers, but
none whose voice ever equalled the volume of Foster's.
It flowed with delicious ease, and yet penetrated every
where. He besides was favored with a noble presence.
Points of difference existed in the theological dogmas of
Foster and Palmer, yet they had the same ends in view;
radicalism and the spread of jacobinical element. Foster's
exordium consisted generally in an invocation to the goddess of liberty, now unshackled, who inhaled nutrition
from heaven, seated on her throne of more than Alpine
heights. Palmer and Foster called each other brother,
and the fraternity was most cordial." [55] Foster remained a
Universalist, although radical even for that liberal sect.
He preached in New York for two or three years, about
1803-1806, "and from that date all trace of him is lost." [56]

[54] *Ibid.*, Vol. II, p. 362.
[55] John W. Francis, *op. cit.*, pp. 136-137.
[56] Abel C. Thomas, *A Century of Universalism in Philadelphia and
New York* (Philadelphia, 1872), p. 268.

To the miserable Paine, the blind Palmer, and the
stentorian Foster must be added the "Walking" Stewart
whose colorful career is matched by his bizarre character.

Stewart was born in London in 1749 of a Scotch family
of respectability.[57]   His originality developed at a very
early age with the result that his "irregularity of conduct,"
as he says, "gained the character of a wicked boy with great
archness or sagacity." [58]   Later at Harrow School, he was
"the blockhead of the class" and "the first player at every
game, and the leader of every enterprise, such as robbing
orchards, fighting the town's-people, and riding jack-asses
to London." [59]   At thirteen he was sent to the Charter-
house where "he obtained a confirmation of his previous
character," [60] with the result that the master advised his
father to send him abroad.   At sixteen, accordingly, he was
sent to India as a writer in the service of the East India
Company.   The drudgery of office work naturally did not
appeal to him and he soon became an interpreter, and suc-
cessively general in command of the troops of Hyder Ally
and prime minister to the Nabob of Arcot.[61]   He lived
through most amazing and perilous experiences, but so
lucrative were these positions that in five years he saved

[57] Anonymous, *The Life and Adventures of the Celebrated Walking
Stewart: including His Travels in the East Indies, Turkey, Germany, &
America. By a Relative.* (London, 1822), p. 3.

[58] John Stewart, *Opus Maximum; or, the Great Essay to reduce the
Moral World from Contingency to System* (London, 1803), Life of the
Author, p. xiv.

[59] John Stewart, *The Scripture of Reason and Nature; The Laws of
Intellect; The Laws of Virtue; The Laws of Policy; The Laws of Physiology; or The Philosophy of Sense; developing the Origin, End, Essence,
and Constitution of Nature* (London, 1813), Life of the Author, p. iv.

[60] *Opus Maximum*, Life of the Author, p. xvi.

[61] Anonymous, *The Life and Adventures of the Celebrated Walking
Stewart*, pp. 4-6.

£4000 with which he bought an annuity on his life.[62] With
financial independence assured before reaching middle age,
he resolved "to travel over all the world, to trace the
causes of human misery, and the causes of human welfare
and its perfectuability." [63]

He left India, travelled through Persia and Turkey on
foot, and finally returned to England. His mother country, however, unfortunately did not appreciate his genius
and he "conjectured that it would suit his purpose best
to travel on the continent. He made the tour of Scotland,
Germany, Italy, and France, on foot, and ultimately settled in Paris. . . ." [64] "I was residing in Paris in the
beginning of the mad revolution," he says, "with the highest reputation of a philosopher, and in possession of the
confidence of the leaders of all parties, occupied in converting my funded property into national domains, when all on
a sudden I perceived the most dreadful symptoms of mob
government, and took my departure with the dereliction of
all my property, to save my liberty and my life, while the
horrid events of the progressive revolution proved the
wisdom of my conduct, and the anticipative discernment of
a thoughtful, prudent, and experienced mind." [65]

He returned to England and finally migrated to America where in 1796 we hear of him in Philadelphia in connection with a *Prospectus of A Series of Lectures, or a*

[62] John Stewart, *The Philosophy of Sense; or, Book of Nature: reveal-
ing the Laws of the Intellectual World, founded on the Laws of the
Physical World: forming the Sun or Source of Moral Truth or Sensitive
Good, as the physical Sun, the Source of Light, Heat, and Motion to this
Planet of the Earth.* (London, n. d.), p. 128; *The Scripture of Reason
and Nature*, pp. v-vi.

[63] *The Scripture of Reason and Nature*, p. vi.

[64] Anonymous, *The Life and Adventures of the Celebrated Walking
Stewart*, pp. 6-8.

[65] *The Scripture of Reason and Nature*, pp. xix-xx.

*New Practical System of Human Reason, calculated to dis-
charge the mind from a great mass of error, and to facilitate its labour in the approximation of moral truth, divested of all metaphysical perplexities and nullities; Ac-
commodated to the Most Ordinary Capacities, in a Simple
Method, which dispenses equally with the study of the
college, or the lecture of musty libraries.*[66] In these remarkable lectures he promised to "teach the man of pleasure how to acquire pleasure; the merchant how to acquire
wealth; the politician social improvement, joined to social
security; the moralist happiness; and the philosopher wisdom: And I call upon the liberal, and enlightened of all
countries, to aid my labours with nothing but their attention." [67]

At about the same time, he published anonymously in
New York "a work of the most important pretensions, and
consummate instruction, that was ever offered to the mind
of man." This was a poem, *The Revelation of Nature,*
and an essay, *The Prophesy of Reason.*[68]

His greatest work however was still to come. It is the
*Opus Maximum; or, the Great Essay to reduce the Moral
World from Contingency to System* (London, 1803).
Coming from the pen of "the first man that ever lived, in
the true category of manhood," it is fittingly presented to

[66] Printed by Thomas Dobson, Philadelphia, 1796. The copy in the
New York Historical Society had apparently never been read. The pages
remained to be cut after 135 years.

[67] *Prospectus of A Series of Lectures, or a New Practical System of
Human Reason,* pp. 3-4.

[68] Printed by Mott & Lyon, New-York, "In the fifth year of intellectual
existence, or the publication of the apocalypse of nature, 3000 years from
the Grecian olympiads, and 4800 from recorded knowledge in the Chinese
tables of eclipses, beyond which chronology is lost in fable." The "Dedication to the Nation of America" reveals (p. xxv) that the book was
published during the presidency of George Washington.

and "worthy of the patronage of the first of potentates, and the first of conquerors," [69] Napoleon, Emperor of the French. "The true philosopher approaches the prince as the sun approaches him in the morning's dawn, not to soothe or flatter, but to awaken to illuminate and to energize his powers." [70] Strangely enough, however, this same volume contains another "Dedication to the American Nation," in which this "exalted and transcendent nation" alone is able to withstand "the immediate dissolution of civilized life" imminent in all other countries of the world. [71]

Stewart's conceit taxes comprehension. He thought that the opportunities which his wide travels had afforded him had made him "the paragon of his species, and the acme of intellectual energy." [72] No other human being, he believed, had ever enjoyed such unique experiences, with the result that none other has ever produced a work comparable to his *Opus Maximum*. It stands in history as the "single work, either ancient or modern, that deserves the character of genius, or authorship, in totality. Many books have, indeed, in a compilation of many pages, suggested one or two new ideas; but there is no instance of any single work that can claim the character of consummate authorship from the beginning to the end." Bacon's *Novum Organum* or Newton's *Principia*, by comparison, merely improved existing sciences without creating any new ones. [73]

A work of "this character of genius, originality, and

[69] *Opus Maximum*, To Napoleon, p. 6.
[70] *Ibid.*, p. 3.
[71] *Opus Maximum*, To the American Nation, pp. iii and vi.
[72] *Ibid.*, p. xviii.
[73] *Ibid.*, pp. xxxiii-xxxiv.

authorship" is of course not likely to be fully appreciated, just as a savage could form no idea of a work of civil legislation. It is a work which future ages will revere, if only it can be preserved for them. "I fear some second Omar will arrive to burn the Alexandrian library of European knowledge, in which the fate of the Opus Maximum will be involved, and the high characteristic of human nature, perfectibility, its subject, will be lost. I recommend this paragon of authorship, which I denominate the Great Essay, or Opus Maximum, to travellers, entreating them, in the name of our common integer, Nature, whose constituent parts in interest, essence, and power, we all form, to transport this book to islands and colonies, and even there to bury some copies, and conceal their place of sepulture, from generation to generation, in oral tradition, that they may escape the fire of persecution, and be preserved, like seed, to be produced at the favorable season of cultivation." [74]

Stewart, like Palmer, had complete faith in human perfectibility, but he differed radically from Palmer in that he thought of individual perfectibility while Palmer thought of human perfectibility in terms of society. "As volition, therefore," says Stewart, "is the cause of moral motion, self is the only agent which the human mind can have any comprehension of, and which claims all the study and reverence of man." [75] Palmer's solution was that man needed simply to rid himself of political despotism and

[74] *Opus Maximum*, p. xl.

[75] [John Stewart], *The Apocalypse of Nature; wherein the Source of Moral Motion is Discovered, and a Moral System established, through the Evidence and Conviction of the Senses, to Elevate Man to intellectual Existence and an enlightened State of Nature* (London, from the aera of the first rising of the Sun of Reason, or the Publication of the Apocalypse of Nature, in the Year of Astronomical Calculation 5000), p. 253.

religious superstition. With these evils out of the way, "knowledge would become universal, and its progress inconceivably accelerated. It would be impossible, in such a case, that moral virtue should fail of a correspondent acceleration, and the ultimate extirpation of vice would become an inevitable consequence." [76]

For Stewart the solution was more intricate. Man must free himself from *all* prejudices and customs. The individual must first of all "uneducate" himself, "and wipe away all the evil propensities and erudite nonsense of school instruction," of which, incidentally, Stewart himself had successfully evaded receiving too much. It is wide travelling, he insisted, not the study of metaphysics, that enables a man to understand all aspects of life, to develop an objective attitude toward the principles to which he had been exposed during his youth. The Persian proverb, *human energy increases in the ratio of travels,* he says, "has formed the motive, conduct, and end of his whole life, . . . not simply to visit and wander over territory, but to know nations by living among their inhabitants, and speaking their languages. This proverb imports, that the man who knows but one, that is, his own nation, is but a simple insulated man of a particular country; that the man who knows two nations, is a double man; three nations, a treble man; four nations, makes a man of quadruple energy; and, progressively, the man who knows all the most important nations of the globe becomes the paragon of his species, and the acme of intellectual energy." [77]   "The incessant contemplation of contradic-

---

[76] Elihu Palmer, *Principles of Nature*, p. 109.

[77] *Opus Maximum*, Life of the Author, pp. xvii-xviii; cf. *Opus Maximum*, pp. 148-150.

tions, errors, absurdities, and superstitious insanity, in religions, laws, customs, and opinions, excited my mind to
the most powerful attention and ratiocination." [78]   "Before I began my travels I was of a very irritable disposition; but, after a very short period, I had found so much
opposition to my will, and so much offence to my feelings,
in the censure and curiosity of strange nations, that I at
length acquired a temperance of toleration that has ever
since formed the greatest cause of my happiness through
life." [79]   ". . . I acquired such habits of benevolence, sincerity, justice, and reason, as elevated me as much above
the noblest of the human species as he was elevated above
the basest." [80]

"Travel being finished, as the first step of virile education, it would be proper next to examine conversation of
books and men, as the last stage of education. Every man
should devote a certain proportion of social intercourse to
the company of enlightened men; with these he should associate, so as to acquire a capacity of thinking, comparing,
and reasoning, to qualify himself for the important functions of life in self-knowledge and happiness. Books of
true philosophy should be read (avoiding all metaphysical
writings), to provide matter for reflection and comparisons
for reason: these books and men are to be made occasional
means, and not habitudes of study, lest they should generate spleen and melancholy. I would recommend these
books to be read, and these conversations to be held, once
only in the week, that the enjoyment of convivial intercourse might not be diminished, and the intellectual pleas-

[78] *Opus Maximum*, p. 185.
[79] *Opus Maximum*, Life of the Author, p. xxiv.
[80] *Ibid.*, p. xxix.

ures of literature, in poetry, history, and belles lettres, might not be depreciated, loathed, and neglected. In short, I would have the all-accomplished man a philosopher in capacity and a man in habitude. And here ends individual education. . . . I prohibit all mention or suggestion of religious mystery in individual education, because it annihilates all discipline of the understanding. Religious faith demands an implicit assent to all propositions, however extravagant and unintelligible." [81]

"To develope and advance this new intellectual creation of moral truth," John Stewart proposed to publish a weekly paper in New York to be entitled, *The New World; or, American Spectator.* To a prospectus of this new periodical, Elihu Palmer devoted nearly the entire issue of the *Prospect* for February 23, 1805. One would scarcely be surprised that Stewart envisaged a most comprehensive undertaking, nor is the prospectus disappointing in this respect: "To investigate without any temporization with opinions, customs, or creeds, and with the most unbounded latitude of elementary inquiry, all subjects, religious, moral, political and philosophical, in order to discover the highest theories of human perfectability (the only distinguishing characteristic of man from the brute species) and to ascertain those practical modes of social institutions which may lead to their accomplishment, through the slow, sure, and safe progress of experimental reform, public instruction, and intellectual improvement. . . . The light of truth, like the fire of the Persians, will be inextinguishable and eternal, when the laws of intellectual power shall be discovered to tear the curtain from the puppet show of deception and credulity, the wires of demo-

[81] *Ibid.*, pp. 152-153.

craft, king-craft, philosophy-craft, and priest-craft, being exposed to the view of the spectators, Punch, and his whole family of moral, political, metaphysical, and theological puppets, will lose their supposed life, and sink into their wooden essences, never more to be resuscitated, by the knaves or dupes of credulity. The interiour, or behind the scenes of the theatre of reason and nature, will then be exposed, where no curtain can conceal deception, and where all mankind will see and understand their true interests, and true happiness, in both theory and practice, in the discovery of the moral, identified with physical science, in *the most just and general relation of things*." [82] "The present state of human imbecility" as evidenced by "the universally defective state of reason" is due to the fact that "man has no discipline of his mental faculties" and reasons like a maniac. Children are reared "in prisons, called schools, where mephitic air and confinement debilitates the nervous system, and the construction of unintelligible sounds, stuffed into memory, is substituted to *sagacity*."

To remedy these deplorable conditions, "The supreme object of the American Spectator will be, *to discover the moral science*, to teach sagacity as a substitute to letter'd knowledge to form the *essential* rather than *technical* powers of the intellect, to enable man through the discipline of his understanding to choose proper ends and accommodative means of human happiness, the true definition of wisdom, developing the moral science as the most just and most general relation of things, which, if once discovered, can never degenerate or be lost in change or contingency."

[82] *Prospect*, February 23, 1805, p. 58.

And like a true evangelist, Stewart combined promise
with threat and denunciation: "Such is the momentous and
inestimable object of this proposed work, calculated to
form the most auspicious concurrence of events, that ever
dignified the human history, viz. *The light of nature meeting the liberty of reason*, and the American who dares not
read or support it with his patronage, can have no manhood in his nature, and is no more fit to be a member or
citizen of the sublime republic of united nations, than a
bladder of air is fit to be the member of a stone arch." [83]
The *American Spectator* was thus grandly conceived but
apparently never born.

This extraordinary person was particularly allied to
Elihu Palmer and Thomas Paine, in some of his religious
views. Such a passage as the following so appealed to
Palmer that he quoted it in the *Prospect:* "Let the bigot,
who would burn a fellow-being at the stake, for not pros-
trating himself before a wafer, as the personified universe,
travel among the Siamese. . . . Let this bigot, if his
superstition is not shaken by this new matter of comparison
and evidence; let him travel into India, and view the ex-
cruciating penance of the Bramins, roasting the living body
between two fires, to conciliate the favour of an idol, that
he made with his own hand but the day before his torture.
If he demands new points of comparison to detect his
bigotry, let him observe, in all parts of the world, where
he extends his travels, inspired idiots, who pretend to
commune with a personified universe, uttering impreca-
tions against each other's tenets, and burning schismatics
at opposite stakes; and if this ultimate demonstration of
human imbecility does not cure his bigotry, he would do

[83] *Ibid.*, February 23, 1805, pp. 59-61.

well to offer himself to the hospital of incurable lunatics for reason could give him no relief." [84] Revealed religion was not worthy of the name. Speaking of one denomination in England, Stewart said, "This sect of mental idolators have formed a tenet, that declares morality inimical to religion, and that a man obtains a recompence of heaven for credulity alone." [85] "In every country that I have travelled into, I have always observed that morality and religion were constantly in enmity, and where the one reigned, the other was exiled. If we begin the parallel of examination in the East, and proceed with it towards the West, we find the oriental nations occupied one half of the day in ceremonies of religion, while the other half of the day is spent in acts of knavery, fraud, and cruelty; sympathy of heart and rectitude of mind are absolutely not only unpractised, but literally unknown. The nations in the West follow the same parallel, and the most religious countries are here; also the most immoral, which Russia and Italy incontestably prove; France and England, as being the least religious, excel in morality, in the same degree they have abandoned religion." [86]

"All the parade of religion that we observe among the middling classes of the community (for that class called gentlemen are men of honour, and above religion, as they prove by duels), in going to church, saying prayers, and singing psalms, is nothing but an observance of external rites to guard against the fears of fancy: it has no effect upon their moral conduct, for we see these pious votaries exact, without any hesitation, the severest labour from

[84] *Opus Maximum*, p. 150. *Cf.*, *Prospect*, December 10, 1803, pp. 5-6.
[85] *The Apocalypse of Nature*, p. 196.
[86] *Ibid.*, pp. 195-196.

their cattle and their peasantry, the most oppressive rents from their tenants, and the hardest bargains from their purchasers. . . . while religion seems to guard mankind from the dangerous evils of ignorance, it increases and perpetuates that very ignorance a thousand fold. Religion demands implicit assent to all propositions upon pain of punishment, which disposes the mind to indolence of examination, ignorance, and a breach of probity. . . . This habit of indolence, fear, and improbity, defeats all discipline of reason, and man becomes a dupe to every kind of imposture." [87]

"These important reflections on religion are not made to recommend its abolition, but only to dispose pious men to tolerate the light of that philosophy, which in the lapse of ages, like water falling on the rock, may wear away the flinty prejudices of error and superstition, without any perceptible shock, or dangerous percussion, to the peace and order of society." [88] In other words, the religion of nature, although practicable only to men of enlightenment, was the ideal to be striven for through the ages.

"The religion of nature," says Stewart, "differs from invented religion, as the former adores the effect of motion, which is comprehensible, and the latter the cause of motion, which is incomprehensible. The effect of moral motion, which is to procure happiness or well-being to all sensitive nature, through the volition and intellectual faculty of man, proves self, or the moral system, the instrument of that motion, to be the only god or intelligence that ought to command the veneration of mankind." [89]

[87] *Opus Maximum*, pp. 202-203.
[88] *Ibid.*, pp. 203-204.
[89] *The Apocalypse of Nature*, pp. 206-207.

Or again, "Self is God—self is religion—self is virtue, wisdom, truth, happiness." [90]

"Self is a material something arising from the aggregate mass of nature and dissolving by separation of the parts into the same mass, which sends forth in other combinations the same something or indestructible matter, eternally connected with its integer, as heat with fire, or any other effect with its cause, which human intellect cannot comprehend, but must assent to." [91] ". . . whatever is hurtful or evil to nature, must be so to self, and vice versa." [92] "When wisdom opens on the mind of man, self feels an inceptive expansion, which in a parallel progress with its cause, leads the mind to a view of the extensive chain of all nature, whose extremes are infinite and undiscoverable; but such a length of it is manifested, as shews the mind how the motion of one link agitates the whole, and that the least violence committed on a fly, agitates the whole chain, and communicates its vibration to all sensitive nature." [93]

"The ignorant and unhappy being, whose volition dares violate the liberty of any sensitive part of nature, causes by that concussion such a vibration on sympathy, or the universal chain of nature, that communicates a dreadful shock of misery to his present, and all future stages of his connection with nature. The cause of these concussions or criminal operations of the animal man, is ignorance; for if he had strength of intellect to comprehend the moral system of self, the center, and sensitive nature, the circle united, it would be as impossible for him to do the least act of violence, by forcing his will upon another, as to

[90] *The Apocalypse of Nature*, p. 75.   [92] *Ibid.*, p. 281.
[91] *Ibid.*, p. 205.   [93] *Ibid.*, p. 207.

bore a hole in the ship on which he is a passenger, or pull down the lower story of a house of which he is an inhabitant, because it was his own apartment. In the religion of nature all idea of merit and demerit is done away, and the only difference between men is, in the degree of wisdom they possess. All men being in pursuit of the same two objects, truth and happiness, they will conduct self thereto, according to the different directions their weaker or stronger mental faculties furnish. The assassin, who murders, and the child of nature, who saves a fellow-creature, have the same view, viz. happiness. The former in a state of ignorance mistakes the means, and the latter, through wisdom, takes the right means, and arrives at the object. The one is an object of pity, which having led a life of misery, is annihilated by the laws of society, and broke in pieces, like an ill-formed vessel, and returned to the great mass of clay, from whence he may be renewed in a more perfect form or existence." [94]

These Hindu ideas reflect the influence of Stewart's sojourn in the Orient. It is a kind of materialism or, more properly, sensationalism, which was so popular at the time and from which utilitarianism developed. His moral system of self is equivalent to an immaterial karma and he conceived of a moral realm as definite and knowable as the laws governing the phenomena of nature. However, his idea of karma, if it can be thus designated, was not spirit. It was an attribute of matter and could not exist apart from matter. "There can be no immortality," he says, "but in matter itself, which, passing alternately through composition and decomposition, must become the multiplied patient of its own agency throughout the dura-

[94] *Ibid.*, pp. 214-216.

tion of the same system of universal organism." [95] "All bodies are constantly changing their substance one with another, which proves the identity of person to be only a duct or mould, through which matter passes in its eternal revolution, and their connection with nature is the same as in the violin producing a melodious air, or the human body producing a virtuous volition, only, that the latter, possessing a more complicated organization, produces consciousness to feel pain and pleasure, and to direct moral motion to convey happiness to matter in time present and future." [96] Thus the human body is composed of ever-changing matter. It differs from inanimate matter in that it possesses consciousness, and it is the operation of this consciousness, involving moral freedom, that is the soul. It is an adaptation of the current French sensationalism of his time that the faculties of the soul have their origin in sensation on which all knowledge is based. To the pure sensationalism of the Abbé de Condillac,[97] however, which implied that personality is an aggregate of sensations and naturally led to a deterministic position, he added the idea that the knowledge obtained through the senses involves "moral motion." Man is a free moral agent.

From this basis of quasi-materialism Stewart developed his ethical principles, similar to those of Helvetius,[98] but now better known as the greatest happiness formula of British Utilitarianism. "This universal idea generates ir-

---

[95] *The Philosophy of Sense; or, Book of Nature*, p. 19.

[96] *The Apocalypse of Nature*, pp. 252-253.

[97] Abbé de Condillac, *Traité des Sensations* (1754), English translation by Geraldine Carr, University of Southern California, Los Angeles, 1930.

[98] Albert Keim, *Helvétius, Sa Vie et Son Œuvre* (Thèse Présentée à la Faculté des Lettres de l'Université de Paris, 1907); Mordecai Grossman, *The Philosophy of Helvetius* (Ph.D. dissertation, Columbia University, New York, 1926).

resistibly in the laws of intellectual power, the notion of analogy, that all organism must be mortal, from the insect to the planet, this to the system, and hence the universe itself; and therefore there can be no eternal or immortal mode of being or organism, and that immortality belongs only to matter itself; and this notion of analogy annihilates at one stroke all the silly errors of superstition, and awakens man to the exercise of his potential energies, to prepare universal good for self and nature in millions of generations, through millions of ages, throughout the duration of the present organism of the universe." [99] "I regard this momentous moral axiom, *to effect the highest degree of indispensable universal good with the least mean of indispensable partial ill*, the most beneficent discovery of intellectual power that ever was made to mankind." [100]

Even suicide is not only justified but demanded under certain conditions: "Universal interest, the great bond or religion of nature, calls, in a voice of thunder and lightning of evidence, upon every being in a state of irremediable misery to execute universal good by destroying his modality [consciousness or personality], and, like the breaking wave, disperse itself into all the waves of the pool or modes of sensitive life; which explains the action of death to be nothing more than a change of attitude in nature's body, or a total loss of one evil modality, and its matter dispersed into the life of all surrounding beings, to enjoy better sensation, and remove the bad, as an agonizing mould of life to universal nature—just as the personal body changes uneasy into easy postures of life." [101]

[99] *The Philosophy of Sense; or, Book of Nature*, p. xxxiv.
[100] *Ibid.*, p. 70.   [101] *Ibid.*, p. xxxii.

By definition, of course, his materialistic philosophy of laws governing both the natural and the moral order can take no account of God or man's relation to God. He frankly admits in his religion of nature that God or, as he expresses it, "the cause of motion," is incomprehensible. Does this mean, however, he asks, that the manifestations of God are also incomprehensible? Not at all. "When hunger propels, does the wise man hesitate to eat till he has discovered the cause of that passion? No, he earnestly sets about procuring its gratification. So does the child of nature, with moral motion or action, he considers not its cause, but studies to conduct it to its end, or the well-being of self. . . ." [102] Like Voltaire, he employs the cosmological argument and affirms the existence of God from the necessity of a first cause. A typical deist, Stewart was no metaphysician. He was satisfied to accept his first cause without speculation and to admit that the origin of man and of the universe is unknowable. The application of knowledge to the practical affairs and needs of life was his conception of philosophy. Scientific agriculture, mathematics and astronomy, and the attempt to get at the underlying principles of economics, politics, and morality were the philosophical interests of eighteenth-century deists. Metaphysics was for them practically synonymous with priestcraft, supernaturalism, and superstition.[103] Says Goethe's Mephistopheles,

> Grau, theurer Freund, ist alle Theorie,
> Und grün des Lebens goldner Baum.

In his political principles, Stewart distinguished sharply between the practical and the theory of the ideal. His

[102] *The Apocalypse of Nature*, p. 199.   [103] See frontispiece.

experiences in the French Revolution had been so unhappy
that he was extremely cautious. "Till nations become
more just and humanized," he explained, "it is necessary
to discover that medium point between democracy and
monarchy, where public energy and individual liberty
unite, and from this enviable and firm position, which
England alone, amongst all the nations of the world, has
had wisdom to discover, and virtue to establish, let her
open the fountain of thought, that only source of moral
perfection, and by establishing the absolute liberty of the
press, inundate the globe, and fertilize the soil of humanity
into intellectual existence; and when this glorious effect
is produced, let her then, and not till then, resign the
power, art and violence have assumed over nature, for her
own benefit, into the hands of enlightened citizens, who
finding wisdom spread to every part of the globe, will
break down the barriers of coercion, and live in universal
fraternity, guided by the religion of nature, having puri-
fied essence into intellectual existence, and elevated civilization, by the virtues of sympathy and probity, to a state
of enlightened nature." [104]   In his political philosophy he
thus echoed the prevailing doctrine of laissez-faire of
Parisian philosophical salons.   The function of government is negative and should extend only to the securing
of a free field for the operation of natural laws.   In the
ideal state, in short, government is unnecessary because
each individual lives in spontaneous harmony with his
fellows.

[104] [John Stewart], *Travels over the Most interesting Parts of the
Globe, to discover the Source of Moral Motion; communicated to lead
Mankind through the Conviction of the Senses to intellectual Existence,
and an enlightened State of Nature* [Probably published in London late in
the 1790's], pp. xx-xxii.

In his cautious counsel for practical purposes of a
"medium point between democracy and monarchy,"
Stewart differed fundamentally from the republicanism of
Thomas Paine and Elihu Palmer who assumed that evil in
government lay solely in a subversive institution, viz.,
despotism. Palmer's faith in man took it for granted that
every man was capable of exercising the political prerogative wisely; just as in the realm of religion he believed
that, freed from superstition, everyone would do justly,
love mercy, and walk humbly with his God. Stewart, on
the other hand, emphasized the necessity of first reform-
ing every individual man. The French Revolution proved
that it is dangerous to humanity to place power in the
hands of men not prepared to exercise it wisely. Even
in America, republicanism, in so far as it was exercised in
1795, seemed unwise to Stewart. Americans, he said,
"have all the vices of England, without its sentiments of
honour, integrity, and knowledge. The land holders, and
opulent men of that country, have no pursuits but study,
dignity, and travel; they have no cares to improve property, which debases the mind; they seek a dignified moral
character, which may distinguish them, and command the
respect and confidence of the plebean multitude." [105] This
appreciating of the English gentleman, free from the necessity of earning a livelihood and incidentally from con-
forming to the traditions and beliefs of clients or employer,
free to travel and philosophize, is fundamental in Stewart's
system of thought.

Thus Stewart attempted to reduce the whole realm of
thought to a simple system. Like all philosophers of the

---

[105] *The Revelation of Nature, with the Prophesy of Reason*, Dedication
to the Nation of America, pp. xxxvi-xxxvii.

enlightenment, he was enchanted by the system and order in the world of nature. By analogy, he was led to believe that the same kind of order prevailed in the moral world. "I observed in the constitution of nature," he said, "that every part had a tendency to harmony or system, in the same order and succession of matter and power, from a mode to an universe, as in the mundane, planetary, and solar systems. This harmony I thought transferable and practicable in the moral world, to execute a system of personal and universal good." [106] These laws of the moral order exist just as the laws of nature existed before man had formulated them. "The modes of operations of the intellect, and the passions which knowledge has taken cognizance of, and become acquainted with, and by that means obtained the dignified title of philosophy, are as easy to be observed, as the motions of outward bodies, and their cause and effect as easily known." [107] True wisdom is therefore the ability to recognize these laws of "moral motion" and happiness is to live according to them.

With the individualism fostered by the needs of the period and rationalized by its philosophers, he was an eccentric character and represented in his thinking an ingenious combination of self-education and erudition, opposition to despotism and distrust of the common man, derision of the Christian tradition and institutions and acceptance of oriental ideas of karma, in addition to the prevailing faith in human progress and coming millennium when each man will have attained the moral and intellectual eminence of John Stewart.

[106] *The Philosophy of Sense; or, Book of Nature,* p. 134.
[107] *The Apocalypse of Nature,* p. 120.

CHAPTER VI

TWILIGHT

THE activities of Palmer, Foster, and Stewart ended at about the same time, 1805-1806. Paine lingered on in ignominy which would have made his championship injurious to even a popular cause. Although the cause of organized deism languished, it was not dead. A few followers still remained and Paine by his death in 1809 again became their leader. They were infused with a new spirit and early in the year 1810 began the publication of *The Theophilanthropist; containing Critical, Moral, Theological and Literary Essays, in monthly numbers.* These lovers of God and man announced in their "Prospectus" that, "The object of this publication is, to present to the public such critical, moral, theological and literary essays, as may tend to correct false opinions, promote the progress of reason, and increase the sum of human happiness." [1]

After a typical anti-clerical harangue, they proceeded to express their own principles in the grandiose language reminiscent of earlier efforts of the same kind: "The last and consummate effort of the soul, is the religion of philosophy: whose only dogma is, that one God superintends the universe; whose mysteries are the means most conducive to human happiness; whose ceremonials are acts of charity, benevolence, generosity, and public spirit; whose

---

[1] *Theophilanthropist* (Printed for the Proprietors, and sold by H. Hart, No. 117, Chatham-Street, New-York, 1810), p. 3.

discipline and designs are to refine the sympathies, direct
the passions, strengthen and enlarge the mind, and facilitate the communication of wisdom and science." [2] As in
former days when they were members of Palmer's Deistic
Society, the true theophilanthropists adored "the great
first cause of all." "When he contemplates the planets as
they roll; the variety, the order, the economy and the
harmony of the little globe he inhabits: he is fired with
devotion, and penetrated with astonishment at the sub-
limity, and grandeur of the scene, and his mind is naturally
elevated to contemplate the all perfect Deity, by whose
wisdom the wonderful system of nature is preserved, and
by whose power it was originally created." [3] In his relations to his fellow men he perceived that his duties "are
in unison with the best affections of the human heart, and
may be comprehended under the general titles of *justice
and benevolence.* From his very nature, he with equal
ease perceives that the duties he owes to himself, consist
in the due regulation of his passions." [4] All of which becomes clear to man through reason, "the best gift of
God." [5]

This "religion of nature," however, first necessitates
"discharging those puerile prejudices"—i.e., religious superstition. "Let the people change, and their teachers will
soon follow. Let the people build temples of reason, and
they will soon find priests to officiate at their altars." [6]
"America is the only country in which 'reason is left free
to combat error.' If we do not profit by this privilege,
the fault will lie at our own door. Let us then think

[2] *Ibid.,* p. 4.
[3] *Ibid.,* p. 6.
[4] *Ibid.,* p. 6.
[5] *Ibid.,* p. 7.
[6] *Ibid.,* p. 7.

freely, and express our thoughts like freemen. We shall on our part endeavour to demonstrate the genial influence of *true religion* upon the morals and social happiness of man; and, at the same time, shall warn our readers against the baneful effects of fostering ignorance and superstition, those deadly enemies to all the joys of life; which, have broken down all the barriers established by Deity, between virtue and vice, right and wrong, and not content with robbing man of the little happiness which this world might afford, insultingly threaten him with an eternity of misery in the world to come." [7] All of which indicates clearly that this last remnant of personal followers of Elihu Palmer and Thomas Paine neither added to nor subtracted from the doctrines of their masters.

They even contented themselves with a reprinting of the old material. The first article featured in the *Theophilanthropist* is a "Discourse upon the festival of Sunday, delivered in the Temple of Reason, by Raisin Pagés, . . . in the 2d year of the French Republic." "With respect to the observance of the Sabbath, it is not highly important to know whether it be of divine origin or not," remark the editors in their introduction to this speech of a by-gone day.[8] "But as we fully agree with our author in regard to the origin of the Sabbath, or day of rest, that it is of human invention; we conceive it perfectly immaterial which of the days has the preference. All we should contend for, therefore, would be, that moral and scientific discourses, which would benefit mankind, should be delivered from the desk on that day, and not such useless and fanatical sermons as are now in vogue." [9]

[7] *Theophilanthropist*, p. 8.　　　　[9] *Ibid.*, p. 10.
[8] *Ibid.*, p. 9.

The first issue of the *Theophilanthropist* also contains
the first installment of extracts from the *Nature and
Origin of Evil* by Soame Jenyns (1703-1787), the English deist. After speaking of "the fable of the triumph
of evil over good, and the consequent fall of man, by eat-
ing the forbidden fruit," the editors explain their anti-
literal interpretation of the book of Genesis. "If it can be
proved by philosophical deductions, that the evils which
man experiences, necessarily originate from the very nature
of his existence, and that those evils could not have been
avoided even by omnipotent power, without withholding
from him a greater good; then the benevolence and goodness of God in the creation of the world will be fully
established, and the story of the fall of man, and the consequent necessity of a redemption, will be no longer worthy
of credit. What joyful tidings would not this be to the
sincere enquirer after truth. If this *fall of man*, this mill-
stone around the necks of mankind, acting as a dead weight
upon human happiness, can be fairly got rid of, and man
left accountable only for his own actions, the road to salvation and happiness would be easy and pleasant." [10]

After this expression of religious latitudinarianism, the
quotations from Jenyns seem reactionary. In good Calvinistic spirit he explains that for God to have created
beings only of the highest and most perfect order would
be as if a painter covered "his whole piece with one single
colour, the most beautiful he could compose." Inferior
beings have their place in the moral order and notwithstanding their imperfections, "more felicity upon the whole
accrues to the universe, than if no such had been created."
Nor is this inconsistent with the benevolence of the Cre-

[10] *Ibid.*, p. 15.

ator, "for though he cannot make all superior, yet, in the dispensations of his blessings his wisdom and goodness both are well worthy the highest admiration; for, amongst all the wide distinctions which he was obliged to make in the dignity and perfection of his creatures, he has made much less in their happiness than is usually imagined, or indeed can be believed from outward appearances. . . . Thus, for example, poverty or the want of riches, is generally compensated by having more hopes, and fewer fears, by a greater share of health, and a more exquisite relish of the smallest enjoyments, than those who possess them are usually blessed with. The want of taste and genius, with all the pleasures that arise from them, are commonly recompensed by a more useful kind of common sense, together with a wonderful delight, as well as success, in the buisy [sic] pursuits of a scrambling world. . . . Ignorance, or the want of knowledge and literature, the appointed lot of all born to poverty, and the drudgeries of life, is the only opiate capable of infusing that insensibility which can enable them to endure the miseries of the one, and the fatigues of the other. It is a cordial administered by the gracious hand of Providence; of which they ought never to be deprived by an ill-judged and improper education. It is the basis of all subordination, the support of society, and the privilege of individuals; and I have ever thought it a most remarkable instance of the Divine Wisdom, that whereas in all animals, whose individuals rise little above the rest of their species, knowledge is instinctive; in man whose individuals are so widely different, it is acquired by education; by which means the prince and the labourer, the philosopher and the peasant, are in some measure fitted for their respective situations.

. . . Thus the Universe resembles a large and well regulated Family, in which all the officers and servants, and even the domestic animals, are subservient to each other in a proper subordination; each enjoys the privileges and perquisites peculiar to his place, and at the same time contributes by that just subordination to the magnificence and happiness of the whole." [11]

This conception of necessary subordination, it seemed to Jenyns, makes evil intelligible. All subordination, he says, implies imperfection, "all imperfection evil, and all evil some kind of inconvenience or suffering; so that there must be particular inconveniences and sufferings annexed to every particular rank of created beings by the circumstances of things and their modes of existence. Most of those [evils] to which we ourselves are liable may be easily shown to be of this kind, the effects only of human nature, and the station man occupies in the universe: and therefore their origin is plainly deducible from necessity; that is, they could not have been prevented without the loss of greater good, or the admission of greater evils than themselves; or by not creating any such creatures as men at all." [12] From which he concludes that most of the natural evils of this world are shown "to be no evils at' all." [13]

As for moral evil, which is not inherent in the order of nature but is subject to man's will, Jenyns is an Utilitarian. "So far as the general practice of any action tends to produce good," he says, "and introduce happiness into the world, so far we may pronounce it virtuous; so much evil as it occasions, such is the degree of vice it contains." [14]

[11] *Theophilanthropist*, pp. 82-86. [13] *Ibid.*, p. 87.
[12] *Ibid.*, p. 122. [14] *Ibid.*, p. 168.

In spite of the fact that it was printed in their columns, this doctrine of acquiescence was not representative of the Theophilanthropists. They followed rather the ardent spirit of social reform and human betterment of Paine and Palmer and devoted themselves to the amelioration of social evils. With their deistic interest in man's life rather than his soul, they wished to improve social conditions, eliminate misery and oppression, and increase human happiness. *The Temple of Reason* had championed at times the cause of unmarried mothers, emphasizing their contribution to the state, and suggesting for their support the taxing of bachelors, who as a class were generally responsible for their plight.[15] But these social evils had been linked with Christian superstition by *The Temple of Reason*. The *Theophilanthropist*, on the other hand, showed a more intelligent interest when it championed prison and temperance reforms on behalf of the Humane Society of New York. In a report of a committee appointed by the Humane Society [16] to inquire into the "sources of vice and misery in this city," we read: "The habit of drinking ar-

---

[15] Nothing, of course, came of these efforts, but late in the year 1811 or early in 1812, the Magdalen Society was established in New York, "which shall afford to repenting victims of seduction the means of support and protection, and be so organized and conducted as to cherish their penitent dispositions, inspire them with the principles of religion and virtue, confirm them in habits of order and industry, and under the divine blessing, produce in them a radical reformation of life."—*The Halcyon Luminary and Theological Repository* (New York, January 1812), Vol. I, p. 43.

[16] For a "Sketch of the Origin and Progress of the Humane Society of the City of New York," see *The American Medical and Philosophical Register* (New York, April 1814), Vol. IV, pp. 632-637. This society had its origin in a "Society for the Relief of Distressed Debtors," founded January 26, 1787. "In 1803, the society, in consequence of the enlargement of its plan, changed its name to that of the Humane Society of the City of New York." The society was incorporated in 1814. It continued its aid to debtors and prisoners, aided the poor in general, and established

dent spirits enervates the mind, sours the disposition, in-
flames the passions, renders the heart callous to the feelings of humanity, and leads to the neglect and violation of
the social duties. It lays the foundations of many diseases,
and makes others terminate fatally which would otherwise yield to the application of remedies. By many whose
opinions deserve weight, it has been thought as destructive
to the human species as the sword: and in this country,
certainly, it furnishes death with more victims than all the
other causes of premature mortality." [17] The committee
also reported on the deplorable conditions in "the Bride-
well or City Prison."

In the same spirit, too, the Theophilanthropists deplored war. "Of all the artificial evils with which civilized
man is cursed," they said, "war is the most afflicting. Its
principles are repugnant to the best feelings of the human
heart, and reason revolts at its horrors. Why then all this
ravage and destruction? Why is the civilized world made
an aceldama and a common charnel-house, and humanity
covered with the habiliments of woe? Why is man the
most inveterate enemy of man, and why do rational beings
thirst for each other's blood? . . . Yes, the ambition of
titled despots and the superstition of mitred knaves have
been the cause of the calamities of war. For the boundary
of a sea, a river or a mountain, could never make mankind

first aid stations for "the resuscitation of persons apparently dead from
drowning."
    The New York society was representative of others of this period. For
example, the Philadelphia Humane Society was established in 1780 (Horace M. Lippincott, *Early Philadelphia*, Philadelphia, 1917, pp. 219-220);
and the Philadelphia Society for Alleviating the Miseries of Public Prisons
in 1787 (Harry Elmer Barnes, *The Story of Punishment*, Boston, 1930,
p. 123).
    [17] *Theophilanthropist*, pp. 55-56.

each other's enemies; but such deeds are still done, and will continue, until Freedom waves her banners over a benighted world." [18]

This kind of pacifism was not, however, internationally minded. It attributed Old World evils to despotism and superstition as Palmer had done and like him, too, believed that America was different. "Were all governments like our own, constituted in legitimate principles, the din of arms would cease, and the whole human family would embrace each other as brethren; but, alas! we cannot even indulge a hope that this happy era is at hand, for the bloody flag of ambition is still unfurled, and self-defence may shortly compel us to raise the hatchet and unsheathe the sword. Should this be our fate; my countrymen, you must be convinced that our virtuous executive have exerted all their energies to avoid its horrors. But should the insults and aggressions of European despots bring us to this issue, we can boldly appeal to the Supreme Being for the justice of our cause. As one man must the nation arouse to arms, and swear at the holy altar of freedom, which was cemented by the best blood of our fathers, 'that we will never relinquish the independence and just rights of our country.'" [19]

At the same time, the Theophilanthropists were much interested in torpedoes, an invention of Fulton's for bombing ships of war which might attempt to attack our shores. An unknown poet sang:

> Sir Isaac Newton from an apple's fall,
> Trac'd the great laws that rule our earthly ball;
> A paper-kite by Franklin taught to rise,
> First drew the lightning from electric skies;

---

[18] *Theophilanthropist*, p. 153.   [19] *Ibid.*, p. 154.

By Fulton's hand the dread *Exploder* hurl'd,
Secures from pirate power an injured world.[20]

In an extract from Robert Fulton's *Torpedo War, and
Submarine Explosions,* it is shown that since the invention
of torpedoes will make war ships ineffective, it may well
be that it will "give to the seas the liberty which shall
secure perpetual peace between nations that are separated
by the ocean. My conviction is, that the means are here
developed, and require only to be organized and practised,
to produce that liberty so dear to every rational and reflecting man." [21] In other words, preparedness for war to
assure peace!

An article on the "Character of Jesus Christ" in the
February issue is of interest. It is similar in point of view
to Dennis Driscol's contribution in *The Temple of Reason*
on "Jesus Christ a Deist and no God," already referred to
above.[22] "Much as we esteem Mr. Volney, and highly as
we prize his literary productions, we cannot agree with
him in doubting the existence of Jesus Christ." [23] Like
Driscol, they feel that Jesus was one of their own kind,
an "obscure *reformer*" who "attempted to uproot that corrupt system of religious mummery, with which they [the
Jewish nation] were oppressed. His political principles
were those of a republican, for he taught the lessons of
political equality. His religious dogmas were those of the
Theophilanthropist, for he inculcated reverence to the
deity, and benevolence towards the whole human family.
. . . Thus the man who had humanely endeavoured to

[20] *Ibid.,* p. 112.
[21] *Ibid.,* pp. 144-145; *cf.,* pp. 111-119, 143-148, 195-198.
[22] *The Temple of Reason,* New York, November 15, 1800, p. 10.
[23] *Theophilanthropist,* p. 69.

ameliorate the condition of his countrymen, and to rescue them from civil despotism and religious tyranny, prematurely fell a victim to the bigotry and superstition of the age in which he lived, and became a martyr in the cause of philanthropy. His character was adorned with an assemblage of amiable virtues, and his ethics were calculated to render his fellow-creatures individually happy, and socially benevolent. Such, in our opinion, are the true characteristics of Jesus Christ. But, several centuries after his death, interested and fanatical men founded a monstrous and impious system of religion in his name.—It is not pretended that he wrote a single line of this himself. His expositors however, to suit their own purposes, taking the heathen mythology as their guide, first deified him, and then intermixed with his rational ethics the most abominable frauds that were ever imposed upon human credulity." [24] Except for their bitterness toward "impostors," the Theophilanthropists were more nearly akin to present-day Protestant modernists than to later nineteenth century freethinkers and militant atheists.

Neither *The Temple of Reason* nor the *Prospect* had been successful financially, but the *Theophilanthropist* seems from the first to have been even less fortunate. On the last page of the second issue, the publisher, Mr. H. Hart [25] of No. 117 Chatham Street, was grateful to those who had "received and paid without hesitation" for the first number, but at the same time, "he regrets the necessity of stating, that a number of his supposed patrons have

---

[24] *Theophilanthropist*, p. 71.

[25] Vol. I of the copy of *The Temple of Reason* in the Long Island Historical Society, Brooklyn, has a rubber stamp on the inside cover: "H. Hart's Circulating Library & Book Store, 117 Chatham St., New York." Mr. Hart had apparently been interested in the promulgation of deism for some time and had been undoubtedly a member of Palmer's society.

mistaken this work for a missionary, evangelical, or won-derful magazine; and besides, when presented with the bill of twenty-five cents, have been struck with horror at the enormity of the charge, for, as they say, so small a book; alledging that they could not think of continuing as subscribers, without first obtaining their wives' consent. Pity has, in most cases of this kind, induced the publisher to erase the names of these unfortunate beings from the list of Theophilanthropists, being convinced that they would be of no use to the cause espoused by this publica-tion. And he thinks it charity to advise them immediately to take shelter under the banners of some superstition." [26]

The third and fourth issues of the *Theophilanthropist* contain articles on a variety of subjects, such as the moral-ity of Mahometanism, the character of John Marshall, thoughts on torpedoes, the poetry of the Osage Indians, and a quotation from Locke on God. This diversity of ideas, often contradictory, may be interpreted as indicating the catholicity of interests of the Theophilanthropists, or that their religious interests were not as ardent as they had been a decade earlier. There are no notices of deist activities, such as public lectures, and one does not feel that the editors are championing a cause. Nevertheless the struggle against superstition remained their real *raison d'être*.

In the May issue in their "Remarks" on Jenyns's *En-quiry into the Nature and Origin of Moral Evil,* their own position is explained. They share the popular interest of deists of this period in comparative religion and conclude that the Christian virtues had been taught long before the advent of Christianity and are not peculiar to the latter

[26] *Theophilanthropist,* p. 80.

system.   After quoting numerous moral precepts and axioms from pagan philosophers, the editors somewhat challengingly remark: "Now, if there be any thing in religion, not contained in the foregoing extracts, we can see no possible reason for desiring to become acquainted with it; because we are convinced that it must consist in the performance of some stupid ceremony, such as *baptism*; or in faith in speculative points, contrary to, or above the comprehension of reason, which an honest man can never assent to; consequently tending to divide mankind into parties, to cherish pride, and promote ill will and animosities, destructive to true religion, and the repose of man. Finally we confidently assert that there is not a single virtue set forth in the Christian system, that is not to be found in the writings of the ancient philosophers, even that (so much boasted of, but little practised) of doing good to, if not loving, our enemies." [27]

Of more than passing interest in the sixth and seventh issues of the *Theophilanthropist* is a hitherto unpublished paper from the pen of Thomas Paine. It is an "Answer to Bishop Watson's Apology for the Bible." Paine had given the manuscript to Mrs. Palmer in 1806 when he was living in her home at the time of his injury.[28] Mr. Conway is indefinite as to the date, but apparently later, "Mrs. Elihu Palmer, in her penury, was employed by Paine to attend to his rooms, etc., during a few months of illness." [29] Paine had also left $100 to Mrs. Palmer in his will,[30] and

---

[27] *Theophilanthropist*, p. 183.

[28] I. N. Phelps Stokes, *The Iconography of Manhattan Island*, Vol. V, p. 1450.

[29] Moncure D. Conway, *The Life of Thomas Paine*, Vol. II, pp. 402-403.

[30] William M. Van der Weyde, *The Life and Works of Thomas Paine*, Vol. X, p. 294.

Mrs. Palmer in gratitude took this first opportunity of publishing another of his essays to perpetuate his work. It is a critical analysis to disprove the statement of Bishop Watson that the book of Genesis is the oldest book in the world "and to show that the book of Job, which is not a Hebrew book, but is a book of the Gentiles, translated into Hebrew, is much older than the book of Genesis." [81]

The last three issues of the *Theophilanthropist* (there were nine altogether) convince the reader that the editors did not limit their opposition to any one religious "superstition." Methodists, Catholics, Mahometans, and Calvinists are all alike exposed. They do not doubt that the majority of the adherents of these faiths are devout—"Ignorance and weakness, though unworthy of respect, are at least entitled to charity"—but the learned who selfishly and designedly foster superstition and bigotry are deserving of contempt and ridicule. Their own position is again well stated: "What can a Doctor of Divinity, who makes theology the peculiar study of his life, know of his maker, which is not known to the illiterate ploughman? The ploughman knows that there is a God, that he is just and good. What more is necessary? The Theologian, impelled by pride and zeal to establish a peculiar doctrine, will perhaps persuade himself that God is partial, vindictive and unjust; electing some to eternal happiness, and reprobating others to eternal misery, without regard to their respective merits. This he believes upon the authority of some obscure unintelligible passage in a book, written by ignorant, though perhaps well meaning men, and compiled and pronounced *holy* by a council of illiterate priests, induced, as spiritual physicians, to represent the

[81] *Theophilanthropist*, p. 220.

malady of their patients as the most frightful and forlorn." [32]

The anti-Catholic outburst of the *Theophilanthropist* came in answer to a mandatum regarding the difficulties of Pope Pius VII with Napoleon, issued by prelates of the Church at Baltimore, November 15, 1810. It is published in full in the *Theophilanthropist* and reads in part: "After suffering with that placid constancy, which only the God of fortitude could inspire, the most disrespectful and insulting treatment, and being stripped of the dominions, which had been held by his predecessors for more than a thousand years, to the immense benefit of the christian world, he was first made a prisoner within the walls of his own palace, and then, as was his immediate and holy predecessor of blessed memory Pius the 6th, forcibly dragged away from the chair of St. Peter, and the sacred ashes of the Apostles; he is detained in a foreign land, as a prisoner, and debarred from communicating to his pastoral care and solicitude." [33]

To which the Theophilanthropists reply: "It is common for religious demogogues to impose their *upsi dixit* [sic] upon their ignorant followers as the word of God, and to represent their enemies as God's enemies. Thus these bishops in the above exposé denominate those who oppose the power of the Pope, the *enemies of Jesus Christ.* Among people of common understanding, this cant now excites only the smile of contempt." [34] "As to the chair of Peter, if he left one, and the ashes of the apostles, if they have been preserved, which is doubtful, we presume that Buonaparte would have no objection to send them after

---

[32] *Theophilanthropist*, p. 278.   [34] *Ibid.*, pp. 309-310.
[33] *Ibid.*, p. 306.

the Pope, should he request it. But it is not the old chair of Peter, nor these ashes, that the Pope and his bishops are so anxious about. Their affections are placed upon power and dominion, earthly riches, which contribute to the gratification of sense, to entice the soul from the pursuit of spiritual graces; and, as Buonaparte justly observes, to disqualify them for the performance of their pastoral duties." [85]

In order to "shew that religious canting is not confined to Catholic bishops, nor Connecticut governors," the editors quote a Turkish proclamation, dated at Pera, July 19, 1810. They conclude that "The Grand Sultan is a proficient in this kind of hoaxing; he can talk about *the holy will of God, unbelievers, and enemies to faith,* as confidently as any of them." [86]

Their attitude toward any theological system is well summarized in the following statement: "The teachers of religion of all denominations assume an arrogant, dictatorial style, in order to convince their followers that they are in possession of the secrets of Heaven, and have a perfect knowledge of the dogmas, and mode of worship which are alone pleasing to the Deity. This confidence gratifies their vanity, and at the same time tends to promote their interest by frightening their flock from straying into other *sheep-folds;* a term in common use with them, and by no means unappropriate. . . . Although it is said that God formerly *chose the fools of this world to confound the wise,* we know of no authority for perpetuating this commission in the hands of any particular order of men." [87]

In spite of the fact that the Theophilanthropists be-

[85] *Ibid.,* pp. 310-311. [87] *Ibid.,* p. 338.
[86] *Ibid.,* p. 316.

lieved that "monkish superstition is fast passing away, and all dogmas which will not bear the investigation of reason are in a fair way of sinking into neglect and contempt," [38] only the first five issues of the *Theophilanthropist* appeared monthly, as planned. The remaining four were not dated, but judging from the fact that the last number contains a letter dated August 21, 1811, (p. 353) it seems that they were issued intermittently between June 1810 and late in the year 1811.[39] As Joel Barlow said in a letter to James Cheetham written in the summer of 1809, the times were not propitious for the dissemination of the principles of Thomas Paine. Not suspecting apparently that Cheetham was writing a defamatory biography of his old friend, Barlow wrote, "It appears to me, that this is not the moment to publish the life of that man in this country. His own writings are his best life, and these are not read at present." [40]

The experience of the editors of the *Theophilanthropist* proved that Joel Barlow was right. Their "conclusion" [41] breathes disappointment rather than hope. The gentlemen who previously to its commencement had volunteered to write for it had failed to do so. Instead of original material, it was necessary to fill the pages with extracts "from works of the greatest merit." The fact was that the principles for which they stood were those of the decade of the 1790's. The *Zeitgeist* of 1810 was of a different temper.

---

[38] *Theophilanthropist*, p. 338.
[39] The fact that the title page of the volume is dated 1810 is misleading.
[40] Letter dated at Kalorama, August 11, 1809. *Theophilanthropist*, p. 366.
[41] *Theophilanthropist*, p. 382.

CHAPTER VII

RESPECTABLE DEISTS

THE dislike for Calvinism which finally led Ethan Allen
and Elihu Palmer to become militantly anti-Christian was
shared by men of respectability and education who knew
how to reconcile the ardor of a new faith to the comforts
of an old society. The difference between Allen and
Palmer, on the one hand, and Joseph Priestley and the
New England Congregational Unitarians on the other,
was primarily the *social* difference between liberalism and
radicalism. Roughly, they agreed in theory, and all alike
had been influenced by the rationalism and naturalism of
the Age of Enlightenment. They were all at least tinged
with deism. But they differed in the practical application
of the new philosophy. "The rich, the well-born, and the
able," as usual, had no sympathy with the demagoguery
which could only incite the masses to forget their place in
the social body. It is one thing to discuss deism and political philosophy in the drawing room, but Elihu Palmer
and his associates were radicals. The distinction between
liberalism and radicalism is very real. It is primarily a
social difference.

The learned, urbane, and well-to-do New Englanders,
unlike their forefathers, now socially and spiritually akin
to their Anglican brethren in the Old World, could adopt
the new without either admitting or proclaiming a change.
Now comfortably established, these descendants of trans-

planted Englishmen recovered the "balance of worldly wisdom and spiritual hypocrisy, which is largely responsible for the charm of English society and the prosperity of the English nation." [1]

Thomas Paine and Elihu Palmer were intellectually *nouveaux riches*. Unable to accept all of the Christian tradition, they would have none of it, and then ironically with the faith and credulity of an evangelical enthusiast accepted literally and preached the faith of deism and republicanism of the 1790's. Intellectually it was alien to the religious tradition of the masses and, once the activities and accompanying fervor of the French Revolution were past, it fell an easy prey to changing circumstances.

As the conditions of life change, man's religion cannot remain the same and permanent orthodoxy is impossible. The Unitarian movement, chronologically accompanying the political revolution and not without similarity to the latter, was thus a continuation of a long heritage of dissent. The American Revolution, as revolutions go, was an extremely conservative political movement, though not without its inevitable social implications and consequences,[2] but the religious revolution in New England was even more conservative. It was perhaps a metamorphosis rather than a revolution, for by 1800 the transformation had taken place in many congregations without change of pastor, house of worship, or break in continuity of tradition. It did justice to the character of the clergy of New England, learned, always respectable, and conservative —in everything except their theology. They resented

---

[1] Herbert W. Schneider, *The Puritan Mind*, p. 14.

[2] See J. Franklin Jameson, *The American Revolution considered as a Social Movement* (Princeton, 1926).

vulgarity, professional reformers, religious enthusiasts, and any radical repudiation of their religious tradition, but in their own dignified and scholarly way were ready to receive whatever new truth God might reveal to them. The liberalism of the New England churches developed from within.

Among these early precursors of Unitarianism was the Rev. Ebenezer Gay, pastor of the First Church in Hingham, Massachusetts, for nearly seventy years. In a convention sermon before the ministers of the Province of the Massachusetts-Bay in 1746 he urged freedom of inquiry and decried the use of man-made creeds and man-made articles of faith. The minister, he said, is ordained to propagate and advance pure and undefiled religion. "A pure Spirit searches impartially after Truth, and is best capable of discovering it: Being free from those corrupt Affections, & vicious Habits, ill Prejudices & base Designs, which cloud and darken the Understanding, bribe and pervert the Judgment." [3] "Ministers are the *Pastors* of the Flock, and it is of greater Consequence, that there should be no Strife between them, than it was of old, that there should be none between *Abraham's Herdsmen and Lot's*. No wonder the Sheep are frighted and scatter'd from them, when they see them biting and devouring one another. They are the Leaders of the People, and if they disagree, how can the People safely follow them?" [4] The deplorable dissension among the clergy which "hath brought much Smoke and Darkness into the Sanctuary,"

[3] Ebenezer Gay, *The True Spirit of a Gospel-Minister represented and urged. A Sermon Preach'd before the Ministers of the Province of the Massachusetts-Bay in New-England, at their Annual Convention in Boston; May 29. 1746* (Boston, 1746), p. 9.

[4] *Ibid.*, p. 25.

is due to "Ministers so often chusing to insist upon the
offensive Peculiarities of the Party they had espous'd,
rather than upon the more weighty Things in which we are
all agreed." [5] In 1751, in his Sermon at the Ordination
of Jonathan Dorby at Scituate, he declared, "And 'tis pity
any man, at his entrance into the ministry, should, in his
Ordination vows, get a snare to his soul, by subscribing,
or any ways engaging to preach according to another rule
of faith, creed or confession, which is merely of human
prescription and imposition." [6]

The deistic influence of the time is particularly reflected
in his Dudleian Lecture delivered at Harvard College, his
Alma Mater, in 1759. "Religion," he says, "is divided
into natural and revealed:—*Revealed* Religion, is that
which God hath made known to Men by the immediate
Inspiration of his Spirit, the Declarations of his Mouth,
and Instructions of his Prophets: *Natural*, that which bare
Reason discovers and dictates." [7] Both are of God, and
both are necessary to man and supplement each other.
The law of nature is purely a law of works and requires
perfect obedience, of which man is not capable. Whether
repentance and humility will obtain the mercy and pardon
of God, cannot be known without a revelation of His will.
Reason renders such pardon not inconsistent with the perfections of God, but cannot infer that God will be merciful. [8] Taken alone natural religion is in fact merely
heathen. "The Law of Nature, like that of *Moses*, may

[5] Ebenezer Gay, *op. cit.*, p. 28.

[6] Quoted in William B. Sprague, *Annals of the American Pulpit* (New
York, 1865), Vol. VIII, p. 6.

[7] Ebenezer Gay, *Natural Religion, as Distinguished from Revealed: A
Sermon preached at the annual Dudleian-Lecture, at Harvard-College in
Cambridge, May 9, 1759* (Boston, 1759), pp. 6-7.

[8] *Ibid.*, p. 17.

be serviceable unto Men, *as a School-Master to bring them to Christ,* for higher Instruction; especially where the Means of such are afforded; and so usher them into a State of Grace. Notwithstanding the Insufficiency of natural Religion to their Salvation, yet it may, in some Measure, prepare them to be Partakers of the Benefit, without any Diminution of the Glory of the Gospel, which is the Grant of it, or Detraction from the Merits of our blessed Redeemer, who is the Author of it." [9]

Just as revealed religion is a necessary supplement to natural religion, the reverse is equally true, for it is essential that reason confirm the truths of revelation. In their purity, natural and revealed religion always coincide. When this is not the case in practice, Ebenezer Gay concludes that, "It must be owing to our Ignorance, or Misapprehension of Things hard to be understood in the Book of Nature, and the holy Bible, that we cannot reconcile them." In such a crisis, he had more than a little faith in reason. "No doctrine, or Scheme of Religion," he says, "should be advanced, or received as scriptural and divine, which is plainly and absolutely inconsistent with the Perfections of God, and the Possibility of Things. Absurdities and Contradictions (from which few human Schemes are entirely free) are not to be obtruded upon our Faith. No Pretence of Revelation can be sufficient for the Admission of them. The manifest Absurdity of any Doctrine, is a stronger Argument that it is not of God, than any other Evidence can be that it is. . . . To say, in Defence of any religious Tenets, reduced to Absurdity, that the Perfections of God, his Holiness, Justice, Goodness, are quite different Things in Him, from what, in an infinitely lower

[9] *Ibid.*, pp. 20-21.

Degree, they are in Men, is to overthrow all Religion both natural and revealed; and make our Faith, as well as Reason vain.—For, if we have no right Notions of the Deity, (as 'tis certain, upon this Supposition, we have none,) as we worship, so we believe, we know not what, or why. We don't know what Respects are due from us to the Perfections of God; or that any are required of us by Him. For, as well as any other moral Perfections, Truth may be quite different in God, from what it is in Men; and so there may be nothing of that which we conceive of as such, in his Assertions and Promises.— He may declare one Thing, and mean another; promise one Thing, and do another:—God may be True and Faithful, and yet deceive us; as well as Holy and Just, and do that which is not Right. Revelation gives us the same (tho' clearer) Ideas of the Attributes of God, which we have from Nature and Reason: And if it taught any Thing contrary thereto, it would unsay what it saith, and destroy its own credibility. To set the Gifts of God at variance, is to frustrate the good Design and deprive ourselves of the Benefit of them. Vehemently to decry Reason as useless, or as a blind Guide, leading Men into Error and Hell; and to run down natural Religion as mere *Paganism*, derogates from the Credit of revealed, subverts our Faith in it, and dissolves our Obligation to practice it." [10]

Dr. Gay was thus only moderately deistic. His theology is a modification of the sterner tenets of Calvinism rather than a thoroughgoing rationalism. He had no thought of rejecting the authority of the Bible and accepted the story of the fall of man as history. The dual

[10] Ebenezer Gay, *op. cit.*, pp. 21-23.

basis of authority of reason and revelation did not trouble him. Both confirm the great body of the Christian tradition to be of God—only those elements which cause dissension among Christians are false. "It is in the Light of Revelation, added to that of Nature, that Things are so plain and easy to our discerning, as that we are ready to think bare Reason must discover them to all Mankind, and that we, un-enlightened by the Gospel, should have known as much of the Principles and Duties of Natural Religion. But, if we are thence insensible of, and unthankful for, *the tender Mercy of our God*, . . . we are stupidly inconsiderate. . . . By Means of Revelation we have the right Use of Reason, in Matters of Religion: And, by the due Exercise of Reason, so excited and directed, we have the inestimable Benefit of Revelation. Both are *good Gifts*, —Rays from *the Father of Lights*, to *enlighten every Man that cometh into the World*." [11] Ebenezer Gay was no Calvinist. The doctrine of predestination finds no place in his theories of either natural or revealed religion. The emphasis is definitely shifted from the glory of God's sovereignty to the dignity and well-being of His creatures.[12]

The Rev. Charles Chauncy, minister of the First Church in Boston for sixty years from 1727 to 1787, published anonymously in London in 1784 an octavo volume, *The Salvation of All Men*. The fact that this learned Bostonian divine and the unlettered Colonel Ethan Allen of Vermont published their doctrine of Universalism in the

[11] *Ibid.*, pp. 31-32.
[12] Melba P. Wilson, *Pre-Revolutionary Liberalism and Post-Revolutionary Unitarianism in America* (MS. master's essay, Columbia University, 1930), p. 29.

same year emphasises the prevalence of the liberal spirit in eighteenth-century New England.

Chauncy had long been of a rationalistic bent. In the 1740's he had been the outstanding critic of the emotionalism of the Great Awakening which he regarded as an unmitigated evil. After the Peace of 1763 when the question of an American bishop for the Episcopal Church agitated the Congregationalists as much as the Stamp Act, there was no limit to the price he would pay for ecclesiastical freedom. "It may be relied on," he threatened, "our people would not be easy, if restrained in the exercise of that 'liberty wherewith Christ has made them free'; yea, they would hazard every thing dear to them, their estates, their very lives, rather than suffer their necks to be put under that yoke of bondage, which was so sadly galling to their fathers, and occasioned their retreat into this distant land, that they might enjoy the freedom of men and christians." [13]

An enemy of both untutored religious emotionalism and episcopacy, he was at the same time becoming more and more a liberal in doctrine. The idea of the salvation of all men is said to have been in Dr. Chauncy's mind for many years before 1784. It was faintly foreshadowed in his sermon at the ordination of Rev. Joseph Bowman in 1762, but he was not the kind of man to jump at a radical idea and shout it from the housetops. It is in fact misleading to speak of him as a radical. His liberalism was primarily an intellectual mitigation of the stern Christian belief in eternal damnation. It is rather because he was so even-

---

[13] Charles Chauncy, *A Letter to a Friend, Containing, Remarks on certain Passages in a Sermon Preached, by the Right Reverend Father in God, John Lord Bishop of Landaff. . . . In which the highest Reproach is undeservedly cast upon the American Colonies* (Boston, 1767), p. 47.

minded that the latter doctrine seemed to him too extreme.
It leaves us with the paradox but not a contradiction that
his liberalism was the natural outcome of his conservatism.

The basis of Chauncy's belief in universal salvation was
the benevolence of God. "As the First Cause of all things
is infinitely benevolent," he said, " 'tis not easy to conceive,
that he should bring mankind into existence, unless he intended to make them finally happy." [14] And if that is
God's aim it cannot be presumed that He should be unable
to carry it into execution.

By "finally happy," however, Chauncy did not mean
that all men would be admitted to "the enjoyment of happiness in the state that next succeeds the present." [15] That
would be in contradiction to the Scriptures, and Chauncy,
unlike Allen, never questioned the authority of the Bible.
The wicked will be punished after death "to a great degree, and for a long time, in proportion to the moral depravity they have contracted in this." [16] This is mentioned
"lest any should foolishly take occasion, from the doctrine
here advanced, to encourage themselves in their evil
ways." [17] But this suffering after death is not strictly
speaking a punishment for evil done, but a process of regeneration. The sin voluntarily engaged in during this
life results in a degeneration of the soul and in a degenerate
state the soul must be miserable. What we think of as
future punishment is the process of delivering the soul
from this misery and fitting it for immortality and happi-

[14] [Charles Chauncy], *The Mystery hid from Ages and Generations,
made manifest by the Gospel-Revelation: or, The Salvation of All Men
the Grand Thing aimed at in the Scheme of God, as opened in the New-
Testament Writings, and entrusted with Jesus Christ to bring into Effect.
By One who wishes well to the whole Human Race* (London, 1784), p. 1.
[15] *Ibid.*, p. 7.   [17] *Ibid.*, p. 10.
[16] *Ibid.*, p. 9.

ness.[18] It may be that some souls will have to go through several stages or processes of punishment "before the scheme of God may be perfected, and mankind universally cured of their moral disorders, and in this way qualified for, and finally instated in, eternal happiness."[19] The inspired authors of the Bible, to be sure, do not say very much about the state *beyond* that following our death, but that, says Chauncy, is only natural. They were interested primarily in promoting our welfare "in the *state that will succeed next after this;* while, at the same time, they have interposed enough to lead an impartial and attentive enquirer into the thought, that the *final result* of the *scheme* of God, conducted by his Son *Jesus Christ,* will be the HAPPINESS OF MANKIND UNIVERSALLY."[20]

It is true, says Chauncy, that this idea makes it necessary to give up doctrines of long standing, but for himself he is glad to be spared the necessity of attempting "to reconcile the doctrine, which dooms so great a number of the human race to eternal flames, with the essential, absolutely perfect, goodness of the Deity."[21] "And 'tis far more reasonable to believe, that the whole human kind, in consequence of his [Christ's] death, will finally be saved, than that the greater part of them should perish. More honor is hereby reflected on God; greater virtue is attributed to the blood of Christ shed on the cross; and, instead of dying in vain, as to any real good that will finally be the event, with respect to the greatest part of mankind, he will be made to die to the best and noblest purpose, even the eternal happiness of a whole world of intelligent and moral beings."[22]

[18] [Charles Chauncy], *op. cit.,* p. 11.
[19] *Ibid.,* p. 12.
[20] *Ibid.,* p. 254.
[21] *Ibid.,* p. 14.
[22] *Ibid.,* p. 22.

Liberal as he thus was with respect to salvation, his very method of proof from the Scriptures emphasises that Charles Chauncy was in no sense the heretic that Ethan Allen was. One looks in vain for any critical analysis of the Bible. He accepted it all literally. For example: "It appears, I would hope," he says, "upon the whole, that the account Moses has given us of the 'fall' of our first parents, far from being trifling, ridiculous, or absurd, and therefore incredible in itself, is grave, solid, and rational; not justly liable to the objections that have been raised against it, but as unexceptionable as any that can be thought of, and therefore an account that no one need be ashamed to own that he receives, as containing the truth." [23]

One has the feeling that despite his Universalism Chauncy remained essentially a Calvinist to the end. His doctrine of salvation seems like a revision of the old faith to bring it into harmony with the democratic spirit of the age.

More rationalistic than Ebenezer Gay, not to say Charles Chauncy, was their younger contemporary, Jonathan Mayhew, who is said to have studied under Dr. Gay for a time. [24] Whether or not Dr. Gay inculcated or merely confirmed his "liberal and rational views," as his biographer believes, the fact remains that the Rev. Mr. Mayhew early attained the reputation of a heretic. When he was to be ordained pastor of the West Church in Boston in 1747 the ordination was postponed because only two of the invited clergymen appeared for the ceremony. A

[23] Charles Chauncy, *Five Dissertations on the Scripture Account of the Fall; and its Consequences* (London, 1785), p. 79.

[24] Alden Bradford, *Memoir of the Life and Writings of Rev. Jonathan Mayhew* (Boston, 1838), p. 21.

new council had to be convoked, but not one of the ten ministers present at the ordination was from Boston.

There is no mistaking Mayhew's rationalistic bent. "Men are naturally endowed," he said, "with faculties proper for distinguishing betwixt truth and error, right and wrong. And hence it follows, that the doctrine of total ignorance, and incapacity to judge of moral and religious truths, brought upon mankind by the apostacy of our *First Parents*, is without foundation. . . . But it is, nevertheless, the manner of vain *Enthusiasts*, when the absurdity of their doctrines is laid open, to fall a railing, telling their opposers that they are in a *carnal state*, *blind*, and unable to judge: but that themselves are *spiritually illuminated*. Thus they endeavour to palm the grossest absurdities upon their neighbours, under the notion of their being divine truths and holy mysteries: So that these enlightened Ideots make inspiration, and the Spirit of truth and wisdom, the vehicle of nonsense and contradictions." [25] "Let us," he pleads, "retain a suitable sense of the dignity of our nature in this respect. It is by our reason that we are exalted above the beasts of the field. It is by this, that we are allied to angels, and all the glorious intelligences of the heavenly world: Yea, by this we resemble God himself. It is principally on account of our reason, that we are said to have been *created in the image of God*. So that how weak soever our intellectual faculties are, yet to speak reproachfully of reason in general, is nothing less than blasphemy against God." [26]

[25] "Men, endowed with Faculties proper for discerning the Difference betwixt Truth and Falshood, &c." in Jonathan Mayhew, *Seven Sermons* preached in the West Meeting-House, Boston, in 1748 (Boston, 1749), p. 38.

[26] *Ibid.*, p. 39.

Mayhew did not, however, reject revelation. He held that "it necessarily follows from the supposition of our rational faculties being *limited*, that there is *room* for our being instructed by revelation. . . . However upon supposition of such a revelation, we must be supposed to be able to see the evidence of its being such. It is the proper office of reason to determine whether what is proposed to us under the notion of a revelation from God, be attended with suitable attestations and credentials, or not. So that even in this case, we may *of ourselves judge what is right*." [27]

This rationalistic view of revelation did not invalidate for Mayhew the authority of the Scriptures. He had no sympathy with vicious men "loth to give up their beloved lusts, and to live that pious and holy life which the gospel injoins upon us." [28] But he did believe that no speculative error will exclude a good man from salvation: "How much soever any man may be mistaken in opinion concerning the terms of salvation; yet if he is practically in the right, there is no doubt but he will be accepted of God, who considers our frame, and knows our weakness. . . . it is certain that such persons shall not be excluded from salvation, merely on account of their erroneous opinion. It is infinitely dishonourable to the all-good and perfect Governor of the world, to imagine that he has suspended the eternal salvation of men upon any niceties of speculation: Or that any one who honestly aims at finding the truth, and at doing the will of his Maker, shall be finally discarded because he fell into some erroneous opinions. He whose heart is

[27] *Ibid.*, pp. 35-36.
[28] Jonathan Mayhew, *Sermons* (Boston, 1755), p. 101.

right with God; he who seeks his will in his word, with an unbiassed mind; and he who conscientiously obeys the gospel, can be guilty of no error for which an infinitely good and merciful Being will condemn him." [29]

Nor is the individual responsible to God for any sin inherited through the fall of Adam. He is accountable only for the sins which he actually and willfully commits himself. "The original apostacy" and the resulting "curse of God" joined flesh and spirit and in this union the flesh is always prone to sin with disastrous consequences to the spirit. As far as the individual is concerned, God himself is responsible for man's proneness to sin. "It was by the ordination of God," says Mayhew, "that we were put into these bodies; which expose us so much to temptation, that it is almost, if not altogether impossible for us, wholly to avoid sinning." It is nevertheless man's duty to avoid sinning. We are the objects of God's wrath only in so far as we individually yield to sin. ". . . no passion or affection, with which we are born, can be in itself sinful; it becomes so, only by wilful or careless indulgence. A creature cannot, strictly speaking, be a sinner, 'till he has violated some law of God, or of nature: for 'sin is the *transgression* of the law.' " [30]

His doctrine of the Trinity is equally radical. His interpretation of the fall of man makes it doubtful that he believed in the necessity of the atonement of Christ. Certainly he was no more an Arminian than a Calvinist. In a footnote in his volume of sermons published in Boston in 1755, his views of the Trinity were repugnant even to those who endorsed his general views, and he himself is

[29] Jonathan Mayhew, *op. cit.*, pp. 103-104.   [30] *Ibid.*, pp. 433-434.

said to have subsequently regretted having written them.[81]
It is not doubted, however, that they did express his personal conviction. "The scripture informs us that the *Logos* had a *body* prepared for him, and that he partook of *flesh* and *blood*, that he might 'thro' death destroy him that had the power of death, that is the *devil*.' But that he took into *personal union* with himself, an human *soul*, my Bible saith not; nor that there is any other true God, besides 'his Father and our Father, his God and our God.' Indeed some who call themselves Christians, have exalted even the *Virgin Mary* above all that is called God in *heaven*, and that is worshipped *there;* saying that she is more *kind* and *merciful* than God himself; and praying to her to *command* her Son to befriend them; styling her the *Mother of God*, &c. It would be no great surprize to me to hear that the *Pope* and a *general Council*, had declared the *B. Virgin* to be the *fourth*, or rather the *first Person*, in the *Godhead*, under the title of *God*, or *Goddess* THE MOTHER; adding that neither the *Persons* are to be *confounded*, nor the *substance divided;* that the Mother is eternal, the Father eternal, the Son eternal, and the Holy Ghost eternal; but yet that there are not *four* Eternals, but *one* Eternal; that this is the *catholic faith*, which except a man *believe* faithfully, he cannot be *saved*—HE THAT HATH AN EAR TO HEAR, LET HIM HEAR! And he that hath a *mouth* given him to *blaspheme*, and a *tongue* to *babble* without ideas, (*understanding not what he says, nor whereof he affirms*) let him *blaspheme* and *babble!* But neither *Papists* nor *Protestants* should imagine that they will be understood by *others*, if they do not understand *themselves:* Nor should they think that nonsense

---

[81] William B. Sprague, *op. cit.*, Vol. VIII, p. 23.

and contradictions can ever be too *sacred* to be *ridiculous.*" [32]

With the learned of his day, Mayhew shared the Newtonian deistic concept of God as "the moral Governor of the world." [33]   Many of the works of God such as earthquakes are incomprehensible and cannot "be methodically calculated, foretold, and accounted for, as we calculate, foretel and account for common tides, eclipses, &c," [34] but "there is doubtless as regular an order and connexion of these facts and effects in nature, whether actually seen and known by us or not; and therefore as truly a course of nature with respect to them, as there is of, and with respect to, the most common and familiar." [35]   "But though human wisdom cannot scan or comprehend the great and marvellous works of God; yet we do, or may know so much, both of Him and them, as may serve the ends of practical religion; which is the end of man.—So that though we should guard against vanity on one hand, yet we should equally guard against false modesty, or scepticism on the other. We are not shut up in a vast, dark labyrinth, without any crevice or clue at all. We see at least some glimmerings of light; and if *Theseus*-like, we follow the clue which is actually given us, it will lead us out of this darkness into open and endless day." [36]

Mayhew was more interested in discovering the truths of natural science than the truths which the mind of man may arrive at through theological speculation. The latter were not important to "serve the ends of practical re-

[32] Jonathan Mayhew, *Sermons,* p. 418, note.
[33] Jonathan Mayhew, *A Discourse Occasioned by the Earthquakes in November 1755* (Boston, 1755), p. 29.
[34] *Ibid.,* p. 25.   [36] *Ibid.,* pp. 32-33.
[35] *Ibid.,* p. 26.

ligion;" a view of religion more than slightly reminiscent
of that "un-Godly Puritan," [37] Benjamin Franklin. Man-
made creeds were not important for Mayhew so long as
man lived according to the laws of God. Not that Mayhew regarded doctrine with indifference, but he saw that
in this respect there was no uniformity among Christians.
"These considerations should," he said, "on the one hand,
keep us from being censorious towards our fellow Christians; and from dealing out our *anathemas* against those
that are in error. On the other hand, they should make
us sincerely inquisitive after the truth ourselves, and
zealous in the defence of it. . . . If we ought to 'contend
earnestly for the *faith* once delivered to the saints;' we
ought certainly to contend with as much earnestness at
least for that practical piety and virtue, without which no
one can be a saint; and which is, in fact, the end of all
faith." [38] Christianity, as he explained on another occasion, is not a fixed set of beliefs but "a practical science; the
art of living piously and virtuously." [39]

Radical as Mayhew was, or was thought to be by his
more orthodox colleagues, he remained a respectable
Christian clergyman instead of becoming an outcast deist
like Palmer. He was not a Trinitarian, but when accused
of "depreciating and lowering the character and merits of
Jesus Christ, after he had written against the Athanasian
creed, he replied, 'My views are misrepresented;' and
added, 'I believe in him as my inspired teacher and Savior;
my soul loves and adores him.' " [40] To which his con-

---

[37] Herbert W. Schneider, *The Puritan Mind*, Ch. VIII.

[38] Jonathan Mayhew, *Sermons*, pp. 105-106.

[39] *Ibid.*, p. 83.

[40] Alden Bradford, *Memoir of the Life and Writings of Rev. Jonathan
Mayhew*, p. 37.

scientious biographer was however constrained to add that on this doctrine, "I cannot but observe, that he is not altogether so clear and definite as on most other subjects." It was after all largely a matter of doctrine, and therefore a matter for the individual to decide for himself or, perhaps better still, to leave undecided. "Let us take pains to find out the truth," he said, "and after we are settled in our judgment concerning any religious tenet or practice, adhere to it with constancy of mind, till convinced of our error in a rational way. Let us despise the frowns and censures of those vain conceited men who set themselves up for the oracles of truth and the standard of orthodoxy; and then call their neighbours hard names—We have not only a right to think for ourselves in matters of religion, but to act for ourselves also. Nor has any man whatever, whether of a *civil* or *sacred* Character, any authority to controul us, unless it be by the gentle methods of argument and perswasion. To Christ alone, the supreme and only head of the christian church, and the final judge of mankind; to him alone we are accountable for not believing his doctrines, and obeying his commandments, as such. And whosoever attempts to restrain or controul us, takes it upon him to rule *another man's servant*, forgetting that he is also *a man under authority;* and must hereafter stand or fall by a sentence from the same mouth with ourselves. Did I say, we have a *right* to judge and act for ourselves? I now add—it is our *indispensible duty* to do it. This is a right which we cannot relinquish, or neglect to exercise, if we would, without being highly culpable; for it is absolutely unalienable in its own nature. We may dispose of our temporal substance if we please; but God and nature and the gospel of Christ injoin it upon us a duty to maintain the right of private judgment, and to worship God according to our consciences." [41]

Christ the final judge of mankind, God and reason are strangely mixed in Mayhew's thought, but there is enough of the old to keep him in the Christian church and enough of the new gradually to transform New England Calvinism into Unitarianism. The prayer quoted in Cotton Mather's *Magnalia,* applied to Harvard College, that it may be "so tenacious of the truth that it shall be easier to find a wolf in England or a snake in Ireland than a Socinian or Arminian in Cambridge," [42] emphasizes how far the sheep had strayed from the fold.

Mayhew died an untimely death in 1766, not yet 46 years of age. The impending revolution which was so successfully to carry out his desires for political emancipation from Great Britain at the same time furthered the extension of his religious liberalism. Such was the beauty of fate, indeed, that the Church of England which was Mayhew's particular *bête noir* was to give America its first Unitarian church!

King's Chapel in Boston, founded in 1686, was the oldest Episcopal church in New England. The Revolution severed its connection with the Church of England and its loyalist minister left the city with the British troops in 1776. In September 1782, James Freeman, a layman and graduate of Harvard in 1777, was invited as a reader. In a letter to his father, dated December 24, 1782, he wrote: "I trust you believe that, by entering into this line, I have

---

[41] Jonathan Mayhew, *Seven Sermons* (Boston, 1749), pp. 85-86.

[42] Quoted in *The Religious History of New England, King's Chapel Lectures* (Cambridge, 1917), pp. 97-98.

imbibed no High Church notions. I have fortunately no temptation to be bigoted, for the proprietors of the Chapel are very liberal in their notions. They allow me to make several alterations in the service, which liberty I frequently use. We can scarcely be called of the Church of England, for we disclaim the authority of that country in ecclesiastical as well as in civil matters." [43]

Freeman soon became known as an outstanding liberal. In 1784 he came under the influence of the English Unitarian minister, William Hazlitt, the father of the essayist, who migrated to Boston after having been unfavorably received in Philadelphia. "While at Boston," confided William Bentley in his Diary, "he attached himself to the ingenious Mr. Freeman, now reader at the King's Chapel, & led that worthy man to some hasty measures in revising the Liturgy, which may prove fatal to his establishment in that Society." [44]

Hazlitt himself was too radical to be acceptable to any church in Boston and vicinity and he finally returned to England in 1785, but he was of great help to Freeman. On the very day on which Hazlitt arrived in Boston, May 15, 1784, he was invited to a meeting of the Boston Association of Ministers at the home of the venerable Dr. Charles Chauncy. [45] The conversation happened to turn to the subject of ordination. Freeman was of course intensely interested. He was still a layman, the Chapel was nominally Episcopalian, and he did not know just what could be done about his ordination. Without reference to

[43] Quoted in Wm. B. Sprague, *op. cit.*, Vol. VIII, p. 164.
[44] *The Diary of William Bentley, D.D., Pastor of the East Church, Salem, Massachusetts* (Salem, Mass., 1905), Vol. I, p. 34.
[45] William B. Sprague, *op. cit.*, Vol. VIII, p. 8.

this particular case, however, Hazlitt stated as his opinion
"that the people or the congregation who chose any man
to be their minister were his proper ordainers. Mr. Freeman, upon hearing this, jumped from his seat in a kind of
transport saying, 'I wish you could prove that, Sir.' The
gentlemen answered that 'few things could admit of an
easier proof.' And from that moment a thorough intimacy
commenced between him and Mr. Freeman. Soon after,
the Boston prints being under no *imprimatur*, he published
several letters in supporting the cause of Mr. Freeman.
At the solicitation of Mr. Freeman he also published a
Scriptural Confutation of the Thirty-nine Articles. . . .
This publication in its consequences converted Mr. Freeman's congregation into a Unitarian church, which, as Mr.
Freeman acknowledged, could never have been done without the labors of this gentleman." [46]

Freeman remained a warm admirer of Hazlitt's. In a
letter to Theophilus Lindsey, dated July 7, 1786, he
wrote, "I bless the day when that honest man first landed
in this country." And in another letter, dated June 1789,
"Before Mr. Hazlitt came to Boston, the Trinitarian dox-
ology was almost universally used. That honest, good
man prevailed upon several ministers to omit it. Since his
departure, the number of those who repeat only scriptural
doxologies has greatly increased, so that there are now
many churches in which the worship is strictly Unitarian." [47]

The congregation of King's Chapel, with few exceptions,

---

[46] Quoted from *Monthly Repository*, Vol. III, p. 305, in George W.
Cooke, *Unitarianism in America* (Boston, 1902), pp. 78-79, note.

[47] Rev. Thomas Belsham, *American Unitarianism* (Boston, 1815), p. 12,
note.

was as liberal as its reader and voted on June 19, 1785, to adopt the amended Unitarian Liturgy of Samuel Clarke, but the question of Freeman's ordination still remained unsolved. The church and its lay pastor both having renounced affiliation with the Episcopal Church, it is scarcely surprising that when Freeman applied for ordination to Bishop Seabury of Connecticut in March 1786, the Bishop replied that, as the case was unusual, the matter would have to be taken up with his presbyters. The Episcopal clergy of Connecticut met at Stratford in June 1786 and examined Freeman. In a long letter to his father filled with interesting details, he says, "Upon the whole, finding me an incorrigible heretic, they dismissed me without granting my request." [48] He would undoubtedly have preferred Episcopal ordination, but finding this impossible, he fell back on first principles, as his colleague and successor the Rev. Mr. Greenwood said, and was ordained by the church itself on November 18, 1787.[49]

This non-clerical ordination was a source of great satisfaction to the liberals. The ceremony was performed "according to a form suggested by Governor Bowdoin, a gentleman, whose learning, good sense, and merit, . . . 'would give a sanction to any sentiment which he expouses. . . . Deep attention was impressed upon every countenance, and many of the advocates for religious liberty, of our own and other churches, could not forbear expressing their sensibility by tears of joy.' " [50] Freeman's friend, William Bentley, spoke of this ordination as "a bold

[48] Letter dated October 31, 1786, quoted in William B. Sprague, op. cit., Vol. VIII, p. 167.
[49] William B. Sprague, op. cit., Vol. VIII, p. 168.
[50] Thomas Belsham, op. cit., pp. 13-14.

stroke at the pride of priestcraft & a just assertion of the right of every religious association." [51]

Because of his association with King's Chapel, Freeman is perhaps more widely known as a liberal than some of the Congregational Unitarians of his time. He himself never claimed the credit of the movement, "but referred to Dr. Mayhew and others as having preached the same doctrine before." [52] Like them, too, he was more conservative than the more extreme English Unitarians like Priestley. It appears that although to his mind the person of Christ did not belong in the Godhead, he was not simply a man. He referred to him as our Savior, Redeemer, Lord, and as one who by his life, death, and resurrection had reconciled us to God. The perfections of Jesus's life are the greatest internal evidence we possess of the truth of the Christian faith, and he is the model to be held up whenever the perfect man is described, the fullest realization of human potentiality. [53] The Christian dispensation is however not an absolute. Man has ever been a free agent, and as "God in no age has left himself without witness," sin has ever been voluntary. [54] The highest standards of life known to man are those of the Christian religion, but it does not therefore follow that there were no virtuous men before the coming of Christ. "Whilst it is a doctrine of the Bible, that God hath appointed us to obtain salvation by our Lord Jesus Christ, it teaches that the way, by which

---

[51] William Bentley, *Diary*, Vol. III, pp. 405-406. For a detailed discussion of Freeman's ordination, *vide*, Henry W. Foote, *Annals of King's Chapel* (Boston, 1896), Vol. II, pp. 383-394.

[52] William B. Sprague, *op. cit.*, Vol. VIII, p. 169.

[53] James Freeman, *Sermons on Particular Occasions* (Boston, 1812), pp. 65, 67, 285.

[54] James Freeman, *Sermons and Charges* (New Edition, Boston, 1832), p. 109.

men enter into this everlasting life, is not by believing in a
mediator, of whom they never heard, and of whom it was
impossible that they should hear, but by keeping the commandments. . . . we dare not consign to everlasting
flames the virtuous heathen of ancient times, who sincerely
and diligently framed their lives according to the light of
nature and the religions which they had received and which
they professed." [55]   The coming of Christ had doomed no
one to destruction.   "The Son of man is come, not to destroy men's lives, but to save them: it [the Gospel] has
depressed no good man, who without any fault of his own
is deprived of its light; but it has exalted all, by whom it
is received and obeyed.   It has created a new order of
beings with enlarged capacities; it has lifted their eyes to
heaven, and enkindled in their souls the flame of divine
love; it has raised the character of human nature higher,
than it ever was before; it has refined and ennobled men,
and made them kings and priests unto God." [56]   Dr. Freeman was not a Calvinist, but he did remain a Christian—
and eminently respectable!

More interesting from the point of view of liberalism,
both religious and political, was the Rev. William Bentley,
for many years pastor of the East Church in Salem, Massachusetts.   He was a Unitarian, a Republican, and a Free-
mason and distinctly influenced by apparently every liberal
current of his time.

He graduated from Harvard College in 1777 in the
same class with James Freeman and was a tutor there from
1780 to 1783.   In 1783 he began his ministry in Salem
where he continued as long as he lived (1819).

[55] James Freeman, *op. cit.*, p. 111.   [56] *Ibid.*, p. 116.

Like Freeman, Bentley was influenced by the sojourn of William Hazlitt and soon adopted Priestley's catechism as a substitute for the Westminster catechism.[57] He was a good deal more militantly anti-Trinitarian than Freeman. On January 9, 1791, he wrote that he had examined the first chapter of the Fourth Gospel and after duly considering the Athanasian, Arian, and Unitarian hypotheses had accepted the Unitarian attitude. A week later, a consideration of the text, "The church of God which he had purchased with his own blood," led him to a summary of arguments to show that Jesus is not God.[58]

He had a high conception of the worth of human life. In 1792, he wrote, "I took the liberty in the most exceptional manner to deliver my sentiments against total depravity as preached at a late lecture."[59] He maintained that infant baptism does not comprise regeneration nor that it has any supernatural effects. It is significant only as marking the resolution of parents to *educate* their children in a Christian way.[60] Man is originally endowed with abilities which are to be developed by means of education.[61] The Calvinistic doctrine of an undemocratic predestination of the elect naturally did not appeal to him. "Heaven and happiness," he said in his memorable sermon in King's

[57] William Bentley, *Diary*, Biographical Sketch, Vol. I, p. xv.
Hazlitt supplied in Salem in 1786, and "in one of his sermons, before the North parish, he openly disavowed his beliefs in the doctrine of the Trinity, much to the surprise of his hearers."—Joseph B. Felt, *Annals of Salem* (Second Edition, Salem, 1849), Vol. II, p. 605.

[58] Samuel A. Eliot, *Heralds of a Liberal Faith* (Boston, 1910), Vol. I, p. 151.

[59] *Ibid.*, Vol. I, p. 151.

[60] William Bentley, *Diary*, Vol. I, pp. 378, 386.

[61] William Bentley, *A Sermon, delivered in the East Meeting House, Salem, on Sunday Morning, March 13 occasioned by the Death of Jonathan Gardner, Esq. Master of the Marine Society in Salem* (Salem, 1791), p. 11.

Chapel,[62] "were not designated by God as the exclusive rights of learned priests, or ingenious doctors; they are the end which God has proposed for all mankind, and are therefore, by the same means, attainable by all men. Riches and honors cannot ensure the purchase; neither can learning, pompous titles, respect nor dignity. Virtue alone is the moral happiness of the world, and personal virtue alone secures heaven."[63] All men will not necessarily get to heaven, but "all men are, and always have been, capable of salvation."[64]

The atmosphere of Salem was one most conducive to breaking down small prejudices and developing a cosmopolitan attitude among its inhabitants. None was more affected by the impact of foreign and particularly oriental ideas than this unusual ship carpenter's son. Coupled with his scholarly inquisitiveness and knowledge of "more than twenty different languages," the contacts which he made through his sea-going parishioners[65] with the religions of India, Arabia, Persia, and China, brought him to a broader view of the merits of Christianity. The shipmasters and merchants themselves from the impact of these new ideas forsook their old theological notions and provided favorable ground for their Reverend Doctor to cultivate.[66] Speaking of one of his parishioners who had been engaged

---

[62] For about thirty years after the Revolution, King's Chapel was generally called Stone Chapel, although the name King's Chapel was neither dropped nor resumed by vote.—Henry W. Foote, *Annals of King's Chapel*, Vol. II, p. 398.

[63] William Bentley, *A Sermon, preached at the Stone Chapel in Boston, September 12, 1790* (Boston, 1790), pp. 8-9.

[64] *Ibid.*, p. 11.

[65] *Cf.*, "Old Salem Sea-Captains," in Thomas W. Higginson, *Travellers and Outlaws* (Boston, 1889).

[66] *Cf.*, George W. Cooke, *op. cit.*, p. 80; Thomas Belsham, *op. cit.*, p. 20; Joseph B. Felt, *op. cit.*, Vol. II, pp. 70, 285, 291, 293-302, 304, 306, 307, 312-314, 318-322, 324, 341, 344, *ff.*

in foreign trade, Bentley said: "He never thought men, who differed from him, were fools or knaves. He had a persuasion that religious opinions depend not on names, but upon sincere inquiry, for their best influence, and that an honest mind might be so circumstanced, as to admit the most absurd doctrines, and be uncharitable in the defence of them, while there might be great benevolence in the native purposes of the heart. He therefore loved all men, who acted in sincerity, and never found his own heart less sensible, nor his hand less ready, from the opinions, condition, or prejudices of any men." [67] "He loved men, rather than opinions, (He professed the Unitarian doctrine.) and he desired to know more of their actions, than of their professions." [68]

"In 1790," says Professor Morison, "the two hundred and twenty-eight heads of families (including widows) in Dr. Bentley's East Church, included thirty-five mariners, fifty-eight master mariners, nine boat- or ship-builders, five rope- or sail-makers, and five fishermen. Even people whose principal occupation was independent of commerce, generally owned a share in a ship, or made private adventures. Nathaniel Richardson, who owned the largest tannery in Essex County, also owned four vessels; and his son Nathaniel, who 'hurried into bold adventures,' died in Malaga at the age of eighteen. Unquestioned social preëminence was enjoyed by the merchant-shipowners, who with few exceptions had commanded vessels on East-India voyages." [69] Twenty out of Salem's twenty-four

[67] William Bentley, *A Funeral Discourse, delivered in the East Meeting-House, Salem, on the Sunday after the Death of Major General John Fiske, who died September 28, 1797 aet 53* (Salem, 1797), p. 16.
[68] *Ibid.*, p. 24.
[69] Samuel Eliot Morison, *The Maritime History of Massachusetts, 1783-1860* (Boston, 1925), pp. 122-123.

most prominent families, all engaged in foreign trade, were Unitarians.[70]

There were as many as sixty or seventy Salem ships engaged in the East India trade,[71] and they brought home much besides the articles of commerce.[72]   While maritime concerns bring a commercial community much profit, says Salem's historian, "they diffuse through its population a knowledge of foreign places, customs, manners, improvements, and character.   They afford a facility of communication with the barbarous and semi-civilized nations of the earth." [73]   More important than such occasional curiosities as when Capt. John Gibaut arrived from India on December 26, 1790, bringing with him a native of Madras,[74] were the rare Persian, Arabic, and Chinese manuscripts and works of art which his friends brought Dr. Bentley from the East.   "The collection of coins and rare books was another of his favorite pursuits, and to gratify him in these respects was a leading object of every ship-master of our parish who went abroad.   Scarcely a vessel arrived that did not bring valuable contributions to his cabinet or library, so that some of his collections were indeed very rare and valuable and often consulted by every virtuoso in the neighborhood." [75]

In 1799, at the suggestion of Captain Gibaut, Bentley

[70] Joseph H. Allen and Richard Eddy, *A History of the Unitarians and Universalists in the United States*, Vol. X in *The American Church History Series* (New York, 1894), pp. 183-184.

[71] Joseph B. Felt, *op. cit.*, Vol. II, p. 75.

[72] Captains were requested by their friends to buy such luxuries as red cornelian necklaces, camel's-hair shawls, bed coverings, and pots of preserved ginger.   An order for a Sanskrit bible suggests an interest in comparative religion.—Samuel Eliot Morison, *op. cit.*, p. 89.

[73] Joseph B. Felt, *op. cit.*, Vol. II, p. 209.

[74] *Ibid.*, Vol. II, p. 295.

[75] William Bentley, *Diary*, Biographical Sketch, Vol. I, p. xvii.

drew up the plans for the East India Marine Society one of whose objectives was to exhibit curios and works of art from the East.[76] Approximately one year after its establishment, this society had fifty-three members, fifty of whom were captains in the Indies.[77] The active membership was limited to those who circumnavigated the Cape of Good Hope.[78] In addition to the museum of this Society, they also began the collection for a library dealing primarily with travel, adventure, and marine affairs.[79]

Another indication of Salem's intellectual liberalism was the Philosophical Library whose inception Bentley describes, as follows: "In the War a Library including Phil. Transactions, &c. was taken, going to Canada, which has laid the foundation of a distinct Philosophical Library."[80] In 1790, the collection contained over two hundred volumes.[81] It was merged with the Salem Athenæum when the latter was established in 1810, and Bentley sadly confided that "there was too much of the Merchant to be seen in this Literary enterprise."[82]

It is evident that Bentley's sea-faring parishioners were on the whole characterized by a relatively wide mental horizon which made it easy for him to judge of the value of religion by its fruits. It seemed to Bentley that man is not depraved by nature; he is worthy of happiness and himself possesses the means to its attainment. Therefore,

---

[76] William Bentley, *Diary*, Oct. 22, 1799, Vol. II, p. 321; Nov. 7, 1799, Vol. II, p. 322.

[77] *Ibid.*, Jan. 13, 1801, Vol. II, p. 362.

[78] *Ibid.*, Aug. 13, 1801, Vol. II, p. 382.

[79] *Ibid.*, Aug. 13, 1801, Vol. II, p. 382; Jan. 4, 1804, Vol. III, p. 68.

[80] *Ibid.*, March 5, 1790, Vol. I, p. 151; *cf.*, Joseph B. Felt, *op. cit.*, Vol. II, pp. 31-32.

[81] William Bentley, *Diary*, April 15, 1790, Vol. I, p. 160.

[82] *Ibid.*, March 2, 1810, Vol. III, p. 502.

wherever virtue is practiced, it is favored of God. "How much more pure," he said, is "the charity of a savage, than the pulpit-anathemas of a priest against churches which differ from his own." [83] God was the friend of Israel that He might advance through them a universal religion. Although the Mohammedan like the Jew may err in detail, we must be convinced that his devotion, zeal, and obedience are acceptable to God, the universal parent of all. Religion in this larger view leads us to consider ourselves "not small societies only, . . . but as belonging to the household of the faithful, who dwell in every nation, and in every clime, with one God and Father, who hateth nothing that he has made, but loveth and cherisheth it." [84] Hence it was inconsistent in Bentley's mind to claim that the true faith could be monopolized by any group distinguished by its own creeds and doctrines. [85] Jesus set a noble example and high standard for other men to follow, but *belief* in him as a divine savior was not necessary.

Like the deists he was concerned not with theological dogmas but with the principle, "by their fruits ye shall know them." His attitude is well expressed in his own words: "I have adopted many opinions abhorrent of my early prejudices, & am still ready to receive truth upon proper evidence from whatever quarter it may come. I think more honor done to God in rejecting Xtianity itself in obedience to my convictions, than in any fervor which is pretended, towards it, & I hope that, no poverty which I can dread, or hope I can entertain, will weaken my resolu-

[83] *A Sermon, preached at the Stone Chapel*, p. 15.
[84] *Ibid.*, pp. 22-23.
[85] He not only preached but also practiced his belief in the brotherhood of religious societies. When the Catholics organized themselves in Salem he welcomed them and entertained the priest in his own house.—Samuel A. Eliot, *op. cit.*, Vol. I, p. 152.

tion to act upon my convictions. The only evidence I wish to have of my integrity is a good life, & as to faith, his can't be wrong whose life is in the right." [86] Or, as he said on another occasion two years later: "However numerous our doctrines, whether simple or mysterious; whether we receive all the dogmas of the Church or not, let us consider that we should produce good fruits. . . . When a man is found, who does not profess much, nor despise all, who is pure from guile, peaceable in his life, gentle in his manners, easily dissuaded from revenge, with an heart to pity and relieve the miserable, impartial in his judgement, and without dissimulation, this is the man of religion." [87] And such a man, thought Bentley, should have the right to choose his opinions for himself.

This emphasis on moral living instead of on beliefs is the same thing as Ethan Allen's or Elihu Palmer's religion of nature. William Bentley used the common term and called it natural religion as distinguished from revelation. "Natural religion," he said, "is still the most excellent religion," [88] but unlike Allen or Palmer, he did not discard revelation. The latter was designed to act in an auxiliary capacity until its assistance becomes unnecessary. Christianity will have done its work when man is brought to the point of acting habitually from his sense of moral responsibility; when it has by its support and encouragement brought his native moral potentialities to full maturity.

Religion for Bentley is thus primarily a temporary instrument for moral education. "The good man," he said, "will scorn to practise the injustice he condemns; to oppress those he professes to love, or to injure those he can

[86] William Bentley, *Diary*, April 22, 1788, Vol. I, p. 98.
[87] *A Sermon, preached at the Stone Chapel*, pp. 19-21.
[88] *Ibid.*, p. 17.

serve. He will not leave wants unsupplied, which he can remove; nor suffer poverty to depart, without hope, from his door. His Religion is his Charity, and he loves God, and the State, by being, as far as he can, the guardian of public virtue." [89] Nor does he look only to the Christian tradition for examples. He quotes with approval from Mahomet and says of Plato, "no one can be entitled to higher respect than Plato, whether we consider his refined speculations on the nature of man, his deep researches into the nature of society, or his more rich speculations on civil institutions." He recognized Rousseau, "with all his indiscretions," as a great authority on education. [90] There is no mistaking Bentley's interest in the good life here and now in contrast to the more orthodox theological emphasis on other-worldliness. Not that he gave no thought to the hereafter. The religious or virtuous man, he believed, is in fact making the best provisions for eternity. He practices what he loves. "A life of affection becomes a life of devotion. Thus we provide for earth and for heaven." [91]

Like the deists, too, Bentley was a republican. He was friendly to the French cause, but came to regret the excesses of the Revolution. On March 25, 1793, he wrote, "The melancholy news of the beheading of the Roi de France is confirmed in the public opinion, & the event is regretted most sincerely by all thinking people. The french loose much of their influence upon the hearts of the Americans by this event." [92]

[89] William Bentley, *A Discourse, delivered in the East Meeting-House in Salem, September 2, 1807, at the Annual Meeting of the Salem Female Charitable Society* (Salem, 1807), p. 3.
[90] *Ibid.*, pp. 14-16.
[91] *Ibid.*, p. 19.
[92] William Bentley, *Diary*, Vol. II, p. 13.

He was a warm admirer of President Jefferson for which he incurred the dislike of the conservatives. On September 20, 1805, he wrote: "I am informed that my friendship for Mr. Jefferson will submit me to great evils." [93] And a few days later, "the abuse which I receive, when called by name in the Federal papers, obliges me to take great satisfaction in the able vindication of the man I esteem as the greatest national benefactor." [94] In a letter to S. H. Smith, January 14, 1806, declining the Presidency of the University of Virginia, he spoke of his "unrivalled esteem" of President Jefferson and admiration for his "wise administration." [95]

The Federalists linked his name with that of Thomas Paine,[96] and not altogether without reason. He had paid for a copy of Paine's song, *Adams and Liberty*, for each member of his singing school.[97] However, he spoke of the *Age of Reason* as a "contemptible publication," [98] although he always maintained a tolerant and understanding spirit towards its author. "The name is enough," said Bentley. "Every person has ideas of him. Some respect his genius & dread the man. Some reverence his political, while they hate his religious, opinions. Some love the man, but not his private manners. Indeed he has done nothing which has not extremes in it. He never appears but we love & hate him. He is as great a paradox as ever appeared in human nature." [99]

His evaluation of Paine is remarkably sane and just:

[93] *Ibid.*, Vol. III, p. 192.
[94] *Ibid.*, September 25, 1805, Vol. III, p. 193.
[95] *Ibid.*, Vol. III, p. 210.
[96] *Ibid.*, Vol. III, p. 371.
[97] *Ibid.*, Vol. II, p. 283.
[98] *Ibid.*, Vol. II, p. 107.
[99] *Ibid.*, August 23, 1803, Vol. III, p. 37.

"The many attempts of this man to degrade Christianity have given him an ill name among Christians who have entirely forgotten their great obligations to him in the American Revolution. Posterity will do justice to his talents, to his services, & to his Character, should it be denied in the present Generation. He had such ideas of the opposition of the religious Orders to the progress of Civil & political society that he opposed everything which involved their existence. It is said that he asked to be buried among the Friends or Quakers with whom he had been educated, but from the prejudices of the times they are said not to have consented. Mr. Paine possessed all the vigour of intellect with all the power of expression. No man had greater ability in assisting the public mind whenever he favoured its inclinations. When he dared openly to insult it, it trembled, it felt, it was silent, it was shaken. He was indeed a wonderful man & he was the first to see in what part every System was most vulnerable. Even in his attacks on Christianity he felt without knowing it, the greatest difficulties which rational Christians have felt. Without their prejudices he found what was simple, powerful, & direct, & what might be renounced without injury to morality, to the reverence of God & the peace of the mind." [100]

Bentley had long been sympathetic with, or at least tolerant of, the deists and certainly was familiar with their writings. He loaned his own copies to friends with unfortunate consequences. He lent his Tindal "to Capt. Jo. W. upon the solemn promise of a private examination. It was left under a pillow, found by a woman, lent to an Aunt, read before her husband, & by him reported to Col.

[100] William Bentley, *op. cit.*, June 18, 1809, Vol. III, pp. 441-442.

Carlton. . . ." His copy of Ethan Allen's *Oracles* created a sensation. He lent it "to Col. C. under solemn promise of secrecy, but by him lent to a Mr Grafton, who was reported to have died a Confirmed Infidel. . . . The book was found at his death in his chamber, examined with horror by his female relations. By them conveyed to a Mr. Williams, whose shop is remarkable for news, & there examined—reported to be mine from the initials W. B., viewed as an awful curiosity by hundreds, connected with a report that I encouraged infidelity in Grafton by my prayers with him in his dying hour, & upon the whole a terrible opposition to me fixed in the minds of the devout & ignorant multitude." [101] How far Bentley had come from orthodoxy is indicated in his simple entry upon hearing of the death of Allen when he spoke of him as "the noted *Col. Ethan Allen*, who distinguished himself in the last war in Canada, & since by a book in his name, called *The Oracles of Reason*." [102] This becomes more pronounced when we contrast it with the reaction of Ezra Stiles who wrote in his *Diary*, "13th Inst died in Vermont the profane & impious Deist Gen Ethan Allen, Author of the *Oracles of Reason*, a Book replete with scurrilous Reflexions on Revelation.—'And in Hell he lift up his Eyes being in Torments.' " [103] It indicates not that Ezra Stiles was bigoted but rather what the deistic influences had done to produce this Bentleian genus of Congregationalism.

William Bentley and his liberal colleagues in the Congregational churches of New England were the product of the same intellectual movement which made those un-

[101] *Ibid.*, November 1787, Vol. I, p. 82.
[102] *Ibid.*, March 25, 1789, Vol. I, p. 120.
[103] Ezra Stiles, *Diary*, February 27, 1789, Vol. III, p. 345.

happy and disreputable deists, Allen, Palmer, and Paine. They liked the deists' dislike of Calvinism and their optimism for the perfectibility and dignity of man. They shared the deists' faith in reason and education. But a man like Bentley did not expend most of his efforts in attacking "superstition" and "priestcraft." His scholarship gave him an enviable perspective and his temperament was such as to keep him from controversy. He was progressive, but not radical; as emancipated from rabid infidelity as from Calvinism and Federalism. In the unofficial amalgamation of deistic principles and Puritanism which he represented, a chemical change rather than a mechanical mixture resulted. In the process they both lost their most virile and extreme features: the "priestcraft," "superstition," and republicanism of the one; the hell fire, election, and piety of the other. Congregational-Unitarianism was deism, refined and respectable, and Puritanism with the dignity of the elect but without the sting of Calvinism.

Strange as it may seem the New England Unitarian movement had no parallel in other sections of the United States. Perhaps one explanation would be that there had been greater religious freedom, i.e., indifference, in the other states and therefore less need for revision of theology and religious practices. The clergy were as a rule either uneducated or, as in the case of a relatively few Episcopalians and Presbyterians in the larger cities, identified with wealthy congregations privately tainted with deism but publicly conservative. Religion in the Middle States and in the South did not profoundly affect the everyday lives of men and women, just as respectability still demands church membership without either obligatory attendance or orthodoxy in belief.

While thus not indigenous to these states, theological radicalism, as distinguished from New England liberalism, came from without. Elihu Palmer, apostate ex-New Englander, is an outstanding example. The well-to-do were not interested in his anti-Calvinism, since the austere principles and practices had never thriven on Manhattan Island or in Philadelphia. On the other hand, they did not like his republicanism, for in spite of a republican governor New York was still controlled by the scions of old, wealthy, and respectable Dutch and English families, in sharp contrast to New England where Unitarianism throve in just such families.

The other importation, which affected Philadelphia primarily and not New York, was English Unitarianism, the chief exponent of which and émigré to America in 1794 was Joseph Priestley.

Priestley was born near Leeds in 1733 of a dissenting family rigidly orthodox and scrupulously pious. While still a boy, however, he became a liberal and dropped one Calvinistic belief after another. While pastor of a large dissenting congregation in Leeds he became a full-fledged Unitarian believing in the humanity of Jesus. Later while pastor of the New Meeting at Birmingham, which had the reputation of being the most liberal congregation in England,[104] he published two of his most important works, *An History of the Corruptions of Christianity*, 2 vols. (1782), and *An History of Early Opinions concerning Jesus Christ, compiled from Original Writers; proving that the Christian Church was at first Unitarian* (1786),

---

[104] Anne Holt, *Life of Joseph Priestley* (London, 1931), p. 132.

in which he held that the earliest belief about Christ was purely Unitarian and that the doctrines which arose later came of the corrupting influence of pagan philosophy upon Christian thought. The orthodox worship of Christ seemed to him sheer idolatry. He summarized the principal corruptions of Christianity, which incidentally were a great cause in leading "philosophical and speculative people" into infidelity, in Part II of his *Letters to a Philosophical Unbeliever* (1787). "The principal of these," he said, "besides the doctrines that are peculiar to the Roman catholics, are those of a trinity of persons in the godhead, original sin, arbitrary predestination, atonement for the sins of men by the death of Christ, and (which has perhaps been as great a cause of infidelity as any other) the doctrine of the plenary inspiration of the scriptures." [105]

There is no question about his opposition to orthodoxy, but he never considered himself anything but a Christian. While in Paris in 1774, where liberal Protestantism was almost unknown and the choice was between Catholicism and infidelity, he wrote to his friend Lindsey, "The more attention I give to the study of the Scriptures, the more attached I am to it; and I hope the time will come when I shall apply myself to it chiefly. At present I read chiefly with a practical view; and the attentive consideration of the facts in the gospel history has certainly the strongest tendency to impress the heart and influence the life in the most favourable manner. The more I read the history of the death of Christ, in particular, the more reasons I think

---

[105] Joseph Priestley, *Letters to a Philosophical Unbeliever. Part II. Containing A State of the Evidence of revealed Religion, with Animadversions on the two last Chapters of the first Volume of 'Mr. Gibbon's History of the Decline and Fall of the Roman Empire'* (Birmingham, 1787), p. 33.

I see why he was to suffer; at least I see the old ones in a stronger light, and feel more of their force. Other studies, and other pursuits, that to many others are very proper and useful, appear to me to be altogether insignificant compared to these. I am here in the midst of unbelievers, and even Atheists. I had a long conversation with one, an ingenious man, and good writer, who maintained seriously that man might arise, without any Maker, from the earth. They may despise me; I am sure I despise and pity them." [106]

He realized that the tenets of orthodox Christianity led either to superstition or to unbelief and endeavored to establish what he believed to be Christianity in its original purity.[107] Pared of "spurious doctrines," he explained, the "christian faith implies a belief of all the great historical facts recorded in the Old and New Testament, in which we are informed concerning the creation and government of the world, the history of the discourses, miracles, death, and resurrection of Christ, and his assurance of the resurrection of all the dead to a future life of retribution; and this is the doctrine that is of the utmost consequence, to enforce the good conduct of men." [108]

In his attack on orthodoxy he anticipated rather than used the historical method, for both his *History of the Corruptions of Christianity* and *History of Early Opinions concerning Jesus Christ* were written to bolster his

---

[106] Letter dated at Paris, October 21, 1774. Joseph Priestley, *Theological and Miscellaneous Works*, edited, with notes, by John Towill Rutt (Hackney, 1817), Vol. I, Part I, p. 254.

[107] "For my own part, I am satisfied that it is only by purging away the whole of this *corrupt leaven*, that we can recover the pristine simplicity and purity of our most excellent and truly rational, though much abused, religion."—Joseph Priestley, *Disquisitions relating to Matter and Spirit*, Preface in *Works*, edited by J. T. Rutt, Vol. III, p. 209.

[108] *Letters to a Philosophical Unbeliever*, Part II, p. 34.

preconceived notions of corrupted theology.[109]　At the same time he retained so much of the supernatural in his own version of Christianity that he was more successful against the defenders of the whole faith than in his apologetics.　Such problems, metaphysical and theological, as "Whether the world we inhabit, and ourselves who inhabit it, had an intelligent and benevolent author, or no proper author at all?　Whether our conduct be inspected, and we are under a righteous government, or under no government at all?　And, lastly, whether we have something to hope and fear beyond the grave?" [110]—are, after all, no more susceptible of proof or disproof than the problems involved in the divinity of Jesus.

His "direct Evidence for the Belief of a God" is the familiar argument of design.　Man must have been caused, and it follows that "the idea of a cause of any thing implies not only something prior to itself, or at least contemporary with itself, but something capable at least of comprehending what it produces. . . . For the same reason that the human species must have had a designing cause, all the species of brute animals, and the *world* to which they belong, and with which they make but *one system*, and indeed all the *visible universe* (which, as far as we can judge, bears all the marks of being *one work*) must have had a cause, or author, possessed of what we may justly call *infinite power and intelligence*." [111]　And that first cause, of

---

[109] Anne Holt, *op. cit.*, pp. 133-138.

[110] Joseph Priestley, *Letters to a Philosophical Unbeliever. Part I. Containing An Examination of the principal Objections to the Doctrines of 'Natural Religion', and especially those contained in the Writings of Mr. Hume* (Bath, 1780), Preface.

[111] *Letters to a Philosophical Unbeliever*, Part I, pp. 17-18.　*Cf., Letters to the Philosophers and Politicians of France, on the Subject of Religion* (London, 1793), Letter II, "Of the Being of God." Priestley's religious ideas are repeated over and over again in all his writings.

course, is God. However, "we *must* acquiesce in our inability of having any ideas on the subject" of "*how* so great a being as this should himself require no cause." [112]

His metaphysical writings, in short, were not original as a few other examples will verify: "That the happiness of the creation was intended by the author of it is just as evident as that the design of the millwright was that the wheels of his machine should keep in motion, and not that they should be obstructed." [113] Pain, storms, tempests, and the other evils in a world controlled by an omnipotent God are "only less evils in lieu of greater." That is, their existence is a greater good than their nonbeing, just as "all diseases are the effort of nature to remove some obstruction, something that impedes the animal functions, and thereby to defer the hour of dissolution, and to recover a state of more perfect health and enjoyment. . . ." And of course it must always be remembered that "past labour and pain is generally pleasing in recollection"! [114] As a good friend of Benjamin Franklin he believed that virtue pays and asks approvingly: "What but common observation has given rise to the common proverb, that *honesty is the best policy?*" [115] "Virtue is, in fact, that which naturally produces the greatest sum of good, and vice is that which produces the greatest sum of evil." [116] We are in a world subjected to "moral government" whose foundation is "*natural religion; that is, there is a system of duty*

[112] *Letters to a Philosophical Unbeliever*, Part I, p. 49.
[113] *Ibid.*, Part I, p. 53.
[114] *Ibid.*, Part I, pp. 55-57.
[115] *Ibid.*, Part I, p. 85. "True religion, not enjoined, or salaried, by the state, but the choice of the individual, you will find a valuable support of public virtue and public spirit; and a great security to your liberty."—*Letters to the Philosophers and Politicians of France, on the Subject of Religion*, p. 41.
[116] *Letters to a Philosophical Unbeliever*, Part I, p. 86.

to which we ought to conform, because there are *rewards and punishments* that we have to expect." [117]

Priestley loved controversy,[118] and as this analysis of his intellectual gymnastics with both the orthodox and unbelievers indicates, his first principles were a mixture of rationalism, materialism, and supernaturalism. He believed that the soul is the sentient principle in man and is therefore identified with the brain, for, he says in his *Disquisitions relating to Matter and Spirit*, first published in 1777, "the powers of sensation or perception, and thought, as belonging to man, have never been found but in conjunction with a certain *organized system of matter*, and, therefore, that those powers necessarily exist in, and depend upon, such a system." [119] "There is no instance of any man retaining the faculty of thinking, when his brain was destroyed. . . ." [120] He noted the close relation between mind and body, that "the faculty of thinking in general ripens and comes to maturity with the body," and that "it is also observed to decay with it." [121]

If the soul is the mind and the mind dies with the body, did Priestley then not believe in immortality? He did, for immortality was to Priestley one of the essential principles of Christianity—and he discarded, what he believed

---

[117] *Letters to a Philosophical Unbeliever*, Part I, p. 88.

[118] John Quincy Adams with insight and a sense of humor aptly recorded in his famous Diary, June 27, 1788, that Priestley's "literary powers may be truly called athletic."—John Quincy Adams, *Life in a New England Town: 1787, 1788* (Boston, 1903), p. 146.

[119] Joseph Priestley, *Disquisitions relating to Matter and Spirit. To which is added, The History of the Philosophical Doctrine concerning the Origin of the Soul, and the Nature of Matter; with its Influence on Christianity, especially with respect to the Doctrine of the Pre-existence of Christ* in *Works*, edited by J. T. Rutt, Vol. III, p. 243.

[120] *Ibid., Works*, Vol. III, p. 244.

[121] *Ibid., Works*, Vol. III, p. 244.

to be, only the untrue. For all the fundamental doctrines of Christianity he relied on revealed religion. He never doubted the doctrine of the judgment day, the reward of virtue, the punishment of vice, the resurrection from the dead, and eternal life. True, the soul dies with the body and death means decomposition. But to God nothing is impossible and "when his [man's] *sleeping dust* shall be re-animated at the resurrection, his power of thinking, and his consciousness, will be restored to him." [122] ". . . we shall be *identically the same beings* after the resurrection that we are at present." [123] Just as a candle may be extinguished without being annihilated and later be lighted again, he explains, so man's death may be only "for a time." In short, "whatever is *decomposed* may certainly be *recomposed,* by the same almighty power that first composed it. . . ." [124] And there you have the resurrection of the body—according to some law of Nature still unknown, to be sure!

As for the remaining principle of that metaphysical trilogy, the freedom of the will, Priestley is almost a Calvinist. Man has the ability to decide or choose, which in orthodox language means to sin or not to sin. His highest good, of course, is to choose the latter which is to act in conformity with the divine will. In fact, viewed aright, everything must be in accordance with the divine will, and this alone would eliminate any possibility of a self-determining will in man, for there is but "one will in the whole universe" and "this one will, exclusive of all chance, or the interference of any other will, disposes of all things,

[122] *Ibid., Works,* Vol. III, p. 276.
[123] *Ibid., Works,* Vol. III, p. 329.
[124] *Ibid., Works,* Vol. III, p. 334.

even to their minutest circumstances, and always for the best of purposes." [125]

Strictly speaking, all things are predetermined by the great Moral Governor of the Universe but, as Priestley says, "No man will refrain from plowing his ground because God foresees whether he will have a harvest or not." [126] He felt himself to be entirely dependent on the will of God. "I am but an instrument in his hands," he says, "for effecting a certain part of the greatest and most glorious of purposes. I am happy in *seeing* a little of this purpose, happier in the *belief* that the operations in which I am concerned, are of infinitely greater moment than I am capable of comprehending, and in the persuasion that, in the continuance of my existence, I shall see more and more of this great purpose, and of the relation that myself and my sphere of influence bear to it." [127]

When one considers the fundamental piety of the man and what he believed of Christianity rather than the dogma he discarded, it is difficult to think of Joseph Priestley as a rationalist. In his own time, whether because of the prevailing orthodoxy or vituperation, or both, he was "under the imputation of absolute Atheism"! [128]

It is doubtful that Priestley's religious liberalism by itself would ever have resulted in anything more serious than the theological controversies which he liked so much. With the advent of the French Revolution, however, the cause of the Dissenters in England, who were deprived of full rights of citizenship, was naturally identified with the

[125] Quoted in Anne Holt, *op. cit.,* p. 119.
[126] *Letters to a Philosophical Unbeliever*, Part I, p. 91.
[127] *Disquisitions relating to Matter and Spirit*, in *Works*, Vol. III, p. 242.
[128] *Ibid.,* Preface to the Edition of 1777, in *Works*, Vol. III, p. 203.

abstract principles of liberty and freedom, religious and political. Priestley entered the new controversy and in his *Letters to the Right Honourable Edmund Burke* clearly allied himself with the republican cause. He charged Burke with joining a "bigotted clergy" in rigorously confining civil offices to the members of the established church, and threatened that the principle that the church and state must forever remain the same while the citizens remain in *"passive obedience and non-resistance, peculiar to the Tories and the friends of arbitrary power"* would no longer be tolerated by Englishmen.[129] Referring to Louis XVI, he asks, "if by a succession of encroachments, the power of *the crown itself* had long been enormous, should that be continued, to the terror and distress of the country, for the sake of the innocent head that happens to wear it?" [130] In support of this rhetorical question he quotes a passage from Thomas Paine's *Rights of Man* explaining that the revolt was against the established despotism of the monarchy and not against the person of the king.[131] He refuted Burke's confusing religion itself with the established church,[132] and denounces him in the typical manner of the eighteenth century pamphleteer: "I the less wonder at this power of imagination and prejudice, and this stupefaction of all your rational faculties in matters of *religion*, as it is apparent that you have been under a similar suspension of your *reason*, and equally under the power of *imagination*, in your views of

---

[129] Joseph Priestley, *Letters to the Right Honourable Edmund Burke occasioned by his Reflections on the Revolution in France, &c.*, Preface (Third Edition, Birmingham, 1791) in *Works*, Vol. XXII, pp. 148-149.
[130] *Ibid.*, Letter II, in *Works*, Vol. XXII, p. 161.
[131] *Ibid.*, Letter II, in *Works*, Vol. XXII, pp. 161-162, note.
[132] *Ibid.*, in *Works*, Vol. XXII, p. 186, *ff*.

the principles of *civil government*. Such, Sir, is your 'proud submission, and the subordination of *your* very heart,' to *princes*, and *nobles;* such your devotion to *rank* and *sex*, in conjunction with your *religious enthusiasm,* that one might suspect that your book was composed after some solemn *vigil*, such as watching your arms at the shrine of the blessed virgin; after which you issued forth the champion, in form, of religion, of monarchy, and of the immaculate virtue of all handsome queens." [133] Cherish your prejudices, he challenged, but added ominously in language tainted with deism: "The spirit of free and rational inquiry is now abroad, and, without any aid from the powers of this world, will not fail to overturn all error and false religion, wherever it is found, and neither the Church of *Rome,* nor the Church of *England,* will be able to stand before it." [134]

In 1791 feeling between Churchman and Dissenter, Tory and Whig, ran high in Birmingham when the friends of the Revolution with more spirit than wisdom decided to celebrate the 14th of July with a dinner. An incendiary handbill, advocating revolution, was secretly printed and circulated and tended to incite the mob against the friends of liberty. Its authorship was never determined. The dinner passed quietly enough, but a crowd hostile to the Revolution gathered about the hotel. Someone suggested the destruction of the New Meeting house and passion and liquor did the rest.

It is difficult to determine to what extent the powers in church and state were responsible for the Birmingham riots but it seems that "the magisterial authority had been

[133] Joseph Priestley, *op. cit.,* Letter VI, in *Works,* Vol. XXII, p. 191.
[134] *Ibid.,* Letter XI, in *Works,* Vol. XXII, p. 219.

wielded in a half-hearted fashion." [135] Certainly the High Church group had not failed to point out the sympathy of the Priestley party with the French Revolution and that the real purpose of the Dissenters was to overthrow the Church of England and dethrone the king. Priestley and his followers, in short, were conspirators and traitors. "It being imagined," he wrote in his *Memoirs*, "though without reason, that I had been the chief promotor of the measures which gave them offence, the clergy, not only in Birmingham, but through all England, seemed to make it their business, by writing in the public papers, by preaching, and other methods, to inflame the minds of the people against me. And on occasion of the celebration of the anniversary of the French revolution on July 14th, 1791, by several of my friends, but with which I had little to do, a mob encouraged by some persons in power, first burned the meeting house in which I preached, then another meeting house in the town, and then my dwelling house, demolished my library, apparatus, and, as far as they could, every thing belonging to me." [136]

He escaped to London where he was safe, although he "continued to be an object of troublesome attention." [137] He enjoyed the company of Lindsey and Belsham, kindred spirits in radicalism in politics and Unitarianism in religion. "I found, however, my society much restricted with respect to my philosophical acquaintances; most of the members of the Royal Society shunning me on account of my religious or political opinions, so that I at length withdrew myself from them." [138]

[135] Anne Holt, *op. cit.*, pp. 170-174.

[136] *Memoirs of Dr. Joseph Priestley, to the Year 1795, written by himself* (Northumberland, 1806), Vol. I, pp. 117-118.

[137] *Ibid.*, Vol. I, pp. 118-119. [138] *Ibid.*, Vol. I, p. 120.

Life in England, "if not hazardous," as he says, "was become unpleasant," and he decided to come to America where his sons had preceded him. While Priestley was crossing the Atlantic, an exile, Lavoisier met an even sterner fate at the guillotine. Europe was not a safe haven for liberalism. "But be cheerful, dear Sir," encouraged the Society of United Irishmen of Dublin, "you are going to a happier world—the world of Washington and Franklin. In idea we accompany you. . . . we participate in your feelings on first beholding Nature in her noblest scenes and grandest features, on finding man busied in rendering himself worthy of Nature, . . . when man will become more precious than fine gold, and when his ambition will be to subdue the elements, not to subjugate his fellow-creatures, to make fire, water, earth and air obey his bidding, but to leave the poor ethereal mind as the sole thing in Nature free and incoercible." [139]

He landed in New York on June 4, 1794, at a most propitious time. The Democratic Society, but recently established, had not yet lost its ardor. Priestley the scientist, the religious liberal, but above all, Priestley the republican, member of the National Convention of France, was more than welcome. Said the President of the Democratic Society, in part: "While the arm of Tyranny is extended in most of the nations of the world, to crush the spirit of liberty, and bind in chains the bodies and minds of men, we acknowledge, with ardent gratitude to the Great Parent of the Universe, our singular felicity in living in a land, where Reason has successfully triumphed

---

[139] Valedictory message to Dr. Priestley from the Society of United Irishmen of Dublin, quoted in Edgar F. Smith, *Priestley in America*, *1794-1804* (Philadelphia, 1920), pp. 14-15.

over the artificial distinctions of European policy and bigotry, and where the law equally protects the virtuous citizen of every description and persuasion. . . . The governments of the old world present to us one huge mass of intrigue, corruption and despotism—most of them are now basely combined, to prevent the establishment of liberty in France, and to affect the total destruction of the rights of man. Under these afflicting circumstances we rejoice that America opens her arms to receive, with fraternal affection, the friend of liberty and human happiness, and that here he may enjoy the best blessings of civilized society." [140]

New York was as hospitable in 1794 as it is to-day. Its citizens from the republican Governor, George Clinton, down delighted to do honor to the distinguished guest. Priestley was no doubt pleased with his fortnight's visit.

His remaining ten years in America were not however uniformly happy. His ministerial work, to which he was more devoted than to science, was not outstandingly successful. His son wrote, "As my father had through life considered the office of a Christian minister as the most useful and honourable of any, [141] and had always derived

[140] From the address of welcome by James Nicholson, President of the Democratic Society of the City of New York, June 7, 1794, quoted in Edgar F. Smith, op. cit., pp. 22-23.

It is interesting to notice that, though a refugee from his native land, Priestley was not particularly anti-British. The English traveller, Henry Wansey, who was in New York at the time, tells us that Priestley's answer to the Democratic Society "pleased every body, except the society itself." The Doctor told them that he did not intend to ally himself with any political party.—Henry Wansey, *An Excursion to the United States of North America in the Summer of 1794* (Second Edition, Salisbury, 1798), pp. 72-75.

[141] "Priestley had always looked on the calling of a minister of the Gospel as the highest that could fall to the lot of man."—Anne Holt, op. cit., p. 44.

the greatest satisfaction from fulfilling its duties, particularly from catechizing young persons, the greatest source of uneasiness therefore to him at Northumberland was, that there was no sufficient opportunity of being useful in that way. Though he was uniformly treated with kindness and respect by the people of the place, yet their sentiments in religion were so different from his own, and the nature and tendency of his opinions were so little understood, that the establishment of a place of unitarian worship . . . was next to impossible." [142]

It was Priestley's intention to spend some time each year in Philadelphia for the purpose of preaching and enjoying intellectual companionship of which there was not much in the backwoods of Northumberland. "My desire, and I think my duty," he wrote to his friend John Vaughan in Philadelphia, "is to appear in my proper character of a Minister of the Gospel, and I will not make any considerable stay in your city, and be reduced to a disgraceful silence by the bigotry and jealousy of the preachers." [143]

Accordingly, in the spring of 1796, he delivered a series of lectures on the "Evidences of Revelation" in the Lombard Street Universalist Church. (No other pulpit had been open to him in New York or Philadelphia in the nearly two years of his residence in America.) The lectures were well "attended by very crowded audiences, including most of the members of the congress of the United States at that time assembled at Philadelphia, and of the executive officers of the government." [144] "He gave uni-

---

[142] *Memoirs*, Vol. I, pp. 190-191. Priestley's *Memoirs* were written by himself to the year 1795 and were then continued by his son, Joseph.

[143] Original letter in the possession of Mrs. Belloc-Lowndes, quoted in Anne Holt, *op. cit.*, p. 193.

[144] *Memoirs*, Vol. I, p. 190.

versal satisfaction," wrote George Thatcher in an enthusiastic letter to Dr. James Freeman of Boston, "for as I
returned in the street it seemed as if every tongue was
engaged in speaking his praise, or answering the clergy
of the City. Can you believe it—not one of the regular
clergy here had civility enough to invite him to
preach. . . ."[145] Thatcher was convinced that Philadelphia had become more liberal. Evidently referring to
Elihu Palmer, he said, "Five years ago a preacher, who
called himself a Unitarian, gave out that on a certain day
he should deny and publicly disprove the Calvinistic idea
of the Divinity of Jesus, in consequence of which declaration the room, which the preacher had engaged by contract
for two or three months, was taken from him, and the
door nailed up, and he was obliged to flee from the City.
But now such a preacher is listened to with pleasing attention, and attended by a thronging multitude."[146]

The large audiences, however, seem to have been at-
tracted by Priestley's reputation rather than by sympathy
for his message. When in the following year (1797), he
delivered a second set of discourses, "partly from the
novelty of the thing being done away, partly from the
prejudices that began to be excited against him on account
of his supposed political opinions, (for high-toned politics
began then to prevail in the fashionable circles) . . . they
were but thinly attended in comparison to his former set.
This induced him to give up the idea of preaching any
more regular sets of discourses."[147]

After his first series of successful lectures in the spring

---

[145] Letter dated at Philadelphia, February 14, 1796, *Massachusetts Historical Society Proceedings* (Boston, 1888), Second Series, Vol. III, p. 39.

[146] *Ibid.*, Second Series, Vol. III, p. 39.

[147] *Memoirs*, Vol. I, pp. 193-194.

of 1796, Priestley established a Unitarian society in Philadelphia which was organized June 12, 1796. Its fourteen original members, described as "nearly all sturdy and free-minded Englishmen, who probably brought their opinions across the water," [148] included John Vaughan, long the librarian of the Philosophical Society, whose family Priestley had known for many years in England.[149] Others were Ralph Eddowes, formerly of Chester; James Wood; James Taylor, a Scotchman and, like Wood, a merchant; William Turner, "who migrated hither to retrieve his fortunes after bankruptcy, eventually paid all his old debts, and left a competency; and William Young Birch, from Manchester, a bookseller. . . . The other original members were William H. Smith, Ralph Eddowes, Jr., Peter Boult, Samuel Darch, Josiah Evans, John Eddowes, Thomas P. Jones, Thomas Astley, and Rev. William Christie, who seems occasionally to have occupied the pulpit. . . . Thus began the first *declared* Unitarian society in America." [150]

The Society, however, was no more successful than Priestley himself.[151] "Inconspicuous and unpopular, the

---

[148] J. Thomas Scharf and Thompson Westcott, *History of Philadelphia, 1609-1884* (Philadelphia, 1884), Vol. II, p. 1405.

[149] Anne Holt, *op. cit.*, p. 185.

[150] J. Thomas Scharf and Thompson Westcott, *op. cit.*, Vol. II, p. 1405.
The fact is, however, that the New York and Philadelphia Unitarians did not become actively established until they identified themselves with the New England Congregational Unitarians in the 1820's. The latter had been nominal Unitarians long before the Philadelphia society was founded.

[151] Priestley died at Northumberland in 1804, ten years after his arrival in America, in relative obscurity. John Bristed's remark that his death excited little more sensation than the dissolution of a German farmer's horse was sheer calumny, but it is typical of the odium attached to Priestley's religious latitudinarianism at a time when religion was "unquestionably gaining ground in the United States; and that cold-blooded

society found no place for years in the lists of city churches, perhaps because it had no abiding place. Its services were held at times in the hall of the University, in the Lombard Street Universalist Church, in a hall once owned by the guild of carpenters, and at several periods in a room in Church Alley." They finally acquired their own church building in 1813, but the society had no settled minister until 1824, twenty-eight years after its establishment.[152]

In New York the Unitarians were still slower in becoming established. The respect and honor accorded Dr. Priestley on his arrival there in 1794 was bestowed apparently in spite of rather than because of his religious liberalism. "The preachers," he said in a letter to Lindsey, "though civil to me, look upon me with dread, and none of them has asked me to preach in their pulpits." [153] The fact is that as late as 1819 no pulpit in New York was open to a Unitarian minister, however distinguished. When William Ellery Channing passed through the city in May of that year, friends succeeded in obtaining per-

compound of irreligion, irony, selfishness, and sarcasm, which the French call *persiflage*," was not as rife as formerly.—John Bristed, *America and Her Resources; or A View of the Agricultural, Commercial, Manufacturing, Financial, Political, Literary, Moral and Religious Capacity and Character of the American People* (London, 1818), pp. 407, 414.

The Duke de la Rochefoucault Liancourt, on the other hand, was of the opinion that Priestley's celebrity was of short duration because Americans were little interested in either science or theology. "They concern themselves but very little about dogmatical discussions of the Bible and the tenets of the Unitarians; and would readily give up all the experiments on air for one good and profitable speculation."—Duke de la Rochefoucault Liancourt, *Travels through the United States of North America, the Country of the Iroquois, and Upper Canada, in the Years 1795, 1796, and 1797* (London, 1799), Vol. I, p. 136.

[152] J. Thomas Scharf and Thompson Westcott, *op. cit.*, Vol. II, p. 1405.

[153] Letter dated at New-York, June 15, 1794. Rev. Thomas Belsham, *American Unitarianism; or a Brief History of the Progress and Present State of the Unitarian Churches in America* (Fourth Edition, Boston, 1815), Appendix, p. 47.

mission to use the lecture hall of the Medical College for a sermon.   Dr. Francis, who was at the time the Registrar of the College, relates an interesting anecdote of the indignation of the Rev. Dr. John M. Mason, "the great theological thunderbolt of the times."   Mason met Francis a few days later in a bookstore and exclaimed, "You doctors have been engaged in a wrongful work; you have permitted heresy to come in among us, and have countenanced its approach.   You have furnished accommodations for the devil's disciples." [154]

Thus, except in New England where Congregational Unitarianism was identified with respectability and wealth and was primarily a civilizing of the old Puritan tradition to meet the needs of the genteel descendants who had prospered on its bleak hills and rock-bound coast, Unitarianism met the fate of Palmer's deism in the first decade of the nineteenth century.   To orthodox Presbyterians and Episcopalians and to evangelical Methodists and Baptists alike, the distinctions between atheism, deism, and Unitarianism were only a quibble.   The age of rationalism and "natural religion" was over and the turning of the century ushered in the Triumph of Fidelity.

[154] John W. Francis, *Old New York*, p. 154.

CHAPTER VIII

THE TRIUMPH OF FIDELITY

WHEN Ezra Stiles wrote in 1759 that the clergy would be put to it to defend religion itself rather than the peculiarity of a particular doctrine, he anticipated correctly the struggle between rationalism and revelation of the half-century to come.

To Stiles himself, the problem seems not to have been unduly disturbing. In a letter to President Clap of Yale who had refused a library from a Newport merchant in schismatic Rhode Island, he wrote on August 6, 1759: "It is true with this Liberty Error may be introduced; but turn the Tables the propagation of Truth may be extinguished. Deism has got such Head in this Age of Licentious Liberty, that it would be in vain to try to stop it by hiding the Deistical Writings: and the only Way left to conquer & demolish it, is to come forth into the open Field & Dispute this matter on even Footing—the Evidences of Revelation in my opinion are nearly as demonstrative as Newton's Principia, & these are the Weapons to be used. . . . *Truth* & this alone being *our* Aim in fact, open, frank & generous we shall avoid the very appearance of Evil." [1]

The conflict between deism and revelation was no abstraction to Ezra Stiles. In "A Birth-Day Memoir" written in 1767 he tells us of his own days of doubt and

[1] Folio volume of Stiles manuscripts in Yale University, p. 460, quoted in I. Woodbridge Riley, *American Philosophy, the Early Schools* (New York, 1907), p. 217.

scepticism. "In 1750," he says, "a conversation with a young gentleman, of an amiable and virtuous character, first raised in me scruples and doubts respecting Revelation, which have cost me many a painful hour. . . . I had a strong doubt whether the whole was not a fable and delusion." [2] He had already begun preaching but, as he says, "my doubts increasing till 1752, I determined to lay aside preaching, and actually adopted the study of law, and took the attorney's oath in 1753." [3] He studied the Bible more assiduously than ever before. "I resolved nothing should determine me in religion but the truth. . . . I made these researches only for the sake of my own personal religion, and that I might be at peace with my God." [4] In 1754 when he had the opportunity of visiting Boston, New York, and Philadelphia he attended the worship of all the religious denominations in these cities, "with a fair and unprejudiced mind," [5] and by 1755 was fully convinced that the Congregational religion in which he had been reared "was nearest the apostolic form, and scripture model." [6] In a sermon soon after his ordination in the same year he said, "No writings of antiquity have come down to the times of printing, with so much evidence of their genuineness, as the Scriptures." [7]

Having himself overcome doubt and deism through study and reasoning, Ezra Stiles earnestly believed that his own method could successfully counteract the rising tide of deism during the Revolution. In his famous Election Sermon in 1783, *The United States elevated to Glory and Honor*, he deplored the fact that, "A general spirit reigns

---

[2] Quoted in Abiel Holmes, *The Life of Ezra Stiles* (Boston, 1798), pp. 35-36.
[3] *Ibid.*, p. 36.   [5] *Ibid.*, p. 41.   [7] *Ibid.*, p. 56.
[4] *Ibid.*, p. 39.   [6] *Ibid.*, p. 42.

against the most liberal and generous establishments in religion; . . . it begins to be a growing idea that it is mighty indifferent, forsooth, not only whether a man be of this or the other religious sect, but whether he be of any religion at all; and that truly deists, and men of indifferentism to all religion, are the most suitable persons for civil office, and most proper to hold the reigns of government. . . . I wish we had not to fear that a neglect of religion was coming to be the road to preferment." [8]

The deism of Tyndal, of Shaftesbury, "the amiable Confucius of deism,—not to mention the smaller and more desultory geniuses of a Hume or a Voltaire," seemed to President Stiles altogether inferior to Christianity.[9] He invited comparison and welcomed the fact that, "Religion may here [in America] receive its last, most liberal, and impartial examination. Religious liberty is peculiarly friendly to fair and generous disquisition. Here Deism will have its full chance; nor need libertines more to complain of being overcome by any weapons but the gentle, the powerful ones of argument and truth. Revelation will be found to stand the test to the ten thousandth examination." [10] But it is doubtful that his even-minded analysis of religious conditions led many of his countrymen to the path over which he himself had come. Ezra Stiles, learned, scholarly, and "no bigot," as he said, was not the man to combat deism. It takes more than reason to neutralize the cult of reason. Certainly during his administration of Yale from 1778 to 1795 the religious tone of the College became worse and worse. Lyman Beecher

---

[8] Ezra Stiles, *The United States elevated to Glory and Honor* (1783) in John W. Thornton, *The Pulpit of the American Revolution: or, the Political Sermons of the Period of 1776* (Boston, 1860), pp. 488-489.
[9] *Ibid.*, p. 498.   [10] *Ibid.*, pp. 470-471.

who entered Yale in 1793 wrote that the "college was in a most ungodly state. The college church was almost extinct. Most of the students were skeptical, and rowdies were plenty. Wine and liquors were kept in many rooms; intemperance, profanity, gambling, and licentiousness were common. I hardly know how I escaped. . . . That was the day of the infidelity of the Tom Paine school. Boys that dressed flax in the barn, as I used to, read Tom Paine and believed him; I read, and fought him all the way. Never had any propensity to infidelity. But most of the class before me were infidels, and called each other Voltaire, Rousseau, D'Alembert, etc., etc." [11]

These conditions of course cannot be charged to President Stiles nor were they peculiar to Yale. William Ellery Channing wrote of Harvard in 1794, "College was never in a worse state than when I entered it. Society was passing through a most critical stage. The French Revolution had diseased the imagination and unsettled the understanding of men everywhere. . . . The tone of books and conversation was presumptuous and daring. The tendency of all classes was to scepticism." [12] At Dartmouth College, one who had been a member of the college between 1785 and 1789 recalled that, "The students, at that early day, were many of them very unruly, lawless, and without the fear of God." [13] "In 1798 the state of religion was so far reduced that but a single member of

---

[11] Lyman Beecher, *Autobiography, Correspondence, etc., of Lyman Beecher, D.D.*, edited by *Charles Beecher* (New York, 1864), Vol. I, p. 43.

[12] William Ellery Channing, *Memoir of William Ellery Channing, with Extracts from his Correspondence and Manuscripts* (London, n. d.), Vol. I, p. 43.

[13] Quoted in Frederick Chase, *A History of Dartmouth College* (Cambridge, 1891), Vol. I, p. 616, from *Sketches of the Life and Times of Elder Ariel Kendrick*, p. 90.

the class of 1799 was publicly known as a professing Christian. . . ." [14] At the College of New Jersey (Princeton) in 1799, "there were only three or four who made any pretensions to piety." Prayer meetings were attended by "none except the tutors and three or four students." [15] And Bishop Meade of Virginia writes, "At the end of the century the College of William and Mary was regarded as the hotbed of infidelity and of the wild politics of France." [16]

It would be misleading, however, to infer that these conditions were associated primarily with institutions of learning. The spirit of lawlessness was in the air. Essential as it was from the point of view of leading to political independence from Great Britain, when carried over into religion the results were deplorable. Comparing conditions with the good old days, the Rev. James Dana of Wallingford, Connecticut, in 1770 bewailed the neglect of family worship. "How are family government and good order, and religious education of children, wherein they [our ancestors] shewed a laudable care, now disregarded? How strict were they in their observation of the Lord's-day? how careless and loose are we? And are not profaneness and intemperance vices continually growing in the land?" [17] On July 1, 1772, Francis Asbury

---

[14] *Ibid.*, Vol. I, p. 617.

[15] John Johnston, *Autobiography*, p. 30. The Rev. Dr. Johnston, graduated from the College of New Jersey in 1801.

This condition had prevailed since Revolutionary days. In 1782 it is said that only two among the students professed themselves Christians.—Leonard W. Bacon, *A History of American Christianity*, Vol. XIII in *The American Church History Series* (New York, 1897), p. 231.

[16] William Meade, *Old Churches, Ministers and Families of Virginia* (Philadelphia, 1910), Vol. I, p. 175.

[17] James Dana, *A Century Discourse, delivered at the Anniversary Meeting of the Freemen of the Town of Wallingford, April 9, 1770* (New-Haven, n. d.), pp. 49-50.

recorded in his *Journal:* "I set off for Philadelphia [from Trenton] with unprofitable company; among whom I sat still as a man dumb; and as one in whose mouth there was no reproof. They appeared so stupidly ignorant, sceptical, deistical, and atheistical, that I thought if there were *no other* hell, I should strive with all my might to shun that." [18]

Nor did the war help to raise the religious tone. In his sermon before the General Assembly of the State of Connecticut on May 13, 1779, the Rev. Dr. Dana warned: "Abuse of prosperity is incident to our lapsed nature. Special divine interpositions often meet with no other returns than unthankfulness, security, and self confidence. Should our deliverances be perverted to the purposes of venality and worldly ambition, infidelity, dissipation, licentiousness and internal dissentions, this would indeed be to *do evil in God's sight.*" [19] "Voluptuousness, pride, and contempt of religion and providence are the natural growth of opulence and military success. . . . For the age of the country we are, perhaps, as degenerate as any people—especially considering the errand of our ancestors hither, and our privileges and deliverances. Profligate manners, during the present war, have *run and been glorified.* Is it not to be feared, that as we multiply, and extend our commerce, a vain magnificence, the lust of power, sensuality, and contempt of all principles of religion and virtue will be imported in as large cargoes as foreign commodities? . . . Methinks I see profusion and luxury coming in like a flood —corruption and bribery invading all ranks—public mea-

[18] Francis Asbury, *Journal* (New-York, 1821), Vol. I, p. 20.

[19] James Dana, *A Sermon, preached before the General Assembly of the State of Connecticut, at Hartford, on the Day of the Anniversary Election, May 13, 1779* (Hartford, 1779), p. 26.

sures carried by influence—houses of worship forsaken, or frequented only by few—the public support of religion withheld, and its ministers despised—the Lord's-day devoted to amusements—family devotion almost universally laid aside—revealed religion generally disbelieved—the present infamy wiped off from the vices of intemperance and uncleanness—our children early taught to set their mouths against the heavens." [20]

These are, of course, the expressions of stern moralists and it might well be argued that they can be duplicated in every age and locality, for the younger generation is perpetually wicked in the eyes of some of their more austere and elderly contemporaries. Nevertheless, students of American social history recognize that the post-revolutionary period was characterized by more than the usual change in habits and institutions. The historian of Windham, Connecticut, says of this period, "Her secular affairs were most flourishing, but religion had sadly declined. It was a transition period—a day of upheaval, overturning, uprootal. Infidelity and Universalism had come in with the Revolution and drawn multitudes from the religious faith of their fathers. Free-thinking and free-drinking were alike in vogue. Great looseness of manners and morals had replaced the ancient Puritanic strictness. . . . Now, sons of those honored fathers and the great majority of those in active life, were sceptics and scoffers, and men were placed in office who never entered the House of God except for town meetings and secular occasions." [21] "It is, however, deeply to be lamented,"

---

[20] *Ibid.*, pp. 30-32.
[21] Ellen D. Larned, *History of Windham County, Connecticut* (Worcester, Mass., 1880), Vol. II, pp. 220-221.

says Bishop Meade of Virginia, "that the successful termi-
nation of the war, and all the rich blessings attending it,
did not produce the gratitude to the Giver which was
promised by the hearts of our people in the day of danger
and supplication. The intimacy produced between infidel
France and our own country, by the union of our arms
against the common foe, was most baneful in its influence
with our citizens generally, and on none more than those
of Virginia. The grain of mustard-seed which was planted
at Williamsburg, about the middle of the century, had
taken root there and sprung up and spread its branches
over the whole State,—the stock still enlarging and
strengthening itself there, and the roots shooting deeper
into the soil." [22]

These conditions were widespread, and a generation
familiar with the aftermath of our own World War finds
it not difficult to agree with Timothy Dwight that, "War
is at least as fatal to morals, as to life, or happiness." [23]
In retrospect two decades afterwards he said, "The pro-
fanation of the Sabbath, before unusual, profaneness of
language, drunkenness, gambling, and lewdness, were exceedingly increased; and, what is less commonly remarked,
but is not less mischievous, than any of them, a light, vain
method of thinking, concerning sacred things, a cold, con-
temptuous indifference toward every moral and religious
subject. In the mean time, that enormous evil, a depreciating currency gave birth to a new spirit of fraud, and
opened numerous temptations, and a boundless field for
its operations; while a new and intimate correspondence

[22] William Meade, *op. cit.*, Vol. I, pp. 174-175.
[23] Timothy Dwight, *A Discourse on Some Events of the Last Century,
delivered in the Brick Church in New Haven, on Wednesday, January 7,
1801* (New Haven, 1801), p. 18.

with corrupted foreigners introduced a multiplicity of loose doctrines, which were greedily embraced by licentious men as the means of palliating and justifying their sins." [24]

The clergy were slow in being aroused. For nearly two centuries in America they had been engaged in their petty doctrinal squabbles and every philosophical and public question in dispute had had its clerical partisans. The early years of the French Revolution were no exception to the rule, and it was therefore not until about 1794 that the excesses of the Revolution in America as well as in France united them as they had never been before in opposition to the principles typically propagated by Thomas Paine and Elihu Palmer, principles which seemed to threaten the very foundations of their existence. They were no longer blind to the fact, says Professor Morse, "that the destruction of the Catholic religion portended, not only the destruction of all religion there [in France], but elsewhere, just as far as the influence of the French Revolution extended." [25]

Most of the English refutations of Thomas Paine's *Age of Reason* were of course imported and usually reprinted in the United States. Nor were American answers lacking. One of the most formidable of these, for there were scores of sermons, was the *Antidote to Deism. The Deist Unmasked; or an ample Refutation of all the Objections of Thomas Paine, against the Christian Religion . . .* published in two volumes in Newark in 1795. The author

[24] *Ibid.*, p. 19; *cf.*, Anson E. Morse, *The Federalist Party in Massachusetts to the Year 1800* (Princeton, 1909), p. 103.

[25] Anson E. Morse, *op. cit.*, p. 98.

For a bibliography and discussion of the effect in America of the anti-religious activities of the French Revolution, see Morse, pp. 80-115, and *passim*, Appendices, pp. 216-225; also Charles D. Hazen, *Contemporary American Opinion of the French Revolution* (Baltimore, 1897), pp. 266-272.

of this work of calumny and abuse was the Rev. Uzal Ogden, Episcopalian minister in Newark. Wakefield's *Examination of the Age of Reason* had just been reprinted in New York and the Rev. Mr. Ogden read it "with disapprobation; Mr. Wakefield having, in a great measure, *betrayed* the cause he undertook to advocate." To sanction his unscriptural tenets, i.e., the errors of Socinianism, he found that Wakefield supported Paine in some respects and that the former's "system of religion, is but *little superior* to some schemes of *deism*." [26]

Instead of attempting to meet the arguments of Thomas Paine, Ogden devoted his energies to determining whether the *Age of Reason* demonstrates most conspicuously the weakness of Paine's intellect, the depravity of his mind, or the impertinence of his conduct.[27] And Paine was convicted on every count!

Ogden admitted that Thomas Paine's writings and services during the American Revolution justly obtained our esteem.[28] He claimed that it was for this reason only that the *Age of Reason* was widely read. If it had been written by Ethan Allen, for instance, "an ignorant and profane deist, in this country, who *undertook* to write against the *bible*, and who *died* with a *mind* replete with *horror* and *despair*," it would have been unnoticed. As it is, in spite of the author's reputation, "it is deemed by every reader of learning and judgment, to be a publication replete, at least, with ignorance and folly!" In France, it was "treated with neglect and contempt, even by deists!" [29]

---

[26] Uzal Ogden, *Antidote to Deism* (Newark, 1795), Vol. I, p. vii, note.
[27] *Ibid.*, Vol. I, p. 16, note.   [29] *Ibid.*, Vol. II, p. 270.
[28] *Ibid.*, Vol. I, p. 13.

The real reason for Paine's infidelity is probably that "the refulgent light of Divine Revelation, gave too much pain to his *reddened* Eyes of intemperance, and, therefore, in hopes of obtaining ease, closed them against the sunbeams of the gospel,[30] it being well known "that Deists in general, are men of *libertine conduct*." [31] For, "when the restraints of religion are dissolved, what can be expected, but that men should *abandon* themselves to the impulse of their passions? Human laws and penalties will be *insufficient* to restrain men from licentiousness, where there is no just sense of the Deity; no regard to a future state, or to the due punishment of vice, and the rewards of virtue hereafter." [32] "But by *some men*, through vice and folly, it [the Gospel] is rejected and even reviled! Though in spiritual thraldom, they reject freedom! Though impure, they despise purity! Though exposed to the vengeance of God, they wish not to be reconciled to him! They endure the terrors of guilt, but spurn from them the blessings of virtue! They are exposed to eternal misery, but disesteem the offer of unceasing happiness! They *believe* their souls shall survive bodies, but 'trouble not themselves' about their everlasting existence! Such is the *conduct* of some Deists! How honorary is it to beings of *reason*! How worthy of *imitation!*" [33] Certain it is, says Ogden almost benevolently, Paine's "*rage* for *revolutions*" seems to have bereft him of his powers, for his *reasonings* "more become a lunatick, than a person in the enjoyment of his rational faculties!" [34]

From all of which Ogden finally draws the following

[30] *Ibid.*, Vol. I, p. 15.
[31] *Ibid.*, Vol. I, p. 15, note.
[32] *Ibid.*, Vol. I, p. 17, note.
[33] *Ibid.*, Vol. II, p. 122.
[34] *Ibid.*, Vol. II, pp. 279-280.

conclusion: "The author having thus *amply refuted* every objection, deserving the least attention, of Mr. Paine, against the christian religion; and having also, besides a variety of other particulars, shewn the *defects* and *impieties* of his *creed;* exhibited the *genius* and *excellence* of *christianity;* demonstrated the *necessity* of divine revelation, and fully *evinced* the truth of the *gospel,* a serious address would now be made to Mr. Paine, with respect to his conduct in renouncing the *christian religion,* and *writing* against it in language of *invective* and *blasphemy,* were it not apprehended that *friendly expostulations* and *reasonings* with Him would be vain, and, in the language of scripture, be like 'casting pearls before swine!' With a mind besotted with liquor; replete with prejudice against christianity; grossly ignorant of its nature; under the domination of vice, and encircled by deistical companions, it is probable he will drag out the remainder of his days in infidelity, guilt and wretchedness, and leave the world, either in stupid insensibility, or in a state of horror, without the least rational hope of future happiness!" [35]

Wretchedly abusive and vulgar as this religious controversy became after the publication of the *Age of Reason,* it descended to still lower levels through its political association. Among the most abusive of the anti-republicans was William Cobbett, better known at that time as Peter Porcupine, who came to this country from England in 1792. At first he taught school in Philadelphia and then became a pamphleteer. The following is typical of the manner of associating religion and politics: "Yet (for, though I hate the very name of Democrat, I would scorn to detract from their merit) there is one character to whom

---

[35] Uzal Ogden, *op. cit.,* Vol. II, pp. 296-297.

they have ever conserved an unshaken attachment. How grateful must it be to thee, injured shade of the gentle *Marat!* whether thou wanderest on the flowery banks of the Stygian Pool, or bathest thy pure limbs in the delightful liquid of Tartarus, or walkest hand in hand with *Jesus Christ* in that Literary Elysium, the *Philadelphia Gazette*,[36]—how grateful must it be to thee, though thou makest Hell more hideous, and frightenest the very furies into fits, to be yet adored by the Democrats of the city *of brotherly love!"* [37] "Oh, base democracy! Why, it is absolutely worse than street-sweepings, or the filth of common-sewers." [38]

In New England, the opposition to infidelity and irreligion was of course led by the clergy. It would not be difficult to show by quotations from a hundred sermons during a century past that the glory of the fathers was no more and that the forces of evil had come to prevail in the land of the Puritans. But it remained for the Rev. Jedidiah Morse of Charlestown, Massachusetts, best known for his *American Geography,* to strike a new and distinctive note. In his fast-day sermon on May 9, 1798, he took specific account of the circumstances that made the period through which the nation was passing "a *day of trouble,* of *reviling and blasphemy."* He saw in our relations with France the main source of American dangers. Here and not elsewhere was to be found the occasion of the unhappy divisions that exist among the citizens of the

[36] In this paper, Marat and Jesus Christ were described as democrats and the greatest benefactors of mankind.

[37] Peter Porcupine, *A Bone to Gnaw for the Democrats* (London, 1797), p. 59. The Preface is dated at Philadelphia, February 19, 1795.

[38] Peter Porcupine, *The Life of Thomas Paine* (Philadelphia, 1797), p. 25.

United States, disturbing their peace, and threatening the overthrow of the government itself. The French, "in conformity to a deep-laid plan, in cherishing party spirit, in vilifying the men we have, by our free suffrages, elected to administer our Constitution . . . have thus endeavoured to destroy the confidence of the people in the constituted authorities, and divide them from the government." [39]

More pernicious by far, however, are the effects of this "plan" on the religious life of the American people. To it, "we may trace that torrent of irreligion, and abuse of every thing good and praise-worthy, which, at the present time, threatens to overwhelm the world." [40] Rulers in all governments, priests and ministers of all religious denominations are reviled and abused as never before. "The existence of a God is boldly denied. Atheism and materialism are systematically professed. Reason and Nature are deified and adored. The christian religion, and its divine and blessed Author, are not only disbelieved, rejected and contemned, but even abhorred, and efforts made to efface their very name from the earth. As the natural fruits of these sentiments, and what we ought to look for where they prevail—fraud, violence, cruelty, debauchery, and the uncontrolled gratification of every corrupt and debasing lust and inclination of the human heart, exist, and are increasing with unaccountable progress." [41]

[39] Jedidiah Morse, *A Sermon, delivered . . . May 9, 1798, being the day recommended by John Adams, President of the United States of America, for Solemn Humiliation, Fasting and Prayer* (Boston, 1798), p. 13.

[40] *Ibid.*, p. 20.   [41] *Ibid.*, p. 18.

But the plan is now unveiled! The Illuminati, an apostate off-shoot of Free Masonry, is back of all these evils. It has "secretly extended its branches through a great part of Europe, and even into America." [42] "There can be little doubt that the *Age of Reason* and the other works of that unprincipled author, as they proceeded from the fountain head of *Illumination*, and have been so industriously and extensively circulated in this country, were written and sent to America expressly in aid of this demoralizing plan. The titles of some of these works, and the tendency of them all, are in exact conformity to the professed principles and designs of the society." [43]

To counteract these evils Morse urged confidence in and support of our government and active support of religious institutions. "If these foundations be destroyed," he asks, "and infidelity and atheism prevail, what will the righteous do?" [44] "Let us examine into the state of our families, 'those little communities which constitute the great public body,' and reform, as far as in us lies, whatever is sinful or wrong in them. Let us exert all our influence and efforts to effect a general reformation, in principles and manners, trusting in the Lord to succeed our endeavours. These are the sure, and only means of our preservation." [45]

Jedidiah Morse, in other words, urged the maintenance of the *status quo*, that mystic union of orthodox Congregationalism or Calvinism and Federalism. His sole authority was John Robison's, *Proofs of a Conspiracy against all the Religions and Governments of Europe*,[46]

---

[42] *Ibid.*, p. 21.
[43] *Ibid.*, p. 24.
[44] *Ibid.*, p. 28.
[45] *Ibid.*, pp. 28-29.
[46] *Supra*, p. 100.

and yet his fast-day sermon was more than merely another
example of Federalist "political preaching." He exaggerated the influence and power of the Illuminati. They
were themselves the product rather than the cause of the
political and religious liberalism of the 1790's. Although
erroneous and unreliable in facts and details, Morse nevertheless interpreted the spirit of the times correctly. Deism
and republicanism were certainly abroad in the land and
whether or not insidiously associated with the movement
in Europe, they were not unrelated. The issues were
clarified as they had not been before. To the hard-pressed
forces of religious and political conservatism, Illuminism
was a new shibboleth eloquently expressive of Jacobinism,
atheism, impiety, and vice.

Of all the New England clergy of the time, the most
influential and dominant, the recognized leader in Federalism and Calvinism, was the Rev. Timothy Dwight
who had succeeded Ezra Stiles as president of Yale in
1795. Timothy Dwight already had an established reputation for the maintenance of the traditions of the "land
of steady habits." His *Triumph of Infidelity,* published
anonymously in 1788, was a scathing attack on heresies
and infidelity since the early days of the Christian Church.
It was dedicated to Voltaire, teacher of the doctrine "that
the chief end of man was, to slander his God, and abuse
him forever." [47] Ethan Allen is described as "the great
Clodhopping oracle of man," who in Satan's cause,
"bustled, bruised, and swore." [48] *The Triumph of Infidelity,* however, like the other literary productions of

---

[47] [Timothy Dwight], *The Triumph of Infidelity* (Printed in the
World, 1788), p. iii.

[48] *Ibid.,* pp. 23-24.

the "Hartford Wits," and even President Dwight's sermons on *The Nature, and Danger, of Infidel Philosophy* [49] lacked the appeal of his sermon preached in New Haven on the Fourth of July, 1798, on *The Duty of Americans, at the Present Crisis.*

Even more entranced than Jedidiah Morse by the idea of Illuminism as the death knell of every New England virtue, President Dwight immediately detected in Robison's *Proofs of a Conspiracy* the explanation of the evil days which had befallen even Connecticut. Now it was clear that "a plan was formed, and to an alarming degree executed, for exterminating Christianity, Natural Religion, the belief of a God, of that immortality of the Soul, and of Moral obligation; for rooting out of the world civil and domestic government, the right of property, marriage, natural affection, chastity, and decency; and in a word for destroying whatever is virtuous, refined or desirable, and introducing again universal savageness and brutism." [50]

In the societies of the Illuminati, he explained "every novel, licentious, and alarming opinion was resolutely advanced. Minds, already tinged with philosophism, were here speedily blackened with a deep and deadly die; and those, which came fresh and innocent to the scene of contamination, became early and irremediably corrupted." [51]

[49] Timothy Dwight, *The Nature, and Danger, of Infidel Philosophy, exhibited in Two Discourses, addressed to the Candidates for the Baccalaureate, in Yale College, September 9th, 1797* (New-Haven, 1798).

[50] Timothy Dwight, *The Nature, and Danger, of Infidel Philosophy,* p. 95, note. He says in this note that after he had sent the discourses to the printer, he saw a copy of Robison's book. The sermon of July 4, 1798, is an elaboration of this idea.

[51] Timothy Dwight, *The Duty of Americans, at the Present Crisis,* July 4, 1798, p. 11.

Doctrines were taught which strike at the root of all human happiness and virtue: God is denied and ridiculed; government is a curse and a usurpation; the possession of property is robbery; chastity is a groundless prejudice; adultery, assassination, and poisoning are lawful and even virtuous actions.[52] Every villainy, impiety, and cruelty is vindicated; every virtue covered with contempt.[53]

To guard against the spread of such evils in America, religion must be maintained. "Where religion prevails, Illuminatism cannot make disciples, a French directory cannot govern, a nation cannot be made slaves, nor villains, nor atheists, nor beasts. To destroy us, therefore, in this dreadful sense, our enemies must first destroy our Sabbath, and seduce us from the house of God." [54] "The sins of these enemies of Christ, and Christians, are of numbers and degrees which mock account and description. All that the malice and atheism of the Dragon, the cruelty and rapacity of the Beast, and the fraud and deceit of the false Prophet, can generate, or accomplish, swell the list. No personal or national, interest of man has been uninvaded; no impious statement, or action, against God has been spared; no malignant hostility against piety, and moral obligation universally, have been, not merely trodden under foot; this might have resulted from vehemence and passion; but ridiculed, spurned, and insulted, as the childish bugbears of drivelling idiocy. Chastity and decency have been alike turned out of doors; and shame and pollution called out of their dens to the hall of distinction, and the chair of state. Nor has any

[52] Timothy Dwight, op. cit., p. 12.   [54] Ibid., p. 18.
[53] Ibid., p. 13.

art, violence, or means, been unemployed to accomplish these evils." [55]

And as he proceeded, the great extemporaneous preacher became increasingly eloquent. His words seem still to thunder from the yellowed page. "For what end shall we be connected with men, of whom this is the character and conduct? Is it that we may assume the same character, and pursue the same conduct? Is it, that our churches may become temples of reason, our Sabbath a decade, and our psalms of praise Marseillois hymns? Is it, that we may change our holy worship into a dance of Jacobin phrenzy, and that we may behold a strumpet personating a Goddess on the altars of Jehovah? Is it that we may see the Bible cast into a bonfire, the vessels of the sacramental supper borne by an ass in public procession, and our children, either wheedled or terrified, uniting in the mob, chanting mockeries against God, and hailing in the sounds of Ca ira the ruin of their religion, and the loss of their souls? Is it that we may see our wives and daughters the victims of legal prostitution; soberly dishonoured; speciously polluted; the outcasts of delicacy and virtue, and the lothing of God and man? Is it, that we may see, in our public papers, a solemn comparison drawn by an American Mother club between the Lord Jesus Christ and a new Marat; and the fiend of malice and fraud exalted above the glorious redeemer?" [56]

But Timothy Dwight's was not a lone voice crying aloud in the wilderness. The same theme reverberated throughout New England from platforms, pulpits, and the press. [57]

[55] *Ibid.*, p. 20.
[56] *Ibid.*, pp. 20-21.
[57] *Cf.* Vernon Stauffer, *New England and the Bavarian Illuminati* (New York, 1918), pp. 252 *ff.*

The Rev. David Tappan, Hollis Professor of Divinity at Harvard, in a discourse before the senior class, cautioned the young men before him against the dangers of speculative principles, the pleasures of idleness and vicious indulgence, and the philosophy of the Order of the Illuminati. He was not prepared to accuse the Illuminati of *all* the wickedness that Robison had attributed to them, but did not doubt that the facts "indicate a real and most alarming plan of hostility against the dearest interests of man." [58]   At Sharon, Connecticut, the orator of the day spoke of, "*a combination long since founded in Europe, by Infidels and Atheists, to root out and effectually destroy Religion and Civil Government,*—not this or that creed of religion,—not this or that form of government, —in this or that particular country,—but all religion,— all government,—and that through the world." [59]

The political possibilities in the situation were early appreciated. Opposition to Federalism and to the established Congregational Church was synonymous with the destruction of all government and all religion. A contributor to the *Connecticut Courant* of Hartford, August 6, 1798, asserted that not until he heard Theodore Dwight's [60] Fourth of July oration were his eyes opened

---

[58] David Tappan, *A Discourse delivered in the Chapel of Harvard College, June 19, 1798, Occasioned by the Approaching Departure of the Senior Class from the University* (Boston, 1798), p. 19.

[59] John C. Smith, *An Oration, pronounced at Sharon, on the Anniversary of American Independence, 4th of July, 1798* (Litchfield, n. d.), pp. 6 ff.

[60] Theodore was a younger brother of Timothy and an equally staunch Federalist. In this *Oration spoken at Hartford, in the State of Connecticut, on the Anniversary of American Independence, July 4th, 1798* (Hartford, 1798), Theodore Dwight said, "I know not who belonged to that society [Illuminati] in this country; but if I were about to make proselytes to illuminatism in the United States, I should in the first place apply to Thomas Jefferson, Albert Gallatin, and their political associates." (p. 30.)

to see in Mr. Jefferson "anything more than the foe of certain men, who were in possession of places to which he might think himself entitled;" but Theodore Dwight convinced him that Jefferson "is the *real Jacobin,* the very child of *modern illumination,* the foe of man, and the enemy of his country." [61] The idea of the insidious Society of the Illuminati undermining the moral and spiritual life of New England accounted so well for the prevalence of what the standing order thought of as vice and irreligion, that they did not resist the temptation to be uncritical in their acceptance of this alluring hypothesis.

Opposition to these spectacular charges was of course not slow in arising. An anonymous contributor to the *Massachusetts Mercury* of Boston, July 27, 1798, assumed a tone of moderation and suggested that the time had come to inquire concerning the authenticity of Professor Robison's sources. It seemed to him that Dr. Morse was not justified, on the unsupported assertion of an individual three thousand miles away, to declare that the Illuminati were responsible for "the torrent of irreligion and the abuse of everything good and praiseworthy which threatens to overwhelm the world. For all these assertions, 'Censor' inquired, where were the evidences?" [62]

Nor were all the clergy in New England Federalists. The Rev. John Cosens Ogden, who had been Episcopal rector in Portsmouth, New Hampshire, from 1786 to 1793, published an anonymous pamphlet in 1799 (Philadelphia), entitled, *A View of the New-England Illuminata: who are indefatigably engaged in Destroying the Religion and Government of the United States; under a feigned regard for their safety and under an impious abuse*

[61] Vernon Stauffer, *op. cit.,* p. 283.   [62] *Ibid.,* pp. 254-255.

of true religion. It is true, said Ogden at the outset, that New England had its Illuminati, though not of the kind represented by Robison and Barruel. The New England societies of the Illuminati were the monthly meetings of the clergy.[63] He professed to see in the dark and obscure questions discussed at these meetings the source of "a strong propensity to deism and scepticism. The clergy exhibited the Christian religion as being full of mysteries and unintelligible opinions. The thoughtful and sagacious discerned such jarrings in sentiments, that they doubted the propriety of the doctrines of the clergy. Argumentations, contradictions, warmths, and dissunion succeeded. . . . In this situation, many of the laity were prepared to attend to deistical writings; and philosophy and liberality became very fashionable."[64] "The head of the Illuminati, Doctor *Dwight*, a divine, has made himself so conspicuous and has been so often animadverted upon publicly, that the nation are very generally acquainted with his character and proceedings. In his sermon preached on the fourth of July, 1798, in New-Haven, he has given us a perfect picture of the Illuminati of Connecticut, under his control, in the representation he has made of the Illuminati of Europe."[65]

This acrimonious discussion intermingled with personal motives and replete with calumny and vituperation was carried over into the presidential election of 1800. Ogden's ingenious attempt to fix the countercharge of Illuminism upon the Federalists immediately met with high favor from the Republicans. A more interesting character and incidentally the most notorious of the New

---

[63] [John C. Ogden], *A View of the New-England Illuminati*, pp. 2-3.
[64] *Ibid.*, p. 5.   [65] *Ibid.*, p. 16.

England Republicans was Abraham Bishop, a graduate of Yale in 1778. In 1787-1738 he visited Europe and, like his classmate Joel Barlow, was profoundly influenced by the political and religious scepticism of those pre-revolutionary days in France. He returned, as President Stiles sourly remarked in his Diary, October 30, 1788, "full of Improvmt & Vanity," [66] but more likely merely impressed with the unprogressive character of Federalist Connecticut.[67]

The presidential election in 1800 naturally found Bishop a Jeffersonian and when the Phi Beta Kappa Society of Yale College appointed him to deliver the annual oration in that year in connection with the commencement exercises, he recognized a rare opportunity for an exposition of his political principles, or perhaps more accurately, his animadversions for the Federalists. He prepared the oration and submitted a copy to the secretary. On the day before the delivery, as Bishop says, "the 'friends of order' in the society, . . . held a conclave, which they called a regular meeting, and without any notice to me, (though I was a member and a party concerned in the object of their convention) proceeded to pass *a rescinding act*, . . ." [68] Bishop, however, was not so easily outmaneuvered. Another hall was procured and according to his own estimate the meeting was attended by about 1500 people among whom were many ladies and certainly eight clergymen.[69]

[66] Ezra Stiles, *Diary*, Vol. III, p. 331.

[67] *Dictionary of American Biography*, edited by Allen Johnson (New York, 1929), Vol. II, p. 294.

[68] Abraham Bishop, *Oration delivered in Wallingford, On the 11th of March 1801, before the Republicans of the State of Connecticut, at Their General Thanksgiving, for the Election of Thomas Jefferson* . . . (New Haven, 1801), Appendix, p. 102.

[69] *Ibid.*, p. 102.

Considering the power, position, and influence of the Federalists in Connecticut at that time, Bishop's address was bold and daring, if not presumptuous. In answer to the charge of the Federalists that the word Republican was synonymous with atheist and libertine, Bishop said that *"there is not an atheist in the state nor a single modern philosopher among the republican party;* Deism is not prevalent, yet there are deists in both parties, whose infidelity has originated from causes wholly unconnected with politics." [70] "How much, think you," he asks, "has religion been benefited by sermons, intended to show that Satan and Cain were jacobins? How much by sermons in which every deistical argument has been presented with its greatest force as being a part of the republican creed? . . . The people, instead of being alarmed lest religion should suffer under a new administration, ought to be infinitely solicitous to wrest the protection of it from those who are using it as a state engine." [71] He minced no words with "that class of clergy, who improperly improve religion to serve political purposes," [72] and with biting sarcasm confessed: "We poor ragged democrats in these truly federal northern states, who read the lying Bee, Aurora and Mercury, and dare not touch the Spectator, the Centinel nor the Connecticut Courant, lest the splendor of truth should destroy our eye-sight: we who meet in barns to settle the

[70] Abraham Bishop, *An Oration on the Extent and Power of Political Delusion, delivered in New-Haven, on the Evening preceding the Public Commencement, September, 1800* (Newark, 1800), Preface, p. iv.

[71] *Ibid.*, p. 22. For a discussion of political sermons of this period, see W. De Loss Love, Jr., *The Fast and Thanksgiving Days of New England* (Boston, 1895), Ch. XXV, "The Political Fast in Massachusetts, 1789-1799."

[72] Abraham Bishop, *An Oration on the Extent and Power of Political Delusion,* p. 23, note.

nation, pray that our littleness may save us from the crushing power of your federal highnesses. We confess that for our sins we deserve to have an everlasting debt fixed upon us, due to men who despise the services for which the debt was contracted. We deserve to be kept under by an army and navy. We deserve to be made the victim of constructive treason. . . . Jails, fines, and gallowses ought to be our portion. We deserve even in the midst of suffering, to be jeered and laughed at by our tormentors; to be traduced in the newspapers of federal truth, and to be ranked in fast and election-sermons among infernal spirits. Though some of us fought and bled for the revolution, yet we have fallen from our first estate into all the guilt and pollution of democracy. . . . Have mercy upon us! Have mercy upon us! ye well-fed, well-dressed, chariot-rolling, caucus-keeping, levee-revelling federalists; for we are poor, and wretched, and ignorant, and miserable." [73]

The Republicans of Connecticut with rare exceptions [74] belonged to the lower social and economic stratum [75] and it is not difficult to believe that Bishop's demagogic address was thoroughly appreciated by them. When in the

---

[73] *Ibid.*, pp. 45-46.

[74] Almost ironically one of the leading Republicans in Connecticut was the Hon. Pierrepont Edwards, youngest child of the famous Jonathan Edwards and uncle of Timothy Dwight. *Cf.*, Richard J. Purcell, *Connecticut in Transition, 1775-1818* (American Historical Association, Washington, D. C., 1918), p. 232; Ch. VI, "Rise of the Democratic-Republican Party," *passim.*

[75] ". . . it must be confessed that the democracy of New England in its beginning raked up and absorbed the chaff of society. It is due to the truth of history to state that men of blemished reputations, tipplers, persons of irregular tempers, odd people, those who were constitutionally upsetters, destructives, comeouters, flocked spontaneously, as if by a kind of instinct, to the banner of democracy, about the period of Jefferson's first election, and constituted, for a considerable period afterward, the staple of the party."—S. G. Goodrich, *Recollections of a Lifetime, or Men and Things I have Seen* (New York, 1857), Vol. I, pp. 119-120.

following March they held a public thanksgiving to celebrate the presidency of Mr. Jefferson, Bishop was invited to address them again. He carried the attack still
further into the enemies' territory. The "friends of
order," he said, talked of jacobinism, atheism, and
philosophism,[76] but it was they who were the real infidels,
enemies of religion: "But when the pretended friends of
religion lead infidel lives; when they carry religion to
market and offer it in exchange for luxuries and honors;
when they place it familiarly and constantly in the columns
of newspapers, *manifestly connected with electioneering
purposes*, and when they are offering it up as a morning
and evening sacrifice on the altar of personal pride or
political party—these men are placing a fire-brand to
every meeting-house and applying a torch to every bible.
They are doing worse; by their hypocrisy they are attacking religion in the heart and life, betraying it and crucify-
ing its author." [77] Those "friends of order" who had so
calumniously predicted that if Mr. Jefferson should be
elected all the meeting-houses and bibles in the country
would be burnt were themselves "among the most open
and profane infidels in our country." [78] Infidel books in
New England, he maintained, were few, but it was through
the writings of Robison and Barruel and the sermons
against infidelity that arguments against revelation were
disclosed and doubts engendered.[79]

[76] Abraham Bishop, *Oration delivered in Wallingford, On the 11th of
March 1801*, p. 28.
[77] *Ibid.*, pp. 36-37.
[78] *Ibid.*, p. 36.
[79] *Ibid.*, pp. 87-88. Bishop proved conclusively by his *Proofs of a Conspiracy, against Christianity, and the Government of the United States;
exhibited in several views of the union of church and state in New-England*
(Hartford, 1802) that in reckless assertions and unrestrained fanaticism the
Republicans were second to none.

The Federalists, of course, responded with their own uninhibited invectives on Bishop and his cause.[80] "Nothing could be clearer," as Dr. Stauffer remarks, "than that the word 'Illuminati' had lost all serious and exact significance and had become a term for politicians to conjure with; or if not that, to give point to the general charge of calloused villainy which Democrats lodged against Federalists at the turn of the eighteenth century."[81] Another student of this long controversy agrees that "both parties, with little attention to the truth, set themselves to invent the most inflammatory and false stories in order to suit their political ends."[82]

The political device of defaming the opposing faction [83] by the charge of Illuminism was not confined to New England, as we have already noticed in connection with John Wood's pamphlet, *A Full Exposition of the Clin-*

[80] See for example, [David Daggett], *Three Letters to Abraham Bishop, Esquire, containing Some Strictures on his Oration, pronounced, in the White Meeting-House, on the Evening Preceding the Public Commencement, September 1800, with some Remarks on his Conduct at the Late Election. By Connecticutensis* (Hartford, 1800).

[Noah Webster, Jun.], *A Rod for the Fool's Back; or Abraham Bishop Unmask'd, By a Citizen of Connecticut* (New Haven, 1800).

Bishop in time became both conservative and respectable. In 1818 he addressed a cordial invitation to Noah Webster, his classmate at Yale, to celebrate the fortieth anniversary of their graduation. "Make my house your home during your stay," he urged and signed himself, "Your friend & classmate." The false spectre of Illuminism had long been happily forgotten.—*Notes on the Life of Noah Webster*, compiled by Emily E. F. Ford and edited by Emily E. F. Skeel (New York, 1912), Vol. II, p. 153.

For a discussion of Bishop's writings, see "Abraham Bishop of Connecticut, and his Writings," in Franklin B. Dexter, *A Selection from the Miscellaneous Historical Papers of Fifty Years* (New Haven, Connecticut, 1918), pp. 257-265.

[81] Vernon Stauffer, *op. cit.*, p. 360.

[82] Anson E. Morse, *op. cit.*, p. 76. *Cf., Ibid.*, p. 114, note 95.

[83] The Federalists and Republicans in 1800 were not parties in the modern sense.

tonian Faction, and the Society of the Columbian Illum-inati.[84] It did not, however, play as important a rôle in New York as did the more direct criticism of the religious views of Mr. Jefferson.

His religious views had been expressed almost a score of years previously in his *Notes on the State of Virginia* which he had written in 1781.[85] Since they were incidental in a volume dealing with the history and geography of Virginia, they did not receive much attention. Nevertheless, they were there and they show the author's faith in human reason.

In his explanations of conditions, he frequently failed to accept Old Testament tradition. He questioned, for example, whether the deluge was universal or merely "probable" in the Mediterranean region.[86] As a matter of fact, the three hypotheses for such an occurrence "are equally unsatisfactory; and we must be content to acknowledge, that this great phenomenon is as yet unsolved. Ignorance is preferable to error; and he is less remote

---

[84] *Supra,* p. 99.

[85] This book was written, "in answer," as he says, "to Queries proposed to the Author, by a Foreigner of Distinction, then residing among us." According to George H. McKee, *Th. Jefferson, Ami de la Revolution Française* (Lorient, 1928), p. 95, the foreigner was Barbé-Marbois, "nominalement secrétaire de la Légation française à Philadelphia, mais, peut-être plus que son chef La Luzerne, l'agent confidentiel de son gouvernement aux Etats-Unis." Many of his friends requested from Jefferson a copy of this work, and after his arrival in France in 1784 to take the place of Benjamin Franklin he had two hundred copies printed. Because of his views on slavery and the Constitution, he purposely wished to restrict the edition. Through the death of one of the owners, however, a copy of the work fell into the hands of a Parisian printer who without authorization published a miserable French translation. Jefferson therefore decided to publish the original text. "C'est cette édition, parue in 1786, qui vulgarisa l'œuvre de Jefferson de part et d'autre de l'Atlantique." (McKee, p. 98.) Other editions of course appeared in the United States.

[86] Thomas Jefferson, *Notes on the State of Virginia* (Philadelphia, 1788), p. 29.

from the truth who believes nothing, than he who believes what is wrong." [87]   There is some doubt in his mind as to whether all men are descended from the original human pair, and he advances the "suspicion" that the inferiority of the blacks may be due to their being originally a distinct race.

Most important of all however is his staunch belief in religious liberty. It is difficult for him to understand that a people, "who have lavished their lives and fortunes for the establishment of their civil freedom," are still willing to submit themselves to "religious slavery." The same principle applies in religion as in politics that "our rulers can have authority over such natural rights only as we have submitted to them. The rights of conscience we never submitted, we could not submit. We are answerable for them to our God. The legitimate powers of government extend to such acts only as are injurious to others. But it does me no injury for my neighbour to say there are twenty gods, or no god. It neither picks my pocket nor breaks my leg." [88]

In fact, difference of opinion in religious matters is a distinct good. Uniformity is unattainable. The effect of attempts at coercion has been "to make one half the world fools, and the other half hypocrites. To support roguery and error all over the earth." [89]   Constraint may fix a man "obstinately in his errors, but will not cure them. Reason and free inquiry are the only effectual agents against error. , Give a loose to them, they will support the true religion, by bringing every false one to their tribunal, to the test of their investigation. They are the

[87] *Ibid.*, p. 31.   [89] *Ibid.*, p. 170.
[88] *Ibid.*, p. 169.

natural enemies of error, and of error only. Had not
the Roman government permitted free inquiry, Christianity could never have been introduced. Had not free
inquiry been indulged, at the æra of the reformation, the
corruptions of Christianity could not have been purged
away. If it be restrained now, the present corruptions will
be protected, and new ones encouraged." [90]

Religion for Jefferson meant not an authentic divine
revelation but a utilitarian moral code. He praises the
religious freedom in New York and Pennsylvania under
which these states "flourish infinitely. Religion is well
supported; of various kinds, indeed, but all good enough;
all sufficient to preserve peace and order: or if a sect arises,
whose tenets would subvert morals, good sense has fair
play, and reasons and laughs it out of doors, without suffering the state to be troubled with it." [91]

[90] Thomas Jefferson, *op. cit.*, p. 169.
[91] *Ibid.*, p. 171.
It was for his published *Notes on the State of Virginia* that Jefferson
was particularly denounced although even more outspoken religious liberalism is found in his correspondence. In a letter to his youthful nephew,
Peter Carr, dated at Paris, August 10, 1787, he said in part: "Your reason
is now mature enough to examine this object [religion]. In the first place
divest yourself of all bias in favour of novelty & singularity of opinion.
Indulge them in any other subject rather than that of religion. It is too
important, & the consequences of error may be too serious. On the other
hand shake off all the fears & servile prejudices under which weak minds
are servilely crouched. Fix reason firmly in her seat, and call to her
tribunal every fact, every opinion. Question with boldness even the existence of a god; because, if there be one, he must more approve of the
homage of reason, than that of blindfolded fear. You will naturally examine first the religion of your own country. Read the bible then, as you
would read Livy or Tacitus. The facts which are within the ordinary
course of nature you will believe on the authority of the writer, as you do
those of the same kind in Livy & Tacitus. The testimony of the writer
weighs in their favor in one scale, and their not being against the laws of
nature does not weigh against them. But those facts in the bible which con-
tradict the laws of nature, must be examined with more care, and under a
variety of faces. Here you must recur to the pretensions of the writer to
inspiration from god. Examine upon what evidence his pretensions are

This common-sense attitude toward religion, practical, if not noble and idealistic, was not peculiar to Jefferson. It was so general that outside of New England the privileged established church was an anachronism by 1800. Various circumstances contrived, however, to bring Jefferson's deistic beliefs into the forefront in the presidential campaign. The decade of the 1790's had left the clergy almost without exception in a hysterical condition. It was not a matter of Arminianism, Calvinism, or Catholicism, but religion itself that was on trial and its very existence seriously threatened. And Jefferson had come to stand as the American symbol for the discredited principles of the French Revolution. It mattered not that John Adams was of practically the same religious persuasions, for the latter was known to be conservative in everything else and had distrusted the French Revolution from the very be-

founded, and whether that evidence is so strong as that its falsehood would be more improbable than a change in the laws of nature in the case he relates. . . . These questions are examined in the books I have mentioned under the head of religion, & several others. They will assist you in your inquiries, but keep your reason firmly on the watch in reading them all. Do not be frightened from this inquiry by any fear of it's consequences. If it ends in a belief that there is no god, you will find incitement to virtue in the comfort & pleasantness you feel in it's exercise, and the love of others which it will procure you. If you find reason to believe there is a god, a consciousness that you are acting under his eye, & that he approves you, will be a vast additional incitement; if that there be a future state, the hope of a happy existence in that increases the appetite to deserve it; if that Jesus was also a god, you will be comforted by a belief of his aid and love. In fine, I repeat that you must lay aside all prejudice on both sides, & neither believe nor reject anything because any other persons, or description of persons have rejected or believe it. Your own reason is the only oracle given you by heaven, and you are answerable not for the rightness but uprightness of the decision."—*The Writings of Thomas Jefferson*, collected and edited by Paul Leicester Ford (New York, 1894), Vol. IV, pp. 429-432.

For an unfriendly discussion of Jefferson's religious views, and therefore emphasizing his unorthodoxy, with numerous references to his *Works*, see Cornélis de Witt, *Jefferson and the American Democracy*, translated by R. S. H. Church (London, 1862), pp. 318-323.

ginning. To these sincere, if illogical, reasons for Jeffersonian opposition must be added the natural proclivities of the Federalists to make political thunder of Jefferson's deism at the time of a rising tide of orthodoxy. The result was the most interesting, if deplorable, openly religious presidential campaign in American history.

Typical of these political sermons was *The Voice of Warning, to Christians, on the Ensuing Election of a President of the United States,* published anonymously. We have already made the acquaintance of its author, the Rev. Dr. Mason, when he reproached Dr. Francis in connection with the preaching of William Ellery Channing in New York in 1819. But Mason was already a forceful and eloquent young preacher in 1800. "I dread the election of Mr. Jefferson," he said, "because I believe him to be a confirmed infidel." [92] "Mr. Jefferson disbelieves the existence of an universal deluge. 'There are many considerations,' says he, 'opposing *this opinion.*' The bible says expressly, '*The waters prevailed exceedingly upon the earth,* and *all the high hills that were under the whole heaven were covered.*' Mr. Jefferson enters into a philosophical argument to prove the fact impossible; that is, he argues in the very face of God's word, and, as far as his reasoning goes, endeavors to convict it of falsehood." [93] "The plain matter of fact is, that he writes like all other infidels, who admit nothing for which they cannot find adequate 'natural agents;' and when these fail them, instead of resorting to the divine word, which would often satisfy a modest enquirer, by revealing the 'arm of Je-

---

[92] [John M. Mason], *The Voice of Warning, to Christians, on the Ensuing Election of a President of the United States* (New-York, 1800), p. 8.
[93] *Ibid.*, p. 11.

hovah,' they shrug up their shoulders, and cry, 'Ignorance is preferable to error.' " [94]

"After these affronts to the oracles of God, you have
no right to be surprized if Mr. Jefferson should preach
the innocence of error, or even of Atheism. What do I
say! He *does* preach it. 'The legitimate powers of government,' they are his own words, 'extend to such acts only
as are injurious to others. *But it does me no injury for
my neighbors to say there are twenty Gods or no God.*
It neither picks my pocket nor breaks my leg.' Ponder
well this paragraph. Ten thousand impieties and mischiefs lurk in its womb." [95] "Pardon me, Christian: this
is the morality of devils, which would break in an instant
every link in the chain of human friendship, and transform
the globe into one equal scene of desolation and horror,
where fiend would prowl with fiend for plunder and blood
—yet atheism 'neither picks my pocket nor breaks my leg.'
I will not abuse you by asking, whether the author of such
an opinion can be a Christian? or whether he has any regard for the scriptures which confines all wisdom and
blessedness and glory, both personal and social, to the fear
and the favor of God?" [96]

The same sentiments are expressed by the Rev. Clement
Clarke Moore.[97] He naïvely remarks that although he
had heard of Jefferson's *Notes on Virginia* from his childhood, he never had curiosity enough to peruse them until
a few weeks since and was then "surprised that a book

[94] *Ibid.*, p. 13, note.
[95] *Ibid.*, pp. 18-19.
[96] *Ibid.*, p. 20.
[97] [Clement Clarke Moore], *Observations upon certain passages in Mr.
Jefferson's Notes on Virginia, which appear to have a tendency to Subvert
Religion, and establish a False Philosophy* (New York, 1804).

tween us and the brutes; and which esteems all religions
'good enough'; can he deny that this book is an instrument
of infidelity? Surely not: it bears the stamp of modern
philosophy as palpably as Le compère Matthieu; not from
its learning or ingenuity, but from the insidious manner in
which it conveys what are called its philosophical doctrines." [102] "Wretched, indeed, is our country, if she is to
be enlightened by these philosophers; philosophers whose
industry is equalled by nothing but their vanity; whose
pursuits are impeded by no danger nor difficulty; by no
law, human or divine; who think nothing too great for
them to grasp, and nothing too minute to be observed: they
dig into the bowels of the earth, and climb the loftiest
mountains; they traverse the ocean, and explore the regions of the air; they search the written records of antiquity, and the traditions of savages; they build up
theories of shells and bones and straws." But the Rev.
Mr. Moore lists these noble endeavours of man not as an
eulogium of the scientific spirit, but asks, "And for what?
Is it to render more stable the uncertain condition of man?
Is it to alleviate one of the miseries which afflict his nature? No; it is to banish civilization from the earth, that
we may be reduced to the state of savages; to pluck from
the wretched their sweetest consolation; to extinguish the
only light by which the Christian hopes to cheer the
gloomy hour of death; to quench the thirst for immortality which the Creator has attached to our nature; to degrade us from the rank of angels, to which we are taught
to aspire, that we may complete the catalogue of
brutes." [103]

[102] [Clement C. Moore], *op. cit.*, pp. 29-30.   [103] *Ibid.*, pp. 30-31.

In spite of the Federalists, however, it was republicanism and not religion that was at stake in the election of
1800. Their attempt to discredit the Jeffersonian faction
by association with deism failed. By obvious overstatement of the facts, by prophecies never to be fulfilled, by
laying themselves open to the charge of the subversion of
religion to politics, it was the Federalists rather than the
Republicans who were irreligious. The fact is that the
triumph of fidelity, the return to orthodox Christianity
at the beginning of the nineteenth century, was largely the
work of men who socially and politically were Republicans. The same uncalculating and unreasoning emotionalism which had characterized the exuberant American republicanism in the heyday of the French Revolution was
decorously transferred to a new channel—evangelical revivalism.

It was the Methodist, Baptist, and Presbyterian
churches, largely republican in their membership, rather
than the more aristocratic Congregationalists or Episcopalians, who led the militant opposition to deism. An
early Methodist historian writes, "About this time [1795]
the minds of many people were corrupted by the deistical
writings of Thomas Paine, whose effusions against the
Bible were received with greater avidity by Americans on
account of the eminent services he had rendered to his
country during the war of the revolution. But Thomas
Paine as a politician and Thomas Paine as a theologian
were very different men. His book, however, against the
Bible, was published by the booksellers, which, together
with others of a kindred character, were widely circulated,
and they were exerting a most deleterious influence upon
the minds of many of our citizens, and threatened to poison

the fountains of knowledge with their pestiferous contents. It could hardly be otherwise, under these circumstances, than that immorality should abound, and the 'love of many wax cold.' " [104]

To counteract these evils, several of the Methodist conferences appointed the first Friday in March 1796, "as a most solemn day of fasting, humiliation, prayer, and supplication. . . . that we should bewail our manifold sins and iniquities—our growing idolatry, which is covetousness and the prevailing love of the world . . . substituting means and opinions for religion," and to call upon the Lord to "stop the growing infidelity of this age, by calling out men who shall preach and live the gospel." [105]

The Methodists were thus as bitterly opposed to deism as the most orthodox Congregationalist, but their clergy, at that time, were not interested in politics. In the language of a by-gone age, they preached Jesus Christ, and Him crucified. By training, or more accurately by the lack of it,[106] the Methodist itinerants were peculiarly qualified to counteract and neutralize the dissemination of deism among the lower classes. They succeeded where the Bishop of Llandaff or the scholars of New England could

---

[104] Nathan Bangs, *A History of the Methodist Episcopal Church* (New-York, 1845), Vol. II, p. 21.

[105] *Ibid.*, Vol. II, p. 22. This was part of a general movement. In 1796, Christians of different denominations in Europe and America united in a quarterly concert of prayer for the revival of religion in the world and for the more general propagation of the gospel.—Samuel Stillman, *A Discourse Preached in Boston before the Massachusetts Baptist Missionary Society, May 25, 1803. Being Their First Anniversary* (Boston, 1803), p. 5; cf. Catharine C. Cleveland, *The Great Revival in the West, 1797-1805* (Ph.D. dissertation, The University of Chicago, 1916), p. 32 and *passim* in Chapter I, "Religious Conditions Prior to 1800."

[106] Learning was in fact regarded as a detriment. S. G. Goodrich tells of a Methodist sermon supposedly delivered in Connecticut: "What I insist upon, my brethren and sisters, is this: larnin isn't religion, and eddication don't give a man the power of the Spirit. It is grace and gifts that

not help but fail. "Had those principles of infidelity," says Nathan Bangs, "with which the minds of many of the leading men of our nation had been infected, and which, at one time, were descending with fearful rapidity to the lower ranks of society, been permitted to operate unchecked by any other barrier than a mere lifeless form of Christianity, or those restraints which a secular and civil education might interpose, is there not reason to apprehend that such streams of moral and intellectual, as well as political pollution, would have poured their poisonous waters over the land, as must have washed our civil and religious institutions into the whirlpool of destruction? . . . it must, I think, be admitted by all who reflect impartially on the subject, that the labors of the itinerating Methodist preachers tended mightily to purify the corrupt mass of mind, and to awaken attention to spiritual and divine things, and to call off the attention of the people from mere secular and political affairs, to the momentous concerns of eternity." [107]

The Presbyterian Church followed the example of the Methodists. In 1798 the General Assembly sounded a note of warning in a pastoral letter: "In this 'solemn crisis,' the Assembly believe that the causes of the calamities felt or feared are traceable to 'a general defection from

---

furnish the rael live coals from off the altar. St. Peter was a fisherman—do you think he ever went to Yale College? Yet he was the rock upon which Christ built his Church. No, no, beloved brethren and sisters. When the Lord wanted to blow down the walls of Jericho, he didn't take a brass trumpet, or a polished French horn: no such thing; he took a ram's horn—a plain, natural ram's horn—just as it grew. And so, when he wants to blow down the walls of the spiritual Jericho, my beloved brethren and sisters, he don't take one of your smooth, polite, college larnt gentlemen, but a plain, natural ram's-horn sort of man like me."—S. G. Goodrich, *Recollections of a Lifetime, or Men and Things I have Seen,* Vol. I, pp. 196-197.

[107] Nathan Bangs, *op. cit.,* Vol. II, p. 146.

God, and corruption of the public principles and morals.'
The evidences of the national guilt were seen in 'a general
dereliction of religious principles and practice amongst
our fellow-citizens; a great departure from the faith and
simple purity of manners for which our fathers were remarkable; a visible and prevailing impiety and contempt
for the laws and institutions of religion; and an abounding
infidelity which in many instances tends to atheism itself,
which contemptuously rejects God's eternal Son, our
Saviour, ridicules the gospel and its most sacred mysteries,
denies the providence of God, grieves and insults the Holy
Spirit; in a word, which assumes a front of daring impiety,
and possesses a mouth filled with blasphemy.' " [108]   In
view of all this, the Assembly solemnly enjoined deep
humiliation, sincere repentance for individual as well as
national sins, supplication for the outpouring of the Spirit
and a revival of God's work.

Before the passing of a year, "the signs of a great
change" were apparent.   "The Assembly of 1799 could
say, that, amid much lukewarmness and formality, they
had 'heard from different parts glad tidings of the outpouring of the Spirit, and of times of refreshing from the
presence of the Lord.' "   And by 1800, "God was 'shak-
ing the valley of dry bones on the frontiers.' 'A spiritual
resurrection' was taking place there.   Hundreds in a short
time, and among them some who had been avowed infidels
and Universalists, had been received into the communion
of the Church.   Thus, the century which was just closing,
and which had threatened to close with dark and dismal
prospects, was destined to leave behind it a brighter record.

[108] Rev. E. H. Gillett, *History of the Presbyterian Church in the United
States of America* (Philadelphia, 1864), Vol. I, p. 297.

A new era had dawned upon the Church—an era of revivals." [109]

While this revivalism is naturally associated primarily with the frontier regions where its manifestations were most pronounced, it affected also the centers of respectability and learning. The well educated clergy naturally tended to look askance at these expressions of religious enthusiasm, just as their predecessors had done in the period of the Great Awakening. Nevertheless, such an upholder of New England's dignity as President Dwight of Yale was in this case not reactionary. Admitting that, "In these seasons the human mind has not unfrequently exhibited many kinds and degrees of weakness, error, and deformity," he said that it does not therefore follow "that nothing exists beyond enthusiasm; and that, amid several irregular and excessive exertions of the mind, there is not to be found a real change of the disposition, a real assumption of piety. To me it is evident, that revivals of religion are often what they are called, if not always; and that the proof abundantly exists (where alone it ought to be looked for) in the real and permanent melioration of the moral character of multitudes, who then become serious and professedly religious." [110] Yale became a different institution under the leadership of Timothy Dwight. "He had the greatest agency in developing my mind," wrote the Rev. Lyman Beecher of the Class of 1797. "Before he came college was in a most ungodly state." [111]

Fittingly enough, Beecher was one of the founders of

[109] *Ibid.*, Vol. I, p. 299.

[110] Timothy Dwight, *A Discourse on Some Events of the Last Century, delivered in the Brick Church in New Haven, on Wednesday, January 7, 1801*, pp. 17-18.

[111] Lyman Beecher, *Autobiography and Correspondence*, Vol. I, pp. 39 *ff.*

the Moral Society in the College in his Senior year.[112] Where in 1795, Thomas Paine had been a good deal of a college hero and students called each other by such names as Voltaire and Rousseau,[113] a little more than half a decade later, infidels were as rare as professing Christians had been when Beecher was a freshman. The change can in part be attributed to President Dwight's powers in refuting rationalism with reason, but a more satisfactory explanation is to be found in Dr. Dexter's simple statement that "an extraordinary revival of religion was experienced in the College, in which the number of professing Christians had been distressingly small." [114] Benjamin Silliman, a tutor in the college, was converted in the great revival of 1802. In a letter to his mother, dated June 11, 1802, he wrote: "It would delight your heart, my dear mother, to see how the trophies of the Cross are multiplied in this Institution. Yale College is a little temple: prayer and praise seem to be the delight of the greater part of the students, while those who are still unfeeling are awed into respectful silence. Pray for me, my dear mother, that while I am attempting to forward others in the journey to heaven, I may not be myself a castaway." [115]

The same metamorphosis transpired at Dartmouth Col-

---

[112] Anson Phelps Stokes, *Memorials of Eminent Yale Men* (New Haven, 1914), Vol. I, p. 54.

[113] These names were extraordinarily popular among the radicals in America during the French Revolution. For example, the unorthodox and anti-clerical Philadelphia merchant, Stephen Girard, named a new brig, launched December 5, 1795, *Voltaire*. Three of his other vessels were named *Montesquieu*, *Rousseau*, and *Helvetius.*—John B. McMaster, *The Life and Times of Stephen Girard, Mariner and Merchant* (Philadelphia, 1918), 2 vols., *passim.*

[114] Franklin B. Dexter, *Biographical Sketches of the Graduates of Yale College with Annals of the College History* (New York, 1911), Vol. V, p. 466.

[115] George P. Fisher, *Life of Benjamin Silliman* (New York, 1866), Vol. I, p. 83.

lege. "In 1801," says Dartmouth's historian, "a permanent Students' Religious Society was for the first time established."[116] At the College of New Jersey "there was apparent among the students an unusual interest in the subject of religion, and this awakening to the importance of personal piety and of a well-founded hope of vital union with Christ gradually increased, until serious thought and feeling seemed to pervade almost the entire body of students. The results were in every view of them most happy. A number, large in proportion to the whole, became hopefully pious, and adorned a profession of their faith in Christ by a godly walk and conversation through life. . . ."[117] The change came later here (1814) than in New England, but it was equally inevitable. Almost ironically, revivalism was the spiritual counterpart of republicanism in politics. The *élan vital* of them both was democracy, freedom, faith, and optimism—the dominant characteristics, in short, of the great American frontier.

This revival movement which thus permeated American society in the first decade of the nineteenth century from Maine to Georgia and westward to the farthest frontier put an end to the cause of militant deism.[118] With the

[116] Frederick Chase, *A History of Dartmouth College* (Cambridge, 1891), Vol. I, p. 617.

[117] John Maclean, *History of the College of New Jersey* (Philadelphia, 1877), Vol. II, p. 162.

[118] Not that every freethinker was converted in the revivals, but after Palmer they remained so as individuals and there was no attempt to carry on as religious societies. The British traveller, John Lambert, gives an account of an impromptu debate or discussion between a Methodist parson and a gentleman who "seemed to doubt the authenticity of revealed religion." This occurred on board a sloop carrying passengers down the Hudson River from the town of Hudson to New York. "For upwards of two hours they combated each other with great ardour, affording the rest of the company high entertainment. The gentleman pointed out all the incongruities in the Old and New Testament, seeming to doubt every thing which had been accomplished by miracles, and challenged the other to

establishment of religious periodicals, tract societies, missionary societies, and the American Bible Society, the forces of orthodoxy were overwhelmingly superior to those small scattered groups of free-thinking followers of Thomas Paine. Times had changed since the decade of the 1790's when the cause of the latter was identified with republicanism and the idealized principles of the French Revolution. After the election of 1800 the struggle between Federalism and Republicanism gradually died out and became irrelevant. The evangelical revivalists were themselves republicans and nothing remained for the deists but the discredited principles and excesses of the French Revolution of which they were regarded as miserable living and anachronistic relics. The second decade of the century, in America as in Europe, was destined to be reactionary.

Napoleon, to be sure, was not a typical symbol of democracy, but his overthrow closed the curtain on the

prove their authenticity. . . . the parson was at times so much perplexed, that he became the butt of the company. He however bore their jokes with great good humour and patience; but finding that he could not satisfy the gentleman's scruples, he began upon politics. We soon discovered that he was a Jeffersonian; and there happened to be a large majority of federalists on board, among whom were the editor and printer of the Albany Balance, a strong anti-democratic paper, the poor parson got most roughly handled; and I perceived that it was a more difficult task for him to keep his temper upon politics than upon religion."—John Lambert, *Travels through Canada, and the United States of North America, in the Years 1806, 1807, & 1808* (Third Edition, London, 1816), Vol. II, pp. 46-47.

In this picture of the informality and intimacy of travel in America one hundred twenty-five years ago, the characters are typical of their time. The Methodist parson was devout, a Jeffersonian, not learned, and undoubtedly poor. The majority of the travellers were conservative politically but sceptical in their religious beliefs. With the advantage of a century's perspective, it is clear that the parson's views were more in accord with the times than those of his "infidel" companions. Federalism was already dead and eighteenth-century reasoning was irrelevant to Methodism.

drama of the French Revolution and the ideals of liberalism which had been so ardently shared on this side of the Atlantic. Eloquently voicing the exultation of the privileged at the demise of democratic ideals, the Hon. Gouverneur Morris, bitterest of the old enemies of Thomas Paine, likened the victorious European rulers to "the Saviour of the world" at the touch of whose garments an obedient subject people "feel sanctified." The pendulum had swung to the other extreme since the fanaticism of 1793 when Marat was linked with Jesus. Where, now, are those "whose envenomed tongues have slavered out invective on all who wear legitimate crowns"? Lost, too, is the cause of those who in self conceit had looked "with affected pity on such as believe in a Saviour." "The Bourbons are restored," he cried. "Rejoice France! Spain! Portugal! You are governed by your legitimate kings. Europe! rejoice. The Bourbons are restored. The family of nations is completed. Peace, the dove descending from heaven, spreads over you her downy pinions. Nations of Europe, ye are brethren once more. Embrace. Rejoice. And thou, too, my much-wronged country! My dear, abused, self-murdered country, bleeding as thou art, rejoice. The Bourbons are restored. Thy friends now reign. The long agony is over. The Bourbons are restored." [119]

Gouverneur Morris was right: the Bourbons were restored. And in American religious life other-worldliness

[119] Gouverneur Morris, *An Oration, delivered on Wednesday, June 29, 1814, at the request of a number of citizens of New-York, in Celebration of the Recent Deliverance of Europe from the Yoke of Military Despotism* (New-York, 1814), pp. 21-23.

again replaced the ideals of Palmer's millennium of the good life here and now." [120]

[120] In spite of his conservative tendencies, it is admitted by M. de Witt that "the men who effected the American revolution were not all of them believers. In different degrees, Jefferson, Franklin, Gouverneur Morris, John Adams, were free-thinkers, but without intolerance or display, without ostentatious irony, quietly, and almost privily; for the masses remained believers. Not to offend them, it was necessary to speak with respect of sacred things; to produce a deep impression upon them, it was requisite to appeal to their religious feelings; and prayers and public fasts continued to be instruments resorted to whenever it was found desirable, whether by agitators or the State, to act powerfully on the minds of the people." —Cornélis de Witt, *Jefferson and the American Democracy*, translated by R. S. H. Church, p. 17. It depends upon one's own view of religion whether to characterize the religious attitude of the fathers of our country as hypocritical or whether they recognized a fundamental truth that there is a necessary difference between the religion of the learned and the "average" man.

CONCLUSION

IT IS a truism more easily forgotten than recalled that religious orthodoxy is an attitude of mind, the spirit of con-
serving a heritage, and that it becomes a problem only
when change is imminent. The philosophy and religion
of a people do not exist in the mind apart from the world
in which this life is lived, and it follows as an inevitable
corollary that where life changes religion cannot remain
the same. Whatever ultimate, disembodied, and absolute
religious truths there may be, man must be trusted to em-
body them in whatever way of life he may follow.

The stern way of life associated with the word Puritanism which has become synonymous with negation was ad-
mirably suited to the needs of the settlers of New England. As the struggle for subsistence became less keen,
denial of pleasures became less necessary, with the result
that orthodox spiritual leaders complained loudly of
worldliness. Gradually even some of the clergy recognized the change in times. The founding of the Brattle
Street Church in Boston is evidence of the fact that the
incoming tides of civilization which had already inundated
the town had reached the sanctuary. Changes in theology
followed. Baptism and the Lord's Supper came to be no
longer reserved for the elect, members of the visible
church of God. John Wise pled forcefully for democracy
in church government. The spirit of equality made the
rigid Calvinistic distinction between the regenerate and

unregenerate untenable. The Great Awakening, the first movement to unite the American colonies from Maine to Georgia in a common experience, opened the doors of salvation to all classes on the same terms.

The dissent from orthodoxy nourished by conditions indigenous to the American scene was supplemented by the importation of heterodox ideas from Europe. Contrary to the rule that the clergy are the last to be influenced by changing thought, they were in this case the first for the reason that as a class they were the best educated and best informed men in their communities. They lost faith in the sanctity of their theological dogmas, just as to-day it is the minister rather than the average layman who finds difficulty in subscribing to Fundamentalism. However, the association of American militiamen with British soldiers in the French and Indian War and later with the French during the Revolution brought the common man into contact with English deism and French scepticism. The necessary spirit of rebellion carried over into restlessness and dissatisfaction with all authority, clerical not excepted. In Ethan Allen we see how these various forces contrived to make an unlettered frontiersman into a thorough-going rebel and iconoclast. He rebelled against the State of New York as well as Great Britain, and the undemocratic temper of Connecticut Calvinism led him to the rejection of Christianity itself. There was no compromising with Arminianism for him.

Ethan Allen was not, however, an important figure in the religious life of his time. Interesting, forceful, and not devoid of truth and sound reasoning though it is, his *Oracles of Reason* offered no substitute for Christianity. It expressed rather the dissatisfaction felt widely by the lower classes with the arrogance of the doctrine and the political power of the established Congregational Church in New England. Allen's work in religion as in government was one of rebellion rather than of construction.

It remained for another son of Connecticut to attempt to establish a new religion expressive of the new age. In the spirit of the French rather than of the American Revolution, he was the champion of ideals. He was the inveterate foe, not of any one nation or of any particular religious sect, but of despotism and superstition everywhere. The Federalists in control in Philadelphia, the Tories in Westminster, and Louis XVI and his followers were all of the same despotic species to Palmer; just as the Congregationalists, Catholics, and Methodists alike stood for priestcraft and superstition. Aside from such unavoidable evils as pain and death inherent in our nature, the evils in this world, thought Palmer, were due to corrupt institutions controlled by unscrupulous and designing men to exploit their fellow creatures.

Contrary to common assertions both then and now, the movement to establish deism as a religion in America had little to do with philosophical materialism. The "Walking" Stewart is the exception that proves the rule. He was more the philosopher; Palmer more the organizer. Stewart was individualistic, concerned with the philosophical reformation of individual men; Palmer was socialistic and striving for a change in human institutions. Stewart tended toward the atheistic; Palmer, like Ethan Allen and Thomas Paine, was theistic.[1] It was the latter

[1] In this period, the words deism and theism were synonymous and were used interchangeably. The meaning of deism seems not to have changed since 1800, but theism is to-day rather associated with orthodoxy in Christianity or Judaism.

that was typical of deism in America, while Stewart, only a visitor to America, represented the prevailing free-thought of continental Europe.[2]　In this country, the movement was really an anti-clerical theism.[3]

But Palmer did not stop with denunciation of despotism and ecclesiasticism.　He envisaged a nascent millennium.[4] It had its inception in the birth of republicanism in the American Revolution, and the fall of the Bastille sig-nalled the collapse of royalty, nobility, and privilege in Europe.　Through a realization of his dignity and power, man would soon attain his full stature.　Palmer, in short, shared the faith of the Age of Enlightenment in education, the sufficiency of reason, and the perfectibility of man.　He believed with Rousseau that man was naturally good and that it is only through the influences of bad education and corrupt government that he becomes depraved.

Palmer's thinking was not original.　His uniqueness lay in his attempt to establish a religion based on the prin-ciples of deism and republicanism.　Many a cultured and educated American shared Palmer's deistic beliefs and thought of Christianity as a superstition, but they differed from him in his faith in republicanism.　They distrusted

---

[2] D'Holbach and La Mettrie are representative of eighteenth-century French atheism and materialism.

[3] It was a period when anti-clericalism was the rule rather than the ex-ception, when most of the learned accepted the generalization expressed by the Duke de la Rochefoucault Liancourt that "Monks are every where the same men, and live by deceiving others; they are every where impostors: in Europe, and in America, men are the same, when placed in the same situation."—Duke de la Rochefoucault Liancourt, *Travels through the United States of North America, the Country of the Iroquois, and Upper Canada, in the Years 1795, 1796, and 1797* (London, 1799), Vol. I, p. 70.

[4] For a detailed discussion of the exuberant optimism and faith of the eighteenth century "that civilisation has moved, is moving, and will move in a desirable direction," see J. B. Bury, *The Idea of Progress* (London, 1920); *cf.*, Carl L. Becker, *The Heavenly City of the Eighteenth-Century Philosophers* (New Haven, 1932).

the common man. Christianity was good for the under dog. By promising him his reward in heaven, Christianity helped him to bear patiently his burdens here below. It kept him in his place. It was a slave's morality. The upper classes, on the other hand, could afford to become enlightened. They had the leisure and the means for education, and their duties called for no opiates of superstition to dull their senses to the realities of life. The immortal words in the Declaration of Independence that "all men are equal" were not to be accepted too literally. As John Adams explained in interpretation of Rousseau's doctrine, all men are men in the sense that they belong to the same species. "But man differs by nature from man almost as much as man from beast. . . . a physical inequality, an intellectual inequality of the most serious kind is established unchangeably by the Author of nature; and society has a right to establish any other inequalities it may judge necessary for its good." [5]   Adams's point of view expressed the conservatism of the fathers of the American Revolution; egalitarianism is a product of the French Revolution. It is not difficult to understand why Palmer received no support for his deistic societies from "the rich,

---

[5] Quoted in Charles D. Hazen, *Contemporary American Opinion of the French Revolution* (Baltimore, 1897), pp. 274-275.

Thomas Jefferson, first and foremost of democrats, wrote in a letter to John Adams, "I agree with you that there is a natural aristocracy among men. The grounds of this are virtue and talents. . . . The natural aristocracy I consider as the most precious gift of nature, for the instruction, the trusts, and government of society. And indeed, it would have been inconsistent in creation to have formed man for the social state, and not to have provided virtue and wisdom enough to manage the concerns of society. May we not even say, that that form of government is the best, which provides the most effectually for a pure selection of these natural aristoi into the offices of government?"—Letter dated at Monticello, October 28, 1813, in *The Writings of Thomas Jefferson*, collected and edited by Paul Leicester Ford (New York, 1898), Vol. IX, p. 425.

the well-born, and the able." Just as to-day, a socialist, however able or altruistic, does not receive the support of men of large means and may on occasion be loosely identified as a communist or Bolshevist, even so Palmer received no money for his cause and was denounced unjustly as an atheist.

The membership of the deistic societies which Palmer organized in New York, Newburgh, Philadelphia, and Baltimore was thus drawn largely from the lower social stratum.[6] Artisans predominated and, probably because of their contact with reading matter, particularly printers and booksellers. The learned professions seem to have

[6] This generalization, as usual, has its exceptions. The British traveller, John Davis, gives us a delightful picture of one Major Howe with whom he quaffed good Madeira in the cool of a shady garden in Cherry-street in the summer of 1798 and discussed religion. "Major Howe after carrying arms through the revolutionary war, instead of reposing upon the laurels he had acquired, was compelled to open a boarding-house in *New-York*, for the maintenance of his wife and children. He was a member of the Cincinnati, and not a little proud of his Eagle." "In principles, my military friend was avowedly a Deist," says Davis, "and by tracing the effect to the cause, I shall expose the pernicious tendency of a book which is read with avidity. The Major was once commanding officer of the fortress at *West Point*, and by accident borrowed of a subaltern the history of the Decline and Fall of the Roman Empire. He read the work systematically, and a diligent perusal of that part which relates to the progress of Religion, caused him to become a Sceptic, and reject all belief in revelation. Before this period the Major was a constant attendant on the Established Church, but he now enlisted himself under the banners of the Infidel *Palmer*, who delivers lectures on Deism at *New-York*, and is securing for himself and followers considerable grants of land in hell."—John Davis, *Travels of Four Years and a Half in the United States of America during 1798, 1799, 1800, 1801, and 1802* (New York, 1909), pp. 22-23. (First published in London in 1803.)

In spite of his rank as major and member of the Cincinnati (who were for the most part Federalists with aristocratic tendencies), his impecuniousness probably tended to make Major Howe socially akin to the more typical follower of Elihu Palmer.

It is interesting to note that Gibbon's famous work was publicly banned in 1791 by the President of Harvard College from that institution.—John Quincy Adams, *Life in a New England Town: 1787, 1788* (Boston, 1903), p. 113, note.

been represented only by physicians, then, as now, apparently tinged with both naturalism and anti-clericalism. Politically, Palmer's followers were all, of course, republicans. They were ardently imbued with the democratic principles of the French Revolution and regarded the wealthy and conservative Federalists as America's counterpart of Europe's royalty and nobility. Although the Republican victory at the polls in the election of 1800 seems to have had the immediate effect of stimulating Palmer's societies, in the long run its effect was weakening. It removed one of their essential grievances and left them instead only a battle of verbal vituperation with the dying Federalist party. The moral support of identification of their cause with the friends of liberty in France had by that time also passed away, and the rapid demise after 1800 of the Society of Ancient Druids in Newburgh indicates how fleeting were the principles for which they stood. With a democratic president in Washington, whom they discovered to be no political innovator, they must have discerned that they were a society left high and dry without a cause. The battle with priestcraft was after all only a sham in view of the fact that no one religious denomination had a monopoly or was in control and religious persecution hence impossible. The New York and Philadelphia societies were longer lived and supported *The Temple of Reason* and later the *Prospect* for several years, but on the religious basis alone Palmer's rationalistic deism was unable to compete with the emotional lure of evangelical revivalism.

One other ideal, shared by Elihu Palmer and orthodox clergymen alike soon seemed irrelevant after 1800, namely, the social and political millennium first heralded by the American Revolution. In the early 1790's it had seemed as if the noble example of American political emancipation was to spread throughout the world, but with the turn of the century it became evident that the salvation of mankind was to be affected not through a reorganization of social institutions but through the individual acceptance of eternal life according to the Christian tradition. The religion of the republican millennium fell with the religion of deism.[7] In its place there arose a curious and most irrational belief in a millennium associated with the end of the world. Preachers agreed that the prophecies in the books of Revelation and Daniel were about to be fulfilled. To the modern reader it seems as if in their reaction to rationalism they vied with one another in proclaiming the fantastic and absurd.[8]

Our story is thus of the rise, the short-lived triumph, and the collapse of an intellectual movement reflected on this side of the Atlantic in the last three decades of the eighteenth century. It is doubtful whether the cosmopolitan spirit has ever prevailed so generally in our history as during that period. Certainly during the French Revolution even the common man was impregnated with

---

[7] Reactionaries were well aware of the fact that political and religious liberalism went hand in hand. "In the present state of the world," wrote John Bristed, "infidelity is closely allied with the *revolutionary* question; and, generally speaking, those who are eager to revolutionize all existing governments, under the ostensible pretence of promoting the *liberty* and *property* of mankind, are alike infidels in precept and in practice."—John Bristed, *America and Her Resources; or A View of the Agricultural, Commercial, Manufacturing, Financial, Political, Literary, Moral and Religious Capacity and Character of the American People* (London, 1818), pp. 403-404.

[8] For a discussion of this movement and numerous references to prophetic sermons, see Oliver W. Elsbree, *The Rise of the Missionary Spirit in America, 1790-1815* (Ph.D. dissertation, Columbia University, New York, 1928), Ch. VI, "Prophecy, Prayer, and Propaganda."

philosophical ideas of the rights of men, the sphere of government, the ideal social order, the origin and function of religion and its relation to morality. The "Triumph of Fidelity," to paraphrase the title of Timothy Dwight's volume of verse, *The Triumph of Infidelity*, written in 1788 when it seemed to him that the powers of evil were sweeping the land, was really the ascendency of those characteristics—intellectual, political, and religious —which have come to be peculiarly identified with and indigenous to the American scene. It marked the road the nation was to follow for over a century to come. In our cultural, intellectual, and religious life, as in our foreign affairs, our policy was strictly one of aloofness, isolation, and non-interference with things European. During the eighteenth century, American men of affairs in church and state, in business as well as in the learned professions, were bound by ties of education, correspondence, and membership in learned societies to kindred spirits abroad. Mrs. Trollope's contrast of our nineteenth-century provincialism to former times was not exaggerated: "Rousseau, Voltaire, Diderot, &c., were read by the old federalists, but now they seem known more as naughty words, than as great names." [9] When Mr. Griswold in the middle of the century apparently remembered Thomas Paine only as a "poor wretch" [10] and wrote of the "littleness, malice, and

[9] Mrs. [Frances] Trollope, *Domestic Manners of the Americans* (London, 1832), Vol. II, p. 122.

[10] Rufus W. Griswold, *The Republican Court*, p. 360. This is a relatively conservative estimate when contrasted with that of Theodore Roosevelt. Roosevelt held that Thomas Paine had no claim to American citizenship and described him as a "filthy little atheist," the kind of infidel who "esteems a bladder of dirty water as the proper weapon with which to assail Christianity."—Theodore Roosevelt, *Gouverneur Morris* (Boston, 1893), p. 289.

insolence" of "Volney, the infidel traveller and essayist,
. . . which have almost invariably marked the class of
thinkers to which he belonged," [11] he expressed the general aversion to deism on the part of American respectability. A typical New England estimate of Thomas Jefferson was that, "He was a man of rare intellectual faculties, but he had one defect—a sort of constitutional atheism
—a want of faith in God and man—in human truth and
human virtue." [12] Bayle's *Dictionnaire Historique et
Critique* was permitted to be in the library of Ohio Wes-
leyan University only because no one could read French! [13]
It exemplifies again the fact that a people's outlook on life
is determined largely by their everyday experiences and
needs. Not even in colonial times were the influences of
the frontier so dominant as during the middle decades of
the nineteenth century. And French thought, which had
dominated the eighteenth century, was incongruous to a
frontier economy.

In the one section of the country—New England—particularly in the older seaboard towns farthest removed
from the frontier in both time and space, the civilizing influences of an older established order asserted themselves.
Neither militant anti-clericalism nor too exuberant revivalism manifested itself there. Many of the Congregational clergy had ceased to believe the Calvinistic principles which the deists attacked. They did not, however,
like Allen, Paine, or Palmer, discard Christianity and rail
against priestcraft. Rather, without much outward change

[11] Rufus W. Griswold, *op. cit.*, p. 332.
[12] S. G. Goodrich, *Recollections of a Lifetime*, Vol. I, p. 109, note.
[13] G. Adolf Koch, *The Growth of Denominational Colleges in the
United States, 1820-1850* (MS. Chanler Historical Prize Essay, Columbia
University, New York, 1927), pp. 80-81.

or overturning of established institutions, they preached
a doctrine which assumed that man was less depraved and
God less exalted. By 1800 many Congregational churches
were in fact Unitarian. The change had been effected with
the dignity and propriety becoming a cultured upper class.
But it needs to be remembered that, while the Unitarian
movement in America is properly thought of as a liberalizing of the older New England religious tradition, para-
doxically, it was also a triumph of conservatism. It was
an upper-class movement for the liberalizing or, perhaps
more correctly, the civilizing of life. It had its roots in
prosperity, urbanity, and worldliness, and was not identified with either republicanism or genuine freethinking.
The principles of the French Revolution were irrelevant
to it. At the time, however, it seems to have acted as a
shock absorber for the Ethan Allen variety of freethought
and safely removed the edge of thorough-going rationalism so that we look in vain for deist societies in New England as in New York or Philadelphia. As has been well
said, "the Unitarians were liberal in theology but conservative in wellnigh everything else." [14]

With the same *savoir faire* the idealism of the 1790's
underwent a peculiarly Puritan metamorphosis in New
England. Their forefathers had felt that in the material
conquest of the wilderness against the odds of heathen
and nature they were battling for the Lord. With the
same zeal and assurance and the same old feeling of self-

[14] William W. Fenn, "The Unitarians" in *The Religious History of
New England* (Cambridge, 1917), p. 113.
  For example, deistic influences tended in other sections of the country
to lead to a disregard of religious exercises. Your respectable New Englander, however, remained by definition, as Dr. Benjamin Rush reminded
John Adams, "a meeting-going animal." *Cf., The Works of John Adams*,
edited by Charles Francis Adams (Boston, 1854), Vol. IX, p. 637, note.

righteousness, New Englanders in the first half of the
nineteenth century engaged in the reformation of their
fellow men and the demolition of evil institutions.
Heathen in distant parts of the world needed to be converted.[15] Protestant colleges had to be founded in the
West to save the frontier from conquest by Romanism,
and preachers needed to be trained for the vast regions
newly opened to settlement.[16] The temperance crusade
was launched against a people long addicted to rum and
spirituous liquors generally.[17] Nowhere were there more
zealous champions of the abolition of slavery than native
or transplanted New Englanders. Fourier's communal
phalanx was tried and found wanting in the Brook Farm
experiment.[18] These and other reforms loosely associated
with New England Transcendentalism was New England's way of giving expression to the heritage of eighteenth century liberalism. And as in the case of Unitarianism, her best citizens led the way.[19] The decade of the
1800's offers a strange contrast to that of the 1790's. One
can epitomize it best perhaps by saying that the republican
spirit of the revolution was replaced by the spirit of re-

[15] Oliver W. Elsbree, *The Rise of the Missionary Spirit in America,
1790-1815;* Peter G. Mode, *Source Book and Bibliographical Guide for
American Church History* (Menasha, Wisconsin, 1921), Ch. XIX, "The
Era of Organization."

[16] *Society for the Promotion of Collegiate and Theological Education
at the West, Permanent Documents of the Society* (Sixteen annual reports
beginning with the year 1844; numerous addresses by prominent clergymen
and educators; abstracts of addresses; and special reports. New York),
2 vols. *Cf.,* Peter G. Mode, *The Frontier Spirit in American Christianity*
(New York, 1923).

[17] *Cf.,* John Allen Krout, *The Origins of Prohibition* (New York,
1925).

[18] Lindsay Swift, *Brook Farm, its members, scholars, and visitors* (New
York, 1900).

[19] Octavius B. Frothingham, *Transcendentalism in New England* (New
York, 1876).

generation. The one believed in man's reason and virtue; the other in his depravity. The former believed in the perfectibility of man and human institutions; the latter in preparing the soul for immortality.

What Unitarianism did for the élite in New England,[20] revivalism did for the lower classes throughout the new nation to save them from the mystic union of deism and republicanism. The evangelical denominations were ideally adapted for this task for which their clergy were as to the manner born. The Baptists, Methodists, and Presbyterians, lay and clerical alike, were "of the people, for the people, and by the people." A painful absence of this world's goods made them republicans to begin with. It divorced politics and religion as far as they were concerned. The lack of money also saved their ministers from the contamination of education and culture. Illiteracy or a very meager acquaintance with books spared them the doubts which had so painfully troubled the learned Ezra Stiles. Deism was never an issue with them to be combated with reason. Convinced that it was a manifestation of the powers below, they fought it as they did all other brands of wickedness and evil by preaching Christ Jesus and Him crucified. With republicanism taken for granted in the cities on the Atlantic seaboard after the election of Mr. Jefferson, as it always had been on the frontier, revivalism remained as the one great emotional outlet of the American people in the first decade of the nineteenth century. It remained the characteristic expres-

[20] In the South, the upper classes were more directly deistical. Never having taken their Anglican faith very seriously, they now disregarded the church altogether or patronized it with the tolerant air of one who understands what is back of the mummery and realizes that, after all, the ignorant must have their superstitions.

sion of the religious life of America for a hundred years to come.

Scotched as it was by 1810, Palmer's and Paine's deistic movement was not dead. In the 1820's a new generation which had not shared their defeat made their ideas articulate again. Abner Kneeland, Robert Owen and his son, Robert Dale Owen, Orestes Augustus Brownson, George Houston, and Frances Wright carried on. On the anniversary of the birth of Thomas Paine in 1827 a toast was drunk "in solemn silence" to "The memory of Elihu Palmer, Voltaire, Hume, and all those deceased philosophers who, by their writings, contributed to subvert superstition, and vindicate the rights of humanity." [21]

But though some of the old shibboleths remained, these crusaders belonged to a new and different day from that of Paine and Palmer. The issues of the French Revolution were no longer dominant and were replaced by new social problems and the beginning of the movement away from the simpler agrarianism with its domestic economy which Thomas Jefferson represented. The story of these later deists and their relation to slavery, rights of women, the labor movement, birth control, prohibition, and Utopian communities still remains to be told.

[21] *The Correspondent*, New York, February 3, 1827, Vol. I, p. 29.

BIBLIOGRAPHY

Source Material

Adams, John, *The Works of John Adams, Second President of the United States, with a Life of the Author, Notes and Illustrations.* Charles Francis Adams, editor. 10 vols. Little, Brown, and Company, Boston, 1850-1856.

Adams, John Quincy, *Life in a New England Town: 1787, 1788. Diary of John Quincy Adams, while a Student in the Office of Theophilus Parsons at Newburyport.* Little, Brown, and Company, Boston, 1903.

Adams, Samuel, *The Writings of Samuel Adams.* Collected and edited by Harry Alonzo Cushing. 4 vols. G. P. Putnam's Sons, New York, 1904-1908.

Allen, Ethan, *A Narrative of Col. Ethan Allen's Captivity. Written by Himself.* Fourth Edition, with Notes. Chauncey Goodrich, Burlington, 1846.

—— *A Narrative of Colonel Ethan Allen's Captivity Containing His Voyages & Travels Written by Himself . . . with An Introductory Note by John Pell, Esq.* Printed for the Fort Ticonderoga Museum by Richard W. Ellis. The Georgian Press, New York, 1930.

—— *Reason the Only Oracle of Man, or a Compenduous System of Natural Religion. Alternately Adorned with Confutations of a variety of Doctrines incompatible to it; Deduced from the most exalted Ideas which we are able to form of the Divine and Human characters, and from the Universe in General.* Printed by Haswell & Russell, Bennington, State of Vermont, 1784.

Allen, Thomas, *A Sermon, preached before His Excellency, James Sullivan, Esq. Governor; His Honor, Levi Lincoln, Esq. Lieutenant-Governor; the Honourable Council, and Both Branches of the Legislature of the Commonwealth of Massachusetts on the day of General Election, May 25th, 1808.* Printed by Adams and Rhoades, Boston, 1808.

Allyn, John, *A Sermon, preached in the Audience of His Excellency Caleb Strong, Esq. Governor, the other Members of the Executive, and the Honorable Legislature of the Commonwealth of Massachusetts, on the Anniversary Election, May 29, 1805.* Printed for Young & Minns, Boston, 1805.

The American Medical and Philosophical Register. Published in New York every three months beginning July 1810. 4 vols. New York, 1811-1814.

ASBURY, REV. FRANCIS, *The Journal of the Rev. Francis Asbury, Bishop of the Methodist Episcopal Church, from August 7, 1771, to December 7, 1815.* 3 vols. Published by N. Bangs and T. Mason, New-York, 1821.

AUSTIN, SAMUEL, *An Oration, pronounced at Worcester, on the Fourth of July, 1798; the Anniversary of the Independence of the United States of America.* Printed by Leonard Worcester at Worcester, 1798.

BACON, JOHN, *Conjectures on Prophecies; written in the fore part of the year 1799.* Printed by David Carlisle, Boston, 1805.

BALDWIN, SIMEON E., *Life and Letters of Simeon Baldwin.* The Tuttle, Morehouse & Taylor Co., New Haven, [1919].

BARRUEL, M. L'ABBÉ, *Abrege des Mémoires pour servir à l'histoire du Jacobinisme.* 2 vols. Chez P. Fauche, Libraire, Hambourg, 1800.

BAYLE, PIERRE, *The Dictionary Historical and Critical of Mr Peter Bayle. The Second Edition, Carefully collated with the several Editions of the Original; in which many Passages are restored, and the whole greatly augmented, particularly with a Translation of the Quotations from eminent Writers in various Languages. To which is prefixed, The Life of The Author, revised, corrected, and enlarged, by Mr Des Maizeaux, Fellow of the Royal Society.* 5 vols. London, 1734-1738.

BEECHER, LYMAN, *Autobiography, Correspondence, etc.* Edited by Charles Beecher. 2 vols. Harper & Brothers, Publishers, New York, 1864.

BELSHAM, REV. THOMAS, *American Unitarianism; or a Brief History of the Progress and Present State of the Unitarian Churches in America.* Fourth Edition. Printed by Nathaniel Willis, Boston, 1815.

BENTLEY, WILLIAM, *The Diary of William Bentley, D.D., Pastor of the East Church, Salem, Massachusetts.* 4 vols. The Essex Institute, Salem, Mass., 1905-1914.

—— *A Discourse, delivered in the East Meeting-House in Salem, September 2, 1807, at the Annual Meeting of the Salem Female Charitable Society.* Printed by Pool & Palfray, Salem, 1807.

—— *A Funeral Discourse, delivered in the East Meeting-House, Salem, on the Sunday after the Death of Major General Fiske, who died September 28, 1797.* Printed by Thomas C. Cushing, Salem, 1797.

—— *Oration, in commemoration of the Birthday of Washington, delivered at Salem, Massachusetts, February 22d, 1793.* Morrisania, N. Y., 1870.

—— *A Sermon, preached at the Stone Chapel in Boston, September 12, 1790.* Printed by Samuel Hall, Boston, 1790.

—— *A Sermon, delivered in the East Meeting-House, Salem, on Sunday Morning, March 13, occasioned by the Death of Jonathan Gardner, Esq. Master of the Marine Society in Salem; who died March 2, 1791, aet. 63.* Printed by Thomas C. Cushing, Salem, 1791.

—— *A Sermon, before the Governor, the Honorable Council, and Both Branches of the Legislature of the Commonwealth of Massachusetts, on the day of General Election, May 27, 1807.* Printed by Adams and Rhoades, Printers to the State, Boston, 1807.

BERNARD, JOHN, *Retrospections of America, 1797-1811.* Harper & Brothers, New York, 1887.

BICHENO, J., *The Signs of the Times: or, the Overthrow of the Papal Tyranny in France, the Prelude of Destruction to Popery and Despotism; but of Peace to Mankind.* First American Edition, from the Second European. Providence, R. I., 1794.

BISHOP, ABRAHAM, *An Oration on the Extent and Power of Political Delusion, delivered in New-Haven, on the Evening preceding the Public Commencement, September, 1800.* The Second Edition. Printed by Pennington and Gould, Newark, 1800.

—— *Oration, delivered in Wallingford, On the 11th of March 1801, before the Republicans of the State of Connecticut, at their General Thanksgiving, for the election of Thomas Jefferson to the Presidency and of Aaron Burr to the Vice Presidency of the United States of America.* Printed by William W. Morse, New Haven, 1801.

—— *Oration, in honor of the election of President Jefferson, and the peaceful acquisition of Louisiana, delivered at the National Festival, in Hartford, on the 11th of May, 1804.* Printed for the General Committee of Republicans, 1804.

BLOUNT, CHARLES, *The Oracles of Reason.* [No Publisher], London, 1693.

BOUDINOT, ELIAS, *The Age of Revelation, or the Age of Reason shewn to be an Age of Infidelity.* Published by Asbury Dickins, Philadelphia, 1801.

BRISTED, JOHN, *America and Her Resources; or A View of the Agricultural, Commercial, Manufacturing, Financial, Political, Liter-*

ary, Moral and Religious Capacity and Character of the American People. Printed for Henry Colburn, London, 1818.

BROWN, WILLIAM, *An Oration, spoken at Hartford, in the State of Connecticut, on the Anniversary of American Independence, July 4th, A.D. 1799.* Printed by Hudson and Goodwin, Hartford, 1799.

[CHALMERS, GEORGE], *The Life of Thomas Pain, the author of Rights of Men. With A Defence of His Writings. By Francis Oldys, A. M. of the University of Pennsylvania.* Printed for John Stockdale, London, 1791. (A hostile account. The pseudonym is wholly fictitious.)

CHANNING, WILLIAM ELLERY, *Memoir of William Ellery Channing, with Extracts from his Correspondence and Manuscripts.* 2 vols. George Routledge and Sons, London, no date.

CHAUNCY, CHARLES, *The Benevolence of the Deity, Fairly and Impartially Considered.* Printed by Powars & Willis, Boston, 1784.

—— *A Discourse on 'the good News from a far Country.' Deliver'd July 24th. A Day of Thanks-giving to Almighty God, throughout the Province of the Massachusetts-Bay in New-England, on Occasion of the Repeal of the Stamp-Act.* Printed by Kneeland and Adams, Boston, 1766.

—— *Five Dissertations on the Scripture Account of the Fall; and its Consequences.* [No Publisher], London, 1785.

—— *A Letter to a Friend, Containing Remarks on certain Passages in a Sermon Preached, by the Right Reverend Father in God, John Lord Bishop of Landaff. . . . In which the highest Reproach is undeservedly cast upon the American Colonies.* Printed by Kneeland and Adams, Boston, 1767.

[CHAUNCY, CHARLES], *The Mystery hid from Ages and Generations, made manifest by the Gospel-Revelation: or, The Salvation of All Men the Grand Thing aimed at in the Scheme of God, as opened in the New-Testament Writings, and entrusted with Jesus Christ to bring into Effect. By One who wishes well to the whole Human Race.* Printed for Charles Dilly, London, 1784.

CHAUNCY, CHARLES, *The Validity of Presbyterian Ordination Asserted and Maintained. A Discourse delivered at the Anniversary Dudleian-Lecture, at Harvard-College in Cambridge New-England, May 12. 1762.* Printed by Richard Draper, Boston, 1762.

CHEETHAM, JAMES, *A dissertation concerning political equality, and the Corporation of New-York.* Printed by D. Denniston, New-York, 1800.

—— *The Life of Thomas Paine.* Printed by Southwick and Pelsue, New York, 1809.

CLARK, PETER, *A Sermon preach'd in the Audience of His Excellency the Governour, the Honourable His Majesty's Council, and the Honourable House of Representatives, of the Province of the Massachusetts-Bay, in New-England, May 30th. 1739. Being the Anniversary for the Election of His Majesty's Council for the Province.* Printed by S. Kneeland, Boston, 1739.

[CLIFFORD, ROBERT], *Application of Barruel's Memoirs of Jacobinism to the Secret Societies of Ireland and Great Britain. By the Translator of that Work.* [No Publisher], London, 1798.

[CLINTON, DE WITT], *A Vindication of Thomas Jefferson, against the charges contained in a pamphlet entitled, 'Serious Considerations,' &c. By Grotius.* Printed by David Denniston, New-York, 1800.

[CLOWES, REV. JOHN], *Remarks on the Assertions of the Author of the Memoirs of Jacobinism respecting the Character of Emanuel Swedenborg. . . .* Printed for John Ormrod, Philadelphia, 1800.

[COBBETT, WILLIAM], *A Bone to Gnaw for the Democrats. By Peter Porcupine.* Printed for J. Wright, London, 1797.

—— *Democratic Principles Illustrated. Part the Second. Containing an Instructive Essay, tracing All the Horrors of the French Revolution to their real Causes, the licentious Politics, and infidel Philosophy of the present Age. By Peter Porcupine.* Seventh Edition. Printed for A. Brown, Aberdeen, 1798.

—— *The History of Jacobinism, its Crimes, Cruelties and Perfidies: comprising an Inquiry into the Manner of Disseminating, under the Appearance of Philosophy and Virtue, Principles which are equally subversive of Order, Virtue, Religion, Liberty and Happiness. With an Appendix, Containing a History of the American Jacobins, commonly denominated Democrats. By Peter Porcupine.* Printed for William Cobbett, Philadelphia, 1796.

—— *The Life of Thomas Paine, interspersed with Remarks and Reflections. By Peter Porcupine.* [No Publisher], Philadelphia, 1797.

—— *Observations, &c. &c. on Dr. Priestley's emigration to America.* [Title page missing], Philadelphia, 1795.

—— *A Twig for a Butting Calf; or Strictures upon remarks on the emigration of Doctor Joseph Priestley, &c. &c. By 'A Brother of the Birch.'* Printed by J. Buel, New-York, 1795.

CONDILLAC, *Condillac's Treatise on the Sensations.* Translated by Geraldine Carr. University of Southern California, Los Angeles, 1930.

CUNNINGHAM, ABNER, *Practical Infidelity Portrayed and the Judgments of God made manifest.* Third Edition. Published by Daniel Cooledge, New-York, 1836.

[DAGGETT, DAVID], *Count the Cost. An Address to the People of Connecticut, on Sundry Political Subjects, and Particularly on the Proposition for a New Constitution. By Jonathan Steadfast.* Printed by Hudson and Goodwin, Hartford, 1804.

DAGGETT, DAVID, *Sun-Beams may be Extracted from Cucumbers, but the Process is Tedious. An Oration, pronounced on the Fourth of July, 1799. At the Request of the Citizens of New-Haven.* Second Edition. Printed by Thomas Green and Son, New-Haven, 1799.

[DAGGETT, DAVID], *Three Letters to Abraham Bishop, Esquire, containing some strictures on his Oration, pronounced, in the White Meeting-House, on the evening preceding the Public Commencement, September 1800, with some remarks on his conduct at the late election. By Connecticutensis.* Printed by Hudson and Goodwin, Hartford, 1800.

DANA, JAMES, *A Century Discourse, delivered at the Anniversary Meeting of the Freemen of the Town of Wallingford, April 9, 1770.* Printed by T. and S. Green, New-Haven, [1770].

—— *The Folly of Practical Atheism. A Discourse, delivered in the Chapel of Yale-College, on Lord's Day, November 23, 1794.* Printed by T. & S. Green, New-Haven, [no date].

—— *A Sermon, preached before the General Assembly of the State of Connecticut, at Hartford, on the Day of the Anniversary Election, May 13, 1779.* Printed by Hudson and Goodwin, Hartford, 1779.

—— *The Wisdom of Observing the Footsteps of Providence. A Sermon, preached at Wethersfield, on the Annual Thanksgiving, November 28, 1805.* Printed by Hudson and Goodwin, Hartford, 1805.

DAVIS, JOHN, *Travels of Four Years and a Half in the United States of America during 1798, 1799, 1800, 1801, and 1802. With an Introduction and Notes by A. J. Morrison.* (First published in London in 1803.) Henry Holt and Company, New York, 1909.

The Deist; or Moral Philosopher. Being an Impartial Inquiry into Moral and Theological Truths: Selected from the Writings of the Most Celebrated Authors in Ancient and Modern Times. 3 vols. Printed and Published by R. Carlile, London, 1819-1826.

DUCHÉ, JACOB, *The Duty of Standing Fast in Our Spiritual and Temporal Liberties, a Sermon, preached in Christ-Church, July 7th, 1775. Before the First Battalion of the City and Liberties of Philadelphia; And now published at their Request.* Printed by James Humphreys, Junior, Philadelphia, 1775.

DUNLAP, WILLIAM, *Diary of William Dunlap (1766-1839). The Memoirs of a Dramatist, Theatrical Manager, Painter, Critic, Novelist, and Historian.* Edited by Dorothy C. Barck. 3 vols. (Collections of the New York Historical Society for the Years 1929, 1930, 1931, Vols. LXII, LXIII, LXIV.) Printed for the New York Historical Society, New York, 1930.

DWIGHT, THEODORE, *The Character of Thomas Jefferson, as exhibited in His Own Writings.* Weeks, Jordan & Company, Boston, 1839.

DWIGHT, TIMOTHY, *A Discourse on Some Events of the Last Century, delivered in the Brick Church in New Haven, on Wednesday, January 7, 1801.* Printed by Ezra Read, New Haven, 1801.

—— *The Duty of Americans, at the Present Crisis, Illustrated in a Discourse, preached on the Fourth of July, 1798.* Printed by Thomas and Samuel Green, New-Haven, 1798.

—— *The Nature, and Danger, of Infidel Philosophy, exhibited in Two Discourses, addressed to the Candidates for the Baccalaureate, in Yale College.* Printed by George Bunce, New-Haven, 1798.

—— *Theology; Explained and Defended, in a Series of Sermons, with a Memoir of the Life of the Author.* 4 vols. Second Edition. Printed and Published by S. Converse, New-Haven, 1823.

—— *Travels; in New-England and New-York.* 4 vols. S. Converse, Printer, New-Haven, 1821-1822.

[DWIGHT, TIMOTHY], *The Triumph of Infidelity: a Poem. Printed in the World,* 1788.

ECKLEY, JOSEPH, *A Discourse, delivered on the Public Thanksgiving Day, November 29, 1798.* Printed by Manning & Loring, Boston, 1798.

FREEMAN, JAMES, *Sermons on Particular Occasions.* Printed by Manning and Loring, Boston, 1812.

—— *Sermons and Charges.* New Edition. Carter, Hendee and Co., Boston, 1832.

GALE, BENJAMIN, *A Brief Essay, or, An Attempt to Prove, from the Prophetick Writings of the Old and New Testament, what Period of Prophecy the Church of God is now under; and from them to shew, What Events Revelationists may expect will take Place during the present Period.* Printed by Thomas and Samuel Green, New-Haven, [no date].

GAY, EBENEZER, *The Devotion of God's People adjusted to the Dispensations of his Providence. A Sermon preached in the first Parish of Hingham, December 6, 1770. The Day observed throughout the Province as a Day of public Thanksgiving and Prayer.* Printed by Richard Draper, Boston, 1771.

GAY, EBENEZER, *Natural Religion, as Distinguished from Revealed: A Sermon preached at the annual Dudleian-Lecture, at Harvard-College in Cambridge, May 9. 1759.* Printed by John Draper, Boston, 1759.

—— *The True Spirit of a Gospel-Minister represented and urged. A Sermon Preach'd before the Ministers of the Province of the Massachusetts-Bay in New-England, at their Annual Convention in Boston; May 29. 1746.* Printed for D. Gookin, Boston, 1746.

GODWIN, WILLIAM, *Enquiry concerning Political Justice, and its Influence on Morals and Happiness.* 2 vols. Third Edition Corrected. Printed for G. G. and J. Robinson, London, 1798.

GOODRICH, S. G., *Recollections of a Lifetime, or Men and Things I have Seen.* 2 vols. Miller, Orton and Mulligan, New York and Auburn, 1857.

GORTON, BENJAMIN, *Plain Dealing with Calvinism: being an Address to Mankind in General, and the Inhabitants of Troy in Particular, on Calvinism Generally: and also, on the subject of a letter to Mr. Jonas Coe, Pastor of the Presbyterian Congregation in Troy: with said letter, and some reasons offered for publishing the same.* (First published in 1803.) Second Edition. Printed by R. Schermerhorn, for the Author, Troy, 1811.

[GORTON, BENJAMIN], *Late Revelations on the Doctrines of Election and Reprobation; or Sheep and Goats; and the Woman Speaking in the Church; also, the Gospel of the Kingdom, the Number of the Beast and Ezekiel's Boiling Pot.* [No date or publisher; bound with *Plain Dealing with Calvinism. . . .*]

GUILD, REUBEN ALDRIDGE, *Early History of Brown University, including the Life, Times, and Correspondence of President Manning. 1756-1791.* [No publisher.] Providence, 1897.

The Halcyon Luminary, and Theological Repository, A Monthly Magazine, devoted to Religion and Polite Literature, conducted by a Society of Gentlemen. 2 vols. Published by Samuel Woodworth & Co. and E. Riley, New York, 1812-1813.

HALL, JOSEPH, *An Oration, pronounced July 4, 1800, at the request of the Inhabitants of the Town of Boston, in commemoration of the Anniversary of American Independence.* Manning & Loring, Boston, 1800.

HALL, ROBERT, *Modern Infidelity Considered with respect to its Influence on Society: in a Sermon, preached at the Baptist Meeting, Cambridge.* First American, from the Third English Edition. Printed by Samuel Etheridge, Charlestown, 1801.

HAMPDEN, *A Letter to the President of the United States, touching the Prosecutions, under his Patronage, before the Circuit Court in the District of Connecticut. . . . By Hampden.* Printed by Oliver Steele and Co., New-Haven, 1808.

HART, LEVI, *Liberty described and recommended; in a Sermon, preached to the Corporation of Freemen in Farmington, at their Meeting on Tuesday, September 20, 1774, and published at their Desire.* Printed by Eben. Watson, Hartford, 1775.

HELVETIUS, CLAUDE ADRIAN, *De l'Esprit: or, Essays on the Mind, and its Several Faculties. Written by Helvetius. Translated from the Edition printed under the Author's Inspection.* London, 1759.

HOLMES, ABIEL, *The Life of Ezra Stiles.* Printed by Thomas & Andrews, Boston, 1798.

—— *A Sermon, on the Freedom and Happiness of America; Preached at Cambridge, February 19, 1795, the day appointed by the President of the United States for a National Thanksgiving.* Printed by Samuel Hall, Boston, 1795.

JEFFERSON, THOMAS, *Notes on the State of Virginia.* Printed by Prichard and Hall, Philadelphia, 1788.

—— *The Writings of Thomas Jefferson.* Collected and edited by Paul Leicester Ford. 10 vols. G. P. Putnam's Sons, New York, 1892-1899.

—— *The Writings of Thomas Jefferson: being his Autobiography, Correspondence, Reports, Messages, Addresses, and Other Writings, Official and Private.* Edited by H. A. Washington. 9 vols. Published by John C. Riker, New York, 1853-1855.

—— *Memoirs of the Hon. Thomas Jefferson, . . . with a View of the Rise and Progress of French Influence and French Principles in that Country.* 2 vols. Printed for the Purchasers, [No place], 1809.

JOHNSTON, JOHN, *The Autobiography and Ministerial Life of the Rev. John Johnston, D. D. Edited and Compiled by the Rev. James Carnahan, D. D., Late President of the College of New Jersey. Together with an Appendix.* M. W. Dodd, New York, 1856.

KINNE, AARON, *A Display, of Scriptural Prophecies, with their events and the Period of their Accomplishment. Compiled from Rollin, Prideaux, Newton, and other eminent writers.* Printed by H. Willard, Stockbridge, 1813.

LAMBERT, JOHN, *Travels through Canada, and the United States of North America, in the Years 1806, 1807, & 1808.* 2 vols.

Third Edition, Corrected and Improved. Printed for Baldwin, Cradock, and Joy, London, 1816.

LATHROP, JOSEPH, *A Sermon, on the Dangers of the Times, from Infidelity and Immorality; and especially from a lately discovered Conspiracy against Religion and Government, delivered at West-Springfield, and afterward at Springfield.* Printed by Francis Stebbins, Springfield, September, 1798.

LELAND, JOHN, *A View of the Principal Deistical Writers that have Appeared in England in the last and present Century; with Observations upon them, and some Account of the Answers that have been published against them. In several Letters to a Friend.* 2 vols. The Third Edition, Improved. Printed for Benj. Dod, London, 1757.

LESLIE, CHARLES, *A Short and Easy Method with the Deists; wherein the Certainty of the Christian Religion is demonstrated by infallible proof, from four rules, which are incompatible with any imposture that ever yet has been, or can possibly be. In a Letter to a Friend. With a Letter from the Author to a Deist, upon his conversion by reading his book.* Printed and Published by the New-York Protestant Episcopal Press, New-York, 1830.

A Letter of Many Ministers in Old England, Requesting The judgement of their Reverend Brethren in New England concerning Nine Positions. Written Anno Dom. 1637. Together with their Answer thereunto returned, Anno 1639. And the Reply made unto the said Answer, and sent over unto them, Anno 1640. Now published (by occasion mentioned in the Epistle to the Reader, following in the next page,) upon the desire of many godly and faithfull Ministers in and about the City of London, who love and seeke the truth. By Simeon Ash and William Rathband. 1 Thes. 5.21. Prove all things; Hold fast that which is good. Printed for Thomas Underhill, at the signe of the Bible in great Woodstreet. London, 1643.

LEWIS, ZECHARIAH, *An Oration, on the Apparent, and the Real Political Situation of the United States, pronounced before the Connecticut Society of Cincinnati, assembled, at New-Haven, for the celebration of American Independence, July the 4th, 1799.* By Zechariah Lewis, A Tutor of Yale-College. Printed by Thomas Green and Son, New-Haven, 1799.

LIANCOURT, DUKE DE LA ROCHEFOUCAULT, *Travels through the United States of North America, the Country of the Iroquois, and Upper Canada, in the Years 1795, 1796, and 1797.* (Translated by H. Neuman.) Printed for R. Phillips, London, 1799.

LINN, WILLIAM, *Discourses on the Signs of the Times.* Printed by Thomas Greenleaf, New-York, 1794.

LONGWORTH, DAVID, *Longworth's American Almanac, New-York Register, and City Directory for the Twenty-sixth Year of American Independence.* Printed and Published by D. Longworth, New York, 1801.

—— *Longworth's American Almanac, New-York Register, and City-Directory, for the Twenty-seventh Year of American Independence.* Printed and Published by D. Longworth, New York, 1802.

LYMAN, JOSEPH, *The Administrations of Providence full of Goodness and Mercy. A Sermon, Delivered at Hatfield, November 7th. A. D. 1793. Being the day of Public Thanksgiving.* Printed by William Butler, Northampton, 1794.

MCKEEN, JOSEPH, *A Sermon, preached before the Honorable the Council, and the Honorable the Senate, and House of Representatives of the Commonwealth of Massachusetts, May 28, 1800, being the day of General Election.* Printed by Young & Minns, Boston, 1800.

MACLAY, WILLIAM, *Journal of William Maclay.* Edited by Edgar S. Maclay. D. Appleton and Company, New York, 1890.

MANWARING, CHRISTOPHER, *Republicanism and Aristocracy contrasted; or, the Steady Habits of Connecticut inconsistent with, and opposed to the Principles of the American Revolution. Exhibited in an Oration, delivered at New-London, (Connecticut) July 4, 1804, on the celebration of American Independence.* Re-printed at Boston, Jan. 1805.

MASON, JOHN M., *The Complete Works of John M. Mason, D. D.* Edited by his son, Ebenezer Mason. 4 vols. Charles Scribner, New York, 1852.

[MASON, JOHN M.], *The Voice of Warning, to Christians, on the Ensuing Election of a President of the United States.* Printed by G. F. Hopkins, New-York, 1800.

Massachusetts Historical Society Collections; Belknap Papers, Fifth Series, Vol. II. Boston, 1877.

MATHER, COTTON, *Diary of Cotton Mather, 1709-1724* in *Massachusetts Historical Society Collections,* Seventh Series, Vol. VIII.

—— *Magnalia Christi Americana; or, the Ecclesiastical History of New England. . . .* 2 vols. Silas Andrus & Son, Hartford, 1853.

MAYHEW, JONATHAN, *A Discourse Occasioned by the Earthquakes in November 1755. Delivered in the West-Meeting-House, Boston, Thursday December 18, following.* Printed by Edes & Gill, Boston, 1755.

—— *Sermons.* Printed by Richard Draper, Boston, 1755.

MAYHEW, JONATHAN, *Seven Sermons upon the Following Subjects;* ... *Preached at a Lecture in the West Meeting-House in Boston, Begun the first Thursday in June, and ended the last Thursday in August, 1748.* Boston, 1749.

—— *The Snare broken. A Thanksgiving-Discourse, preached At the Desire of the West Church in Boston, N. E. Friday May 23, 1766. Occasioned by the Repeal of the Stamp-Act.* Printed by R. & S. Draper, Boston, 1766.

MELISH, JOHN, *Travels in the United States of America in the Years 1806 & 1807, and 1809, 1810, & 1811.* .... 2 vols. Printed for the Author by Thomas & George Palmer, Philadelphia, 1812.

MILLER, SAMUEL, *A Brief Retrospect of the Eighteenth Century. Part First; in Two Volumes: containing a Sketch of the Revolutions and Improvements in Science, Arts, and Literature during that Period.* 2 vols. Printed by T. and J. Swords, New-York, 1803.

—— *A Sermon, preached in New-York, July 4th, 1793. Being the Anniversary of the Independence of America: at the request of the Tammany Society, or Columbian Order.* Printed by Thomas Greenleaf, New-York, 1793.

Minutes of the Common Council of the City of New York, 1784-1831, Vol. II, April 8, 1793 to June 12, 1801. Published by the City of New York, New York, 1917.

[MOORE, CLEMENT CLARKE], *Observations upon certain passages in Mr. Jefferson's Notes on Virginia, which appear to have a tendency to Subvert Religion, and establish a False Philosophy.* [No publisher.] New York, 1804.

MORE, HANNAH, *Remarks on the Speech of M. Dupont, made in the National Convention of France, on the Subjects of Religion and Public Education.* Second Edition. Printed for T. Cadell, London, 1793.

MORRIS, GOUVERNEUR, *An Oration, delivered on Wednesday, June 29, 1814, at the request of a number of citizens of New-York, in Celebration of the Recent Deliverance of Europe from the Yoke of Military Despotism.* Printed and Published by Van Winkle and Wiley, New-York, 1814.

MORSE, JEDIDIAH, *The present Situation of other Nations of the World, contrasted with our own. A Sermon, delivered At Charlestown, in the Commonwealth of Massachusetts, February 19, 1795; being the day recommended by George Washington, President of the United States of America, for Publick Thanksgiving and Prayer.* Printed by Samuel Hall, Boston, 1795.

—— *A Sermon, delivered at the New North Church in Boston, in the morning, and in the afternoon at Charlestown, May 9th, 1798, being the day recommended by John Adams, President of the United States of America, for Solemn Humiliation, Fasting and Prayer.* Printed by Samuel Hall, Boston, 1798.

—— *A Sermon, preached at Charlestown, November 29, 1798, on the Anniversary Thanksgiving in Massachusetts. With An Appendix, Designed to illustrate some parts of the Discourse; exhibiting proofs of the early existence, progress, and deleterious effects of French intrigue and influence in the United States.* Second Edition. Printed by Samuel Hall, Boston, 1799.

Nelson, Rev. David, *The Cause and Cure of Infidelity: including a notice of the Author's Unbelief, and the Means of his Rescue.* Published by the American Tract Society, New-York, 1841.

New-York Society Library, *A Catalogue of the Books belonging to the New-York Society Library, together with the Charter and the By-laws of the Same.* Printed by C. S. Van Winkle, New York, 1813.

Nott, Eliphalet, *A Discourse delivered in the North Dutch Church, in the City of Albany, occasioned by the ever to be lamented Death of General Alexander Hamilton, July 29, 1804.* Printed by Charles R. and George Webster, Albany, 1804.

Offen, Benjamin, *A Legacy to the Friends of Free Discussion: being a review of the Principal Historical Facts and Personages of the books known as the Old and New Testament; with remarks on the Morality of Nature. By Benjamin Offen, Formerly Lecturer to the Society of Moral Philanthropists, at Tammany Hall, New York.* Printed and Published by J. P. Mendum, Boston, 1846.

[Ogden, John Cosens], *A View of the New-England Illuminati: who are indefatigably engaged in Destroying the Religion and Government of the United States; under a feigned regard for their safety and under an impious abuse of true religion.* Printed by James Carey, Philadelphia, 1799.

Ogden, Uzal, *Antidote to Deism. The Deist Unmasked; or an ample Refutation of all the Objections of Thomas Paine, against the Christian Religion; as contained in a Pamphlet, intitled, The Age of Reason; addressed to the Citizens of these States.* 2 vols. Printed by John Woods, Newark, 1795.

Oldys, Francis—see Chalmers, George

Osgood, David, *The Wonderful Works of God are to be remembered. A Sermon, delivered on the day of Annual Thanksgiving, November 20, 1794.* Printed by Samuel Hall, Boston, 1795.

Paine, Thomas, *The Life and Works of Thomas Paine.* Patriots'
Edition, edited by William M. Van der Weyde.   10 vols.
Thomas Paine National Historical Association, New Rochelle,
N. Y., 1925.

Palmer, Elihu, *An Enquiry relative to the Moral & Political Im-
provement of the Human Species. An Oration, delivered in the
City of New-York on the twenty-first anniversary of American
Independence.* Printed by John Crookes, New-York, 1797.

[Palmer, Elihu], *The Examiners Examined: being a Defence of the
Age of Reason.* Printed for the Author by L. Wayland and J.
Fellows, New-York, 1794.

Palmer, Elihu, *Extracts from an Oration, delivered by Elihu Palmer,
the 4th of July, 1793* in a pamphlet entitled *Political Miscellany.*
Printed by G. Forman, New-York, 1793.

—— *The Political Happiness of Nations; an Oration. Delivered at
the City of New-York, on the Fourth of July, Twenty-fourth
Anniversary of American Independence.* [New York, 1800.]

—— *Posthumous Pieces. By Elihu Palmer, being three chapters of
an unfinished work intended to have been entitled 'The Political
World.' To which are prefixed a Memoir of Mr. Palmer by his
friend Mr. John Fellows of New York, and Mr. Palmer's 'Principles of the Deistical Society of the State of New York.'* Printed
and Published by R. Carlile, London, 1826.

—— *Principles of Nature; or, a Developement of the Moral Causes of
Happiness and Misery among the Human Species.* Third Edition. [New York], 1806.

—— *Principles of Nature; or, a Developement of the Moral Causes of
Happiness and Misery among the Human Species.* America
Printed. Re-Printed and Published by R. Carlile, London, 1823.

—— *Prospect; or, View of the Moral World, for the Year 1804.*
Printed for the Editor, New York. (This was a weekly paper
edited by Elihu Palmer from December 10, 1803 to March 30,
1805.)

Payson, Seth, *Proofs of the Real Existence, and Dangerous Tendency
of Illuminism. Containing an abstract of the most interesting
parts of what Dr. Robison and the Abbe Barruel have published
on this subject; with collateral proofs and general observations.*
Printed by Samuel Etheridge, Charlestown, 1802.

—— *A Sermon preached at Concord, June 6th, 1799, before His
Excellency the Governor, the Honorable Council, Senate, and
House of Representatives, of the State of New-Hampshire.*
Printed by John Melcher, Portsmouth, N. H., 1799.

Pigott, Charles, *A Political Dictionary: explaining the True Meaning of Words. Illustrated and exemplified in the Lives, Morals,*

Character and Conduct of the following Most Illustrious Personages, among many others. . . . Printed for Thomas Greenleaf, New York, 1796.

PORCUPINE, PETER—see Cobbett, William

PRIESTLEY, JOSEPH, *An Appeal to the Public, on the Subject of the Riots in Birmingham.* Printed by J. Thompson, Birmingham, 1791. *Ibid.,* Part II. Printed for J. Johnson, London, 1792.

[PRIESTLEY, JOSEPH], *An Appeal to the serious and candid Professors of Christianity.* 1771. [No publisher or place given.]

PRIESTLEY, JOSEPH, *Defences of Unitarianism for the Year 1787, containing Letters to the Rev. Dr. Geddes, to The Rev. Dr. Price, Part II. and to The Candidates for Orders in the Universities.* . . . Printed for the Author by Pearson and Rollason, Birmingham, 1788.

—— *An History of the Corruptions of Christianity.* 2 vols. Birmingham, 1782.

—— *An History of Early Opinions concerning Jesus Christ, compiled from Original Writers; proving that the Christian Church was at first Unitarian.* Birmingham, 1786.

—— *Letters to the Members of the New Jerusalem Church formed by Baron Swedenborg.* Printed by J. Thompson, Birmingham, 1791.

—— *Letters to the Philosophers and Politicians of France, on the Subject of Religion.* Printed for J. Johnson, London, 1793.

—— *Letters to a Philosophical Unbeliever. Part I. Containing an Examination of the principal Objections to the Doctrines of 'Natural Religion,' and especially those contained in the Writings of Mr. Hume.* Printed by R. Cruttwell, Bath, 1780.

—— *Letters to a Philosophical Unbeliever. Part II. Containing A State of the Evidence of revealed Religion, with Animadversions on the two last Chapters of the first Volume of 'Mr. Gibbon's History of the Decline and Fall of the Roman Empire.'* Printed by Pearson and Rollason, Birmingham, 1787.

—— *Memoirs of Dr. Joseph Priestley, to the Year 1795, written by himself: With a continuation, to the time of his decease, by his Son, Joseph Priestley: And Observations on his Writings, by Thomas Cooper, Presiding Judge of the 4th District of Pennsylvania: and the Rev. William Christie.* 2 vols. Printed by John Binns, Northumberland, 1806.

—— *Observations on the Increase of Infidelity. Third Edition. To which are added, Animadversions on the Writings of several modern Unbelievers, and especially the Ruins of Mr. Volney.* Printed for Thomas Dobson, Philadelphia, 1797.

—— *Two Sermons. viz. I. The present State of Europe compared with Antient Prophecies; preached on the Fast-Day in 1794; with a Preface, containing the Reasons for the Author's Leaving England. II. The Use of Christianity, especially in difficult Times; being the Author's Farewell Discourse to his Congregation at Hackney.* Printed by Thomas Dobson, Philadelphia, 1794.

PRIESTLEY, JOSEPH, *Theological and Miscellaneous Works.* Edited with Notes by John Towill Rutt. 25 vols. Hackney, 1817-1832.

[PRIESTLEY, JOSEPH], *The Triumph of Truth; being an account of the Trial of Mr. E. Elwall, for Heresy and Blasphemy, at Stafford Assizes, before Judge Denton. To which are added, Extracts from some other Pieces of Mr. Elwall's, concerning the Unity of God. And a few Additional Illustrations.* Sold by John Binns, Leeds, 1771.

Prisoner of Hope, Newspaper published in 1800 in the City of New York in the interest of "The Society of the Relief of Distressed Prisoners."

RAYNAL, ABBÉ, *The Revolution of America.* Printed for Lockyer Davis, Holborn London, 1781.

ROBISON, JOHN, *Proofs of a Conspiracy against all the Religions and Governments of Europe, carried on in the Secret Meetings of Free Masons, Illuminati, and Reading Societies.* Fourth Edition. Printed by George Forman, New-York, 1798.

SHERWIN, W. T., *Memoirs of the Life of Thomas Paine.* Published by R. Carlile, London, 1819.

Society for the Promotion of Collegiate and Theological Education at the West, Permanent Documents. 2 vols. John F. Trow, Printer, New York, 1852.

SPRING, SAMUEL, *A Sermon, delivered before the Massachusetts Missionary Society, at their Annual Meeting May 25, 1802.* Printed by E. M. Blunt, Newburyport, 1802.

STEADFAST, JONATHAN—see Daggett, David.

[STEWART, JOHN], *The Apocalypse of Nature; wherein the Source of Moral Motion is Discovered, and a Moral System is established, through the Evidence and Conviction of the Senses, to Elevate Man to intellectual Existence and an enlightened State of Nature.* Printed for J. Ridgway, London, no date.

STEWART, JOHN, *The Moral or Intellectual Last Will and Testament of John Stewart, the Traveller, the only Man of Nature that ever appeared in the world.* Printed for the Author, London, 1810.

—— *Opus Maximum; or, the Great Essay to reduce the Moral World from Contingency to System, In the following new Sciences:*

Psyconomy; or, the science of the moral powers: In Two Parts: 1st, containing the Discipline of the Understanding; 2d, the Discipline of the Will: Mathemanomy; or, the laws of knowledge: Logonomy; or, the science of language: Anagognomy; or, the science of education: Ontonomy; or, the science of being. Printed for J. Ginger, London, 1803.

—— *The Philosophy of Sense; or, Book of Nature: revealing the Laws of the Intellectual World, founded on the Laws of the Physical World: forming the Sun or Source of Moral Truth or Sensitive Good, as the physical Sun, the Source of Light, Heat, and Motion to this Planet of the Earth. By John Stewart, the Traveller. From the Era of its own Publication, in the 7000th Year of Astronomical History, taken from Chinese Tables.* Printed for the Author, London, no date.

—— *Prospectus of A Series of Lectures, or a New Practical System of Human Reason, calculated to discharge the mind from a great mass of error, and to facilitate its labour in the approximation of moral truth, divested of all metaphysical perplexities and nullities; Accomodated to the Most Ordinary Capacities, in a Simple Method, which dispenses equally with the study of the college, or the lecture of musty libraries.* Printed by Thomas Dobson, Philadelphia, 1796.

—— *The Scripture of Reason and Nature; The Laws of Intellect; The Laws of Virtue; The Laws of Policy; The Laws of Physiology; or The Philosophy of Sense; developing the Origin, End, Essence, and Constitution of Nature. By John Stewart, the Traveler. In the 7000th Year of Astronomical History, in the Chinese Tables.* Printed for T. Egerton, London, 1813.

—— *The Sophiometer; or, Regulator of Mental Power; Forming the Nucleus of the Moral World, To convert Talent, Abilities, Literature, and Science, into Thought, Sense, Wisdom, and Prudence, 'the God of Man'; to form those Intermodifications of Good and Evil, whose Preponderancy marks the Characters of Virtue and Vice. By John Stewart, the only man of nature that ever appeared in the world. In the 7000th Year of Astronomical History, and the first Day of Intellectual Life or Moral World, from the Era of this Work.* London, no date.

[STEWART, JOHN], *Travels over the Most interesting Parts of the Globe, to discover the Source of Moral Motion; communicated to lead Mankind through the Conviction of the Senses to intellectual Existence, and an enlightened State of Nature. In the Year of Man's retrospective Knowledge, by astronomical Calculation 5000.* [No place, no date.]

—— *The Life and Adventures of the Celebrated Walking Stewart:*

including His Travels in the East Indies, Turkey, Germany, &
America. By a Relative. With a Portrait. Printed for E.
Wheatley, London, 1822.

STILES, EZRA, *The Literary Diary of Ezra Stiles.* Edited by Franklin B. Dexter. 3 vols. Charles Scribner's Sons, New York, 1901.

STILLMAN, SAMUEL, *A Discourse, delivered before the Members of the*
Boston Female Asylum, Friday, Sept. 25, 1801, Being Their
First Anniversary. Printed by Russell and Cutler, Boston, 1801.

—— *An Oration, Delivered July 4th, 1789, at the request of the*
inhabitants of The Town of Boston in Celebration of The Anni-
versary of American Independence. Printed by B. Edes & Son,
Boston, 1789.

—— *Thoughts on the French Revolution. A Sermon, delivered No-*
vember 20, 1794: being the Day of Annual Thanksgiving.
Printed by Manning & Loring, Boston, 1795.

STRONG, NATHAN, *Political Instruction from the Prophecies of God's*
Word. A Sermon, preached on the State Thanksgiving, Nov. 29,
1798. Printed by Hudson and Goodwin, Hartford, 1798.

The Temple of Reason, a deistic weekly paper published in the City
of New York from November 8, 1800 to February 7, 1801;
and in Philadelphia from April 22, 1801 to February 19, 1803.

The Theophilanthropist; containing Critical, Moral, Theological and
Literary Essays, in Monthly Numbers. By a Society. Printed
for the Proprietors, and Sold by H. Hart, No. 117, Chatham-
Street, New-York, 1810.

Theophilanthropy: or, the spirit of Genuine Religion, displayed in
Thirty-nine Articles, and published for the consideration of all
rational and liberal minds, and for promoting universal benevo-
lence. By a Layman. Printed by Wm. Hamilton, Lancaster,
1799.

THORNTON, JOHN WINGATE, *The Pulpit of the American Revolution:*
or, the Political Sermons of the Period of 1776. Gould and
Lincoln, Boston, 1860.

TROLLOPE, MRS. [FRANCES], *Domestic Manners of the Americans.*
2 vols. Printed for Whittaker, Treacher, & Co., London, 1832.

TRUMBULL, BENJAMIN, *A Discourse, delivered at the Anniversary*
Meeting of the Freemen of the Town of New-Haven, April 12,
1773. Printed by Thomas and Samuel Green, New-Haven,
1773.

TRUMBULL, JOHN, *Autobiography, Reminiscences and Letters of John*
Trumbull, from 1756 to 1841. B. L. Hamlen, New Haven,
1841.

VOLNEY, M., *Volney's Answer to Dr. Priestley, on a pamphlet entitled Observations on the Increase of Infidelity.* Printed for the Author and sold at the Office of the *Aurora,* Philadelphia, 1797.

—— *Les Ruines, ou Méditation sur les Révolutions des Empires; par M. Volney, Député à l'Assemblée Nationale de 1789.* Paris, 1791.

WAKEFIELD, GILBERT, *A Reply to Thomas Paine's Second Part of the Age of Reason.* Printed for H. D. Symonds, London, 1795.

WANSEY, HENRY, *An Excursion to the United States of North America in the Summer of 1794.* Second Edition with Additions. Salisbury, 1798.

WATSON, R., *An Address to the People of Great Britain.* By the Lord Bishop of Landaff. Second Edition. London, 1798.

—— *An Apology for the Bible, in a Series of Letters, addressed to Thomas Paine, Author of a Book entitled, The Age of Reason, Part the Second, being an Investigation of True and of Fabulous Theology.* Printed by John Bull, New-York, 1796.

WHITING, SAMUEL, *An Oration, delivered at the celebration of American Independence, at Sheffield, July 4th, 1796.* Printed by Loring Andrews, Stockbridge, 1796.

WHITTINGHAM, W. R. (Editor), *Standard Works Adapted to the Use of the Protestant Episcopal Church in the United States. Vol. I. Leslie on Deism. West on the Resurrection. With a General and Special Prefaces, Biographical Memoirs, and Notes.* Published by the New-York Protestant Episcopal Press, New-York, 1830.

The Whole Duty of Man, laid down in a Plain and Familiar Way for the Use of All, especially the Meanest Readers. Printed for John Eyre, London, 1733.

WILLIAMS, REV. DAVID, *Lectures on Education. Read to a Society for promoting Reasonable and Humane Improvements in the Discipline and Instruction of Youth.* 3 vols. Printed by John Bell, Bookseller to His Royal Highness the Prince of Wales, London, 1789.

WILLIAMS, SAMUEL, *The Natural and Civil History of Vermont.* Isaiah Thomas and David Carlisle, Jun., Walpole, Newhampshire, 1794.

WOLLASTON, WILLIAM, *The Religion of Nature Delineated.* Fifth Edition. Printed for James and John Knapton, London, 1731.

WOOD, JOHN, *A Full Exposition of the Clintonian Faction, and the Society of the Columbian Illuminati; with an account of the writer of the Narrative, and the characters of his Certificate Men, as also remarks on Warren's Pamphlet.* Printed for the Author, Newark, 1802.

SECONDARY WORKS

ADAMS, BROOKS, *The Emancipation of Massachusetts.* Houghton, Mifflin and Company, Boston, 1893.

ADAMS, HENRY, *History of the United States of America During the First Administration of Thomas Jefferson.* 2 vols. (Being the first 2 vols. of his *History of the United States of America.* . . . 9 vols.) Charles Scribner's Sons, New York, 1921.
—— *The Life of Albert Gallatin.* J. B. Lippincott & Co., Philadelphia, 1879.

ALLEN, JOSEPH HENRY and EDDY, RICHARD, *A History of the Unitarians and the Universalists in the United States.* (Vol. X in *The American Church History Series.*) The Christian Literature Company, New York, 1894.

ALLISON, WILLIAM HENRY, *Inventory of Unpublished Material for American Religious History in Protestant Church Archives and Other Repositories.* Published by the Carnegie Institution of Washington, 1910.

Appleton's Cyclopedia of American Biography. Edited by James Grant Wilson and John Fiske. 6 vols. New York, 1887-1889.

AREY, HENRY W., *The Girard College and its Founder: containing the Biography of Mr. Girard, the History of the Institution, . . . and the Will of Mr. Girard.* C. Sherman, Printer, Philadelphia, 1854.

The Atlantic Monthly, "Thomas Paine's Second Appearance in the United States," July, 1859, Vol. IV, pp. 1-17.

BACON, LEONARD WOOLSEY, *A History of American Christianity.* (Vol. XIII in *The American Church History Series.*) The Christian Literature Company, New York, 1897.

BALDWIN, ALICE M., *The New England Clergy and the American Revolution.* Duke University Press, Durham, N. C., 1928.

BANGS, NATHAN, *A History of the Methodist Episcopal Church.* 4 vols. Published by G. Lane & C. B. Tippett, New York, 1845.

BECKER, CARL L., *The Heavenly City of the Eighteenth-Century Philosophers.* Yale University Press, New Haven, 1932.

BEER, WILLIAM, *Checklist of American Periodicals, 1740-1800.* Reprinted from the *Proceedings of the American Antiquarian Society,* Worcester, Mass., 1923.

BENEDICT, ROBERT DEWEY, "Ethan Allen's Use of Language" in *Proceedings of the Vermont Historical Society,* 1901-1902.

BEST, MARY AGNES, *Thomas Paine, Prophet and Martyr of Democracy.* Harcourt, Brace & Company, New York, 1927.

BLAND, J. P., *President Roosevelt and Paine's Defamers.* Boston Investigator Co., Boston, 1903.

BRADFORD, ALDEN, *Memoir of the Life and Writings of Rev. Jonathan Mayhew, D. D.* C. C. Little & Co., Boston, 1838.

BRIGHAM, CLARENCE S., "Bibliography of American Newspapers, 1690-1820" in *Proceedings of the American Antiquarian Society.* Eighteen installments, New Series, Vols. 23-37, *passim.* Published by the Society, Worcester, Mass., 1913-1927.

BURY, J. B., *The Idea of Progress. An Inquiry into its Origin and Growth.* Macmillan and Co., Limited, London, 1920.

Cambridge History of American Literature. Edited by W. P. Trent, John Erskine, Stuart P. Sherman, and Carl Van Doren. 4 vols. G. P. Putnam's Sons, New York, 1918-1921.

CHASE, FREDERICK, *A History of Dartmouth College and the Town of Hanover, New Hampshire.* Edited by John K. Lord. 2 vols. John Wilson and Son, Cambridge, 1891.

CHESTERTON, G. K., *William Cobbett.* Hodder and Stoughton, Ltd., London, no date.

CHINARD, GILBERT, *Volney et l'Amérique d'après des documents inédits et sa correspondance avec Jefferson.* (The Johns Hopkins Studies in Romance Literatures and Languages, Vol. I.) The Johns Hopkins Press, Baltimore, 1923.

CLARK, JOSEPH B., *Leavening the Nation.* The Story of American Home Missions. The Baker and Taylor Company, New York, 1903.

CLEVELAND, CATHARINE C., *The Great Revival in the West, 1797-1805.* (Ph.D. dissertation, University of Chicago), The University of Chicago Press, Chicago, 1916.

COAD, ORAL SUMNER, *William Dunlap.* (Ph.D. dissertation, Columbia University), The Dunlap Society, New York, 1917.

COBB, SANFORD H., *The Rise of Religious Liberty in America.* The Macmillan Company, New York, 1902.

CONWAY, MONCURE DANIEL, *The Life of Thomas Paine with a history of his literary, political and religious career in America, France, and England. To which is added a sketch of Paine by William Cobbett.* 2 vols. G. P. Putnam's Sons, New York, 1892.

COOKE, GEORGE WILLIS, *Unitarianism in America, A History of its Origin and Development.* American Unitarian Association, Boston, 1902.

DE TOCQUEVILLE, ALEXIS, *The Old Regime and the Revolution.* Translated by John Bonner. Harper & Brothers, Publishers, New York, 1856.

DE WITT, CORNÉLIS, *Jefferson and the American Democracy.* Translated by R. S. H. Church. Longman, Green, Longman, Roberts & Green, London, 1862.

DEXTER, FRANKLIN BOWDITCH, *Biographical Sketches of the Graduates of Yale College with Annals of the College History, 1701-1815.* 6 vols. Henry Holt and Company, New York, 1885-1912.

—— *A Selection from the Miscellaneous Historical Papers of Fifty Years.* The Tuttle, Morehouse & Taylor Company, New Haven, 1918.

Dictionary of American Biography. 9 vols. to date. Vols. I-III, edited by Allen Johnson; Vols. IV-VII, edited by Allen Johnson and Dumas Malone; Vols. VIII-IX, edited by Dumas Malone. Charles Scribner's Sons, New York, 1928-1932.

DUER, JOHN, *A Discourse on the Life, Character, and Public Services of James Kent.* D. Appleton & Company, New-York, 1848.

ELIOT, SAMUEL A., *Heralds of a Liberal Faith.* 3 vols. American Unitarian Association, Boston, 1910.

ELSBREE, OLIVER WENDELL, *The Rise of the Missionary Spirit in America, 1790-1815.* (Ph.D. dissertation, Columbia University), The Williamsport Printing and Binding Co., Williamsport, Pa., 1928.

EMERSON, CHARLES FRANKLIN, *General Catalogue of Dartmouth College and the Associated Schools, 1769-1910, including a Historical Sketch of the College.* Printed for the College, Hanover, N. H., 1910-1911.

EVANS, CHARLES, *American Bibliography by Charles Evans. A Chronological Dictionary of all Books Pamphlets and Periodical Publications printed in the United States of America from the Genesis of Printing in 1639 down to and including the Year 1820 with Bibliographical and Biographical Notes.* 11 vols. Privately Printed for the Author, Chicago, 1903-1931.

FAŸ, BERNARD, *Bibliographie Critique des Ouvrages français relatifs aux Etats-Unis (1770-1800).* Librairie Ancienne Edouard Champion, Paris, 1924.

—— *The Revolutionary Spirit in France and America.* Translated by Ramon Guthrie. Harcourt, Brace & Company, New York, 1927.

FELT, JOSEPH B., *Annals of Salem.* 2 vols. Second Edition. Salem, 1845-1849.

FISHER, GEORGE P., *Life of Benjamin Silliman, M.D., LL.D.* 2 vols. Charles Scribner and Company, New York, 1866.

FOOTE, G. W., *Infidel Death-Beds.* The Truth Seeker Co., New York, 1892.

FOOTE, HENRY WILDER, *Annals of King's Chapel.* 2 vols. Little, Brown and Company, Boston, 1882-1896.

FORBES, HARRIETTE M. (Compiler), *New England Diaries, 1602-1800; a Descriptive Catalogue of Diaries, Orderly Books and Sea Journals.* Privately printed at The Perkins Press, Topsfield, Mass., 1923.

FOSDICK, LUCIAN J., *The French Blood in America.* The Baker & Taylor Co., New York, 1911.

FOX, DIXON RYAN, *The Decline of Aristocracy in the Politics of New York.* (Ph.D. dissertation, Columbia University), New York, 1918.

FRANCIS, JOHN W., *Old New York: or, Reminiscences of the Past Sixty Years.* W. J. Widdleton, Publisher, New York, 1866.

FREELAND, REV. DANIEL NILES, *Chronicles of Monroe in the Olden Time, Town and Village, Orange County, New York.* The De Vinne Press, New York, 1898.

FROTHINGHAM, OCTAVIUS BROOKS, *Transcendentalism in New England.* G. P. Putnam's Sons, New York, 1876.

GEWEHR, WESLEY M., *The Great Awakening in Virginia, 1740-1790.* Duke University Press, Durham, N. C., 1930.

GILLESPIE, JAMES E., *The Influence of Oversea Expansion on England to 1700.* (Ph.D. dissertation, Columbia University), New York, 1920.

GILLETT, REV. E. H., *History of the Presbyterian Church in the United States of America.* 2 vols. Revised Edition. Presbyterian Board of Publication, Philadelphia, 1864.

GILMAN, M. D., *The Bibliography of Vermont or A List of Books and Pamphlets Relating in any way to the State. With Bibliographical and Other Notes.* Printed by the Free Press Association, Burlington, 1897.

GOODRICH, PROF., "Narrative of Revivals of Religion in Yale College, from its Commencement to the Present Time" in *The American Quarterly Register* (February, 1838), Vol. X. Published by The American Education Society, Boston.

GREEN, MASON A., *Springfield, 1636-1886, History of Town and City.* C. A. Nichols & Co., Publishers [No place], 1888.

GREENE, EVARTS B. and MORRIS, RICHARD B., *A Guide to the Principal Sources for Early American History (1600-1800) in the*

City of New York. Columbia University Press, New York, 1929.

GREENE, M. LOUISE, *The Development of Religious Liberty in Connecticut*. Houghton, Mifflin and Company, Boston and New York, 1905.

GREENLEAF, JONATHAN, *A History of the Churches, of all Denominations, in the City of New York, from the first Settlement to the Year 1846*. E. French, New York, 1846.

GRIFFIN, APPLETON PRENTISS CLARK (Compiler), *List of works relating to the French alliance in the American revolution*. Government Printing Office, Washington, 1907.

GRISWOLD, RUFUS WILMOT, *The Republican Court or American Society in the Days of Washington*. New and Revised Edition. D. Appleton and Company, New York, 1856.

GROSSMAN, MORDECAI, *The Philosophy of Helvetius with Special Emphasis on the Educational Implications of Sensationalism*. (Ph.D. dissertation, Teachers College, Columbia University), New York, 1926.

HALL, HENRY, *Ethan Allen, the Robin Hood of Vermont*. D. Appleton and Company, New York, 1892.

HALL, THOMAS C., *The Religious Background of American Culture*. Little, Brown, and Company, Boston, 1930.

HAMMOND, JABEZ D., *The History of Political Parties in the State of New-York, from the ratification of the Federal Constitution to December, 1840*. 2 vols. Fourth Edition, Corrected, and Enlarged. Published by H. & E. Phinney, Cooperstown, 1846.

HANDSCHIN, CHARLES HART, *The Teaching of Modern Languages in the United States*. United States Bureau of Education, Bulletin, 1913, No. 3. Government Printing Office, Washington, 1913.

HANSEN, ALLEN OSCAR, *Liberalism and American Education in the Eighteenth Century*. The Macmillan Company, New York, 1926.

HASTINGS, JAMES (Editor), *Encyclopædia of Religion and Ethics*. 13 vols. Charles Scribner's Sons, New York, 1908-1927.

HAZEN, CHARLES DOWNER, *Contemporary American Opinion of the French Revolution*. (Johns Hopkins University Studies in Historical and Political Science, Extra Volume XVI), The Johns Hopkins Press, Baltimore, 1897.

HEARNSHAW, F. J. C. (Editor), *The Social & Political Ideas of Some Great French Thinkers of the Age of Reason*. F. S. Crofts & Co., New York, 1930.

HENDRICKSON, WM. H., *A Brief History of the First Presbyterian Church of Newtown, Long Island*. [No place], 1902.

HOLT, ANNE, *A Life of Joseph Priestley. With an Introduction by Francis W. Hirst.* Oxford University Press, London, 1931.

HUMPHREY, EDWARD FRANK, *Nationalism and Religion in America, 1774-1789.* Chipman Law Publishing Company, Boston, 1924.

ISHAM, EDWARD SWIFT, "Ethan Allen, A Study of Civic Authority" in *Proceedings of the Vermont Historical Society,* October and November, 1898.

JAMESON, J. FRANKLIN, *The American Revolution considered as a Social Movement.* Princeton University Press, Princeton, 1926.

JONES, ADAM LEROY, *Early American Philosophers.* (Ph.D. dissertation, Columbia University), New York, 1898.

JONES, HOWARD MUMFORD, *America and French Culture, 1750-1848.* The University of North Carolina Press, Chapel Hill, N. C., 1927.

KADISON, ALEXANDER, "An Unfamiliar Figure in American Rationalism" in *The Rationalist Press Association Annual for the Year 1926,* pp. 76-80. London, 1926.

KEEP, AUSTIN BAXTER, *The Library in Colonial New York.* (Ph.D. dissertation, Columbia University), The De Vinne Press, New York, 1909.

KEIM, ALBERT, *Helvétius, Sa Vie et Son Oeuvre.* (Thèse Présentée à la Faculté des Lettres de l'Université de Paris), Librairies Félix Alcan et Guillaumin Réunies, Paris, 1907.

KILROE, EDWIN PATRICK, *Saint Tammany and the Origin of the Society of Tammany or Columbian Order in the City of New York.* (Ph.D. dissertation, Columbia University), New York, 1913.

KILROE, EDWIN P. ET AL., *The Story of Tammany.* Issued by the Democratic Organization, New York County, Tammany Hall, 1924.

King's Chapel Lectures. The Religious History of New England. Harvard University Press, Cambridge, 1917.

KOCH, G. ADOLF, *The Growth of Denominational Colleges in the United States, 1820-1850.* MS. Chanler Historical Prize Essay, Columbia University, New York, 1927.

LAMSON, ALVAN, *A History of the First Church and Parish in Dedham, in three discourses, delivered on occasion of the completion, November 18, 1838, of the Second Century since the gathering of said Church.* Printed by Herman Mann, Dedham, 1839.

LARNED, ELLEN D., *History of Windham County, Connecticut.* 2 vols. Published by the Author, Worcester, Mass., 1874-1880.

LEAVITT, EMILY WILDER, *Groups of Palmer Families*. Privately printed. David Clapp & Son, Boston, 1901.

LOTHROP, SAMUEL KIRKLAND, *A History of the Church in Brattle Street, Boston*. Wm. Crosby and H. P. Nichols, Boston, 1851.

LOVE, W. DE LOSS, JR., *The Fast and Thanksgiving Days of New England*. Houghton, Mifflin and Company, Boston, 1895.

MCBAIN, HOWARD LEE, *De Witt Clinton and the Origin of the Spoils System in New York*. (Ph.D. dissertation, Columbia University), New York, 1907.

M'CLINTOCK, REV. JOHN and STRONG, REV. JAMES, *Cyclopædia of Biblical, Theological, and Ecclesiastical Literature*. 10 vols. Harper & Brothers, Publishers, New York, 1871-1881.

MCKEE, GEORGE H., *Th. Jefferson, Ami de la Révolution Française*. Imprimerie Al. Cathrine, Lorient, 1928.

MACLEAN, JOHN, *History of the College of New Jersey*. 2 vols. J. B. Lippincott & Co., Philadelphia, 1877.

MCMASTER, JOHN BACH, *A History of the People of the United States, from the Revolution to the Civil War*. 8 vols. D. Appleton and Company, New York, 1883-1913.

—— *The Life and Times of Stephen Girard, Mariner and Merchant*. 2 vols. J. B. Lippincott Company, Philadelphia, 1918.

MALONE, DUMAS, *The Public Life of Thomas Cooper, 1783-1839*. Yale University Press, New Haven, 1926.

MARTIN, KINGSLEY, *French Liberal Thought in the Eighteenth Century: A Study of Political Ideas from Bayle to Condorcet*. Little, Brown, and Company, Boston, 1929.

MATHEWS, LOIS KIMBALL, *The Expansion of New England: The Spread of New England Settlement and Institutions to the Mississippi River, 1620-1865*. Houghton Mifflin Company, Boston, 1909.

MATHIEZ, ALBERT, *La Théophilanthropie et le Culte Décadaire, 1796-1801, essai sur l'histoire religieuse de la révolution*. Félix Alcan, Éditeur. Paris, 1904.

MEADE, BISHOP, *Old Churches, Ministers and Families of Virginia*. 2 vols. J. B. Lippincott Company, Philadelphia; Vol. I, 1910; Vol. II, 1906.

MELVILLE, LEWIS, *The Life and Letters of William Cobbett in England and America*. 2 vols. John Lane, London, 1913.

MESICK, JANE LOUISE, *The English Traveller in America, 1785-1835*. (Ph.D. dissertation, Columbia University), Columbia University Press, New York, 1922.

MITCHELL, JULIA POST, "Jean Pierre Tétard" in *Columbia University Quarterly*, June 1910, Vol. XII, pp. 286-289.

Mode, Peter George, *The Frontier Spirit in American Christianity*. The Macmillan Company, New York, 1923.
—— *Source Book and Bibliographical Guide for American Church History*. The Collegiate Press, George Banta Publishing Company, Menasha, Wisconsin, 1921.
Moore, Hugh, *Memoir of Col. Ethan Allen*. Published by O. R. Cook, Plattsburgh, N. Y., 1834.
Morison, Samuel Eliot, *The Life and Letters of Harrison Gray Otis, Federalist, 1765-1848*. 2 vols. Houghton Mifflin Company, Boston, 1913.
—— *The Maritime History of Massachusetts, 1783-1860*. Houghton Mifflin Company, Boston, 1925.
Morse, Anson Ely, *The Federalist Party in Massachusetts to the Year 1800*. (Ph.D. dissertation, Princeton University), The University Library, Princeton, 1909.
Mott, Frank Luther, *A History of American Magazines, 1741-1850*. D. Appleton and Company, New York, 1930.
Myers, Gustavus, *The History of Tammany Hall*. Boni & Liveright, Inc., New York, 1917.

Nevins, Allen (Compiler and Editor), *American Social History as Recorded by British Travellers*. Henry Holt and Company, New York, 1923.
—— *The American States during and after the Revolution, 1775-1789*. The Macmillan Company, New York, 1924.
Nokes, G. D., *A History of the Crime of Blasphemy*. Sweet & Maxwell, Limited, London, 1928.

Osgood, Herbert L., *The American Colonies in the Eighteenth Century*. 4 vols. Columbia University Press, New York, 1924.

Parrington, Vernon Louis, *The Colonial Mind, 1620-1800* and *The Romantic Revolution in America, 1800-1860*. (Vols. I and II in *Main Currents in American Thought, an Interpretation of American Literature from the Beginnings to 1920*.) Harcourt, Brace and Company, New York, 1927.
Pell, John, *Ethan Allen*. Houghton Mifflin Company, Boston, 1929.
Purcell, Richard J., *Connecticut in Transition, 1775-1818*. American Historical Association, Washington, 1918.
Putnam, Samuel P., *400 Years of Freethought*. The Truth Seeker Company, New York, 1894.

Quincy, Josiah, *The History of Harvard University*. 2 vols. Published by John Owen, Cambridge, 1840.

RANDALL, HENRY S., *The Life of Thomas Jefferson.* 3 vols. Derby & Jackson, New York, 1858.

REMSBURG, JOHN E., *Thomas Paine, the Apostle of Religious and Political Liberty.* Second Edition. Published by J. P. Mendum, Boston, 1889.

RIKER, JAMES, *The Annals of Newtown, in Queens County, New-York: containing Its History from its first Settlement.* Published by D. Fanshaw, New-York, 1852.

RILEY, I. WOODBRIDGE, *American Philosophy; The Early Schools.* Dodd, Mead & Company, New York, 1907.

ROBERTSON, J. M., *A History of Freethought in the Nineteenth Century.* Watts & Co., London, 1929.

ROBINSON, HOWARD, *Bayle the Sceptic.* Columbia University Press, New York, 1931.

ROBINSON, WILLIAM A., *Jeffersonian Democracy in New England.* Yale University Press, New Haven, 1916.

ROOSEVELT, THEODORE, *Gouverneur Morris.* (*American Statesmen Series,* edited by John T. Morse, Jr.) Houghton Mifflin and Company, Boston, 1893.

RUSK, RALPH LESLIE, *The Literature of the Middle Western Frontier.* 2 vols. Columbia University Press, New York, 1925.

RUTTENBER, E. M., *History of the County of Orange: with a History of the ⅃own and City of Newburgh: General, Analytical and Biographical.* F. M. Ruttenber & Son, Printers, Newburgh, N. Y., 1875.

SCHARF, J. THOMAS and WESTCOTT, THOMPSON, *History of Philadelphia, 1609-1884.* 3 vols. Philadelphia, 1884.

SCUDDER, HORACE E., *Noah Webster.* (*American Men of Letters Series,* edited by Charles D. Warner.) Houghton Mifflin and Company, Boston, 1882.

SHEA, JOHN GILMARY, *Life and Times of the Most Rev. John Carroll, Bishop and First Archbishop of Baltimore. Embracing the History of the Catholic Church in the United States, 1763-1815.* John G. Shea, New York, 1888.

SIGSBEE, RAY ADDISON, *Das philosophische System Joseph Priestleys.* (Ph.D. dissertation, Heidelberg), Heidelberg, 1912.

SMITH, EDGAR F., *Priestley in America, 1794-1804.* P. Blakiston's Son & Co., Philadelphia, 1920.

SMITH, J. E. A., *The History of Pittsfield, (Berkshire County), Massachusetts, from the Year 1734 to the Year 1800.* Lee and Shepard, Boston, 1869.

—— *The History of Pittsfield, (Berkshire County), Massachusetts, from the Year 1800 to the Year 1876.* C. W. Bryan & Co., Springfield, 1876.

SMITH, THOMAS E. V., *The City of New York in the Year of Washington's Inauguration, 1789.* Anson D. F. Randolph & Co., New York, 1889.

SPARKS, JARED, *Life of Ethan Allen* in *The Library of American Biography*, conducted by Jared Sparks, Vol. I. Hilliard, Gray, and Co., Boston, 1834.

SPRAGUE, WILLIAM B., *Annals of the American Pulpit; or Commemorative Notices of Distinguished American Clergymen of Various Denominations*. . . . 9 vols. Robert Carter and Brothers, New York, 1857-1869.

—— *The Life of Jedidiah Morse, D.D.* Anson D. F. Randolph & Company, New York, 1874.

STAUFFER, VERNON, *New England and the Bavarian Illuminati.* (Ph.D. dissertation, Columbia University), New York, 1918.

STEPHEN, LESLIE, *History of English Thought in the Eighteenth Century.* 2 vols. Third Edition. Smith, Elder & Co., London, 1902.

STOKES, ANSON PHELPS, *Memorials of Eminent Yale Men.* 2 vols. Yale University Press, New Haven, 1914.

STOKES, I. N. PHELPS, *The Iconography of Manhattan Island, 1498-1909.* 6 vols. Robert H. Dodd, New York, 1915-1928.

SWEET, WILLIAM WARREN, "John Wesley, Tory" in *Methodist Quarterly Review*, 1922, pp. 255-268.

—— *The Story of Religions in America.* Harper & Brothers, Publishers, New York, 1930.

SWIFT, LINDSAY, *Brook Farm, its members, scholars, and visitors.* The Macmillan Company, 1900.

THOMAS, ABEL C., *A Century of Universalism in Philadelphia and New York.* [No publisher], Philadelphia, 1872.

TODD, CHARLES BURR, *Life and Letters of Joel Barlow, LL.D. Poet, Statesman, Philosopher with Extracts from his Work and hitherto unpublished poems.* G. P. Putnam's Sons, New York, 1886.

TRENT, WILLIAM P., *English Culture in Virginia: a study of the Gilmer letters, and an account of the English professors obtained by Jefferson for the University of Virginia.* (Johns Hopkins University Studies in Historical and Political Science, Seventh Series, V-VI), Baltimore, 1889.

TYLER, MOSES COIT, *The Literary History of the American Revolution.* 2 vols. G. P. Putnam's Sons, New York, 1897.

—— *Three Men of Letters.* G. P. Putnam's Sons, New York, 1895.

VALE, G., *The Life of Thomas Paine.* J. P. Mendum, Boston, 1859.

VAN BECELAERE, L., *La Philosophie en Amérique depuis les origines jusqu'à nos jours*, (*1607-1900*). The Electic Publishing Co., New York, 1904.

VOSSLER, OTTO, *Die Amerikanischen Revolutionsideale in ihrem Verhältnis zu den Europäischen untersucht an Thomas Jefferson.* Verlag von R. Oldenbourg, München und Berlin, 1929.

WATERMAN, WILLIAM RANDALL, *Frances Wright.* (Ph.D. dissertation, Columbia University), New York, 1924.

WEBSTER, NOAH, *Notes on the Life of Noah Webster*, compiled by Emily E. F. Ford and edited by Emily E. F. Skeel. 2 vols. Privately printed, New York, 1912.

WESTCOTT, THOMPSON, *The Life of John Fitch, the Inventor of the Steamboat.* J. B. Lippincott & Co., Philadelphia, 1857.

WILBUR, JAMES BENJAMIN, *Ira Allen, Founder of Vermont, 1751-1814.* 2 vols. Houghton Mifflin Company, Boston and New York, 1928.

WILSON, MELBA PAXTON, *Pre-Revolutionary Liberalism and Post-Revolutionary Unitarianism in America.* MS. Master of Arts thesis, Columbia University, New York, May 1930.

WOODWARD, E. M. and HAGEMAN, JOHN F., *History of Burlington and Mercer Counties, New Jersey, with Biographical Sketches of many of their Pioneers and Prominent Men.* Everts & Peck, Philadelphia, 1883.

INDEX

9 781606 085875